Disclosures to a Stranger

Social Worlds of Childhood

General Editor: Rom Harré

Disclosures to a Stranger
Adolescent Values in an Advanced Industrial Society

Tom Kitwood

Routledge & Kegan Paul
London, Boston and Henley

First published in 1980
by Routledge & Kegan Paul Ltd
39 Store Street, London WC1E 7DD,
Broadway House, Newtown Road,
Henley-on-Thames, Oxon RG9 1EN and
2 Park Street, Boston, Mass. 02108, USA
Set in 10 on 11pt Times by
Rowland Phototypesetting Ltd
Bury St Edmunds, Suffolk
and printed in Great Britain by
Redwood Burn Ltd
Trowbridge & Esher
© Tom Kitwood 1980

British Library Cataloguing in Publication Data

Kitwood, Thomas Morris
Disclosures to a stranger. – (Social worlds
of childhood).
1. Social values
2. Adolescence
I. Title   II. Series
310.43'15'0941   HQ799.2.S/   79-41253

ISBN 0 7100 0463 X

Contents

Acknowledgments

I wish to express my thanks to all those who contributed to the formation of this book:

to Rom Harré, Ralph Ruddock, and Alan Smithers for their advice and encouragement;

to Steve Holtzman for his very thorough reading of the typescript, and many detailed suggestions;

to Sylvia Pilling and Sheila Clark for their work when the research was in its early stages;

to Carol Borrill for her assistance given in many ways; had chapters 5 and 8 been published as papers, this would have been under our joint authorship;

to those who facilitated the carrying out of interviews in youth clubs, schools, and elsewhere;

and especially to the boys and girls who took part in the research. The research project of which this book is a part is financed by a grant from the Leverhulme Trust Fund.

T.K.

General Editor's Preface

For most of us childhood is a forgotten and even a rejected time. The aim of this series is to recover the flavour of childhood and adolescence in a systematic and sympathetic way. The frame of mind cultivated by the authors as investigators is that of anthropologists who glimpse a strange tribe across a space of forest and millennia of time. The huddled group on the other side of the school playground and the thumping of feet in the upstairs rooms mark the presence of a strange tribe. This frame of mind is deliberately different from that of the classical investigators of child psychology, who have brought adult concepts to bear upon the understanding of children's thoughts and actions, and have looked at childhood primarily as a passage towards the skills and accomplishments and distortions of adults. In these studies the authors try to look upon the activities of children as autonomous and complete in themselves. Of course, not all the activities of childhood could be treated in this way. Rather than being in opposition to the traditional kind of study, the work upon which this series is based aims to amplify our understanding by bringing to light aspects of childhood which usually remain invisible when it is looked at in the traditional way. The ethogenic method is in use throughout the studies represented in this series, that is the children themselves are the prime sources of theories about their actions and thoughts and of explanations of the inwardness of their otherwise mysterious activities.

Introduction

The inquiry reported in this book turned out on completion to be very different from the project that was at first envisaged. I had planned to carry out a study of adolescent values within one of the main research traditions of social psychology, developing, validating, and then applying a testing instrument which might be more powerful than some of those currently in use. As the research progressed I found that it was impossible to keep to my initial aims and engage with the issues, both theoretical and practical, that began to appear to be central. The most important of these related to the character of an empirical social psychology of the person; a science in which there would be as full as possible an acknowledgment of individual human powers, the social nature of human life, and the relationship between consciousness and the conditions of everyday existence. Many of my initial assumptions about how to proceed had to be abandoned, and the research seemed almost to take on a life and character of its own. As happens from time to time in scientific endeavour, a person begins by searching for one kind of thing, guided by expectations derived from previous research, but finds another, and comes to interpret past knowledge in that light.

There were several reasons for making adolescence the focus of a piece of research concerned with values. It is commonly supposed, for example, that the period of life between about twelve and twenty years of age is one of the most critical for the social and moral development of the individual. Work that has grown out of two great psychological traditions—psychodynamic theory and cognitive–developmentalism—strongly suggests that this is so; though in neither case have the resulting theories proved convincing to those who take a more sociological standpoint. There is also the fact that adolescents are particularly subject to stereotyping, some of it allegedly concerned with their 'values'. This process occurs not only in everyday encounters in schools and youth clubs, and in conflict with established authority; it is also the case that simplistic assumptions about adolescents and their values have crept into social research, the consequence being that existing stereotypes have tended to be reinforced, with the added weight of 'scientific' authority. Moreover, a great deal of the research carried out with this age group has begun by characterizing adolescence in terms of 'problems' of some kind; if nothing else, funds are more easily obtained for research projects that might lead to a reduced disruption of the social order. In contrast to this I wished to make a contribution to the social psychology of 'normal' adolescence, in the hope of providing a background against which some of the so-called 'problems' and 'abnormalities' might be reinterpreted.

It quickly became apparent in pilot studies that a thorough treatment of the phenomena related to 'values', even when largely at a descriptive level, would necessitate a more socialized conception of the person than is commonly found in psychological research. It was important to take into account not only immediate relationships, but also a person's broader location in the social structure. In contrast to a considerable volume of research, it seemed that the objective conditions of existence, which often were clearly related to social class position, were of paramount importance in the study of values. Putting this another way, it would be mistaken to interpret evidence as if it were not affected by the continuous movement of history; there is no 'social psychology of values', no 'developmental theory of adolescence' in an absolute sense. Thus the end-product of the inquiry would be a description and interpretation of some aspects of values in the lives of English adolescents of the latter part of the 1970s, a period when advanced industrial societies are in a time of transition, facing economic and social conditions for which there is no clear historical precedent. If any broad generalizations emerged these would be not so much about adolescence in itself as about method, and the ways in which values are related to the circumstances of everyday life.

About twenty years ago a great interest in adolescent values was developing, particularly under the growing influence of the idea of a distinct and pervasive 'youth culture'. The assumption was that a division within society based on age was becoming, or had become, more significant than any that was based on social class. Talcott Parsons had given sociological authority to such a view some years earlier, though it required a time of general prosperity, in which social class differences tended to be obscured, for it to gain a wide plausibility. Adolescence in modern industrial society was often characterized by psychologists and sociologists as a period when boys and girls are both denied the roles of children and barred from access to the adult world; in response to this situation, it was suggested, they develop social and cultural forms that are peculiarly their own. Whether or not those years spent in a kind of limbo were beneficial was a matter of dispute. The balance of opinion among psychologists was that it was good for young people to undergo such an experience, since this made possible a more complete and less constrained personal development.

It is still the case that boys and girls have to pass through a period during which they are, apparently, neither children nor adults. Over the last fifteen or twenty years, however, their position has changed in a number of ways.

Although there has been no great alteration in human physiology, the period socially defined as 'adolescence' has tended to grow longer, with the raising of the school-leaving age and the extension of provision for further and higher education. In addition, whereas only a few years ago the majority of those who left school at the first opportunity could look forward to finding employment virtually at once, this is no longer the case; with the shortage of jobs many have to wait some time longer, and in some areas there is the prospect of prolonged unemployment. There has been an extended period of inflation whose main effect, as with society at large, has been to sharpen existing but latent inequalities. Official provision for youth has been expanded, with a tendency to institutionalize patterns of adolescent behaviour observed during the 1960s and assumed to be manifestations of the natural characteristics of young people. At the same time the pub, in which people of all ages above the legal threshold are treated on equal terms, has emerged as a major focus of adolescent life. The position of women in British society has begun to shift, partly no doubt as a result of radical reappraisal of the woman's role, but perhaps in the short term more significantly as a result of changing opportunities for women in paid employment. There have also been subtle transformations in the 'normal', taken-for-granted world that forms the background to adolescent life. The days when television was a novelty, for example, have faded into history; and whereas formerly to be in active political revolt appeared to critically minded youth to be a rational response to current conditions (since there was an underlying belief that peace and progress were real possibilities), it is often now more plausible to believe that on the large scale nothing can be radically changed.

In such ways as these both the objective and subjective conditions of adolescent life in Britain have altered since the time
when the idea of a 'youth culture' with its own distinctive values
captured the attention of social scientists. Little now remains of that
conception, which has proved to be inadequate in the light of more
discerning research. In this general area, however, psychology has
tended to lag behind, owing in part, perhaps, to the development
of highly coherent but somewhat restricted traditions, which have
limited the character of empirical inquiry. The psychological study
of values (and the closely associated domain demarcated as
morality) requires not only the extension of existing work, but also
the development of more sensitive and open approaches, in which
there is a careful study of the character of everyday life, and the
way this impinges on the person. This book is intended as a
contribution in that direction.

Within these general terms of reference, the work described
here is tentative and incomplete. The research produced such
a wealth of data that to do it justice would require perhaps
twenty monographs, each one dealing in depth with a particular
topic. For the purposes of this book four main themes have been
taken, and discussed in as much detail as space has permitted:
relationships in the home, social life among peers, experiences of
formal and informal work, and the development of the self-image.
There are important values related to each of these. The most
obvious omission from this book is a discussion of schooling. The
decision not to deal with this, despite the fact that there was an
abundance of relevant material, was based on two main considerations. First, there has been a great deal of research directly
concerned with this topic, though admittedly not such a large
amount from a theoretical standpoint similar to that which has been
adopted here; second, it is possible to exaggerate the significance of
school in adolescent life, while failing to take into account other
aspects which are not so well understood. If one main section of
the data was to be excluded, this seemed to be the one. Nevertheless, the influence of both the content and process of formal
education is certainly acknowledged; as will be seen, schooling is a
hidden presence in much of the discussion surrounding the four
selected themes.

This study is limited also in several other ways. The 'sample' of
153 boys and girls was designed so that it would approximately
match the distribution in the social stratification system. This
means that the proportion of participants in the 'middle' part,
roughly corresponding to the Registrar General's category III, is
large, whereas that of those at either end is smaller. In this there is
something of a contrast with a good deal of research on adoles-

cence, which has tended to concentrate on the two extremes. While the centre of gravity of this study is where, statistically, it rightly belongs, this policy has necessitated many omissions. For example, it is relatively deficient in its treatment of those in the upper middle class, who form about 20 per cent of the whole population. Those who are educated at boarding schools, and generally come from the most affluent part of society, have not been included at all; indeed, the great majority of the 'sample' either were at, or had been at, comprehensive schools. Another limitation concerns the age-range. Although those who took part in the research covered a span of about five years, from fourteen and a half upwards, the material presented in this book is more restricted in its scope. The inquiry involved retrospective accounts, so that the main body of data relates to an earlier and narrower age-range. In effect, this book presents a developmental study covering the years from about fourteen to seventeen and a half. Some of the information given by older boys and girls was particularly useful here, since they could look back on the period with a clear memory, but also with some degree of detachment.

The research is yet further constrained by its urban bias. A few boys and girls from genuinely rural environments were included; their accounts provided ground for thinking that the experience of adolescents from such backgrounds, especially if they are working-class, is very different from that which is presented in this book as typical, and that the study of their values merits a separate inquiry. Finally, this research was confined to indigenous English adolescents, living in a variety of areas, the northern-most limit of which was approximately the line from Lancaster to York.

The method of research is that of the loosely structured interview, designed in such a way as to provide data relevant to the study of values. Considering the conditions within which the inquiry was conducted, the accounts that the participants gave of themselves may be characterized as 'disclosures to a stranger', implying that the context of the interview, and the way the researchers were perceived, affected the nature of what was said. One of the features of the research instrument was that it left the choice of topic for discussion largely in the hands of the partici-pants themselves; the framework provided by the interview schedule was extremely flexible, in some respects being almost like a clinical psychologist's 'projective test'. There are some topics that a person is prepared to talk about with a stranger, whose possession of highly personal information will not become an embarrassment at a later stage; it is also the case that there are certain aspects of life that are too delicate or too difficult to explain to someone who is virtually unknown. In this way, too, it is acknowledged that the data are far from complete.

The book begins with a lengthy chapter summarizing the theoretical background to the inquiry, showing how it is related to two main traditions of psychological work in the same general field. It is possible, however, to begin at chapter 2, which describes the evolution of the research method without going into technicalities. Anyone who does this, having a greater liking for empirical material than for methodology and theory, will probably find that the meaning of the main concepts used in the interpretation of data gradually becomes clear from their use.

The setting out of a finished piece of work in this way, with a theoretical section at the beginning and the report of the actual research following it, could be misleading, as I have already hinted. For it was not a case of first working out a theoretical position, and then operationalizing it for the purpose of empirical inquiry. Throughout this research 'theory' and 'fact' have been in a dialectical relationship, such that what was observed was constantly modifying theory, and the result was providing fresh schemata for the interpretation of data. Those of us who carried out the research came to each new group of interviews with subtly changed expectations, and returned from them with fresh insights to be incorporated into theory. It was only near to the end of the whole inquiry that a tentative 'closure' was established. Such a view of scientific activity may not commend itself to all methodologists, since it accords with the view that theories are not totally determined by objects and events in the world itself. At any rate, to present scientific work as if it had no individual character arising from the foibles of those engaged upon it can be highly misleading. I have tried, on the contrary, to make plain some of the practical difficulties and limitations of interpersonal research, as well as the hazards involved in developing a theoretical framework. For the research did not provide data of that deceptively neat and tidy sort that can easily be transmuted into numbers. It did not deal with adolescents' answers to hypothetical questions, but with values developed in facing the realities of everyday life, where there is great (and methodologically inconvenient) variety. Unlike many types of psychological work, it has deliberately avoided that kind of abstraction through which the character of human existence disappears from view.

There is always the danger that the outcome of research of this kind will merely be the replacing of one set of stereotypes by another, equally inadequate. Some of the generalizations blandly presented in the later chapters as if they were 'facts' may well be incorrect, even as first approximations, and important distinctions have probably been obscured. But at any rate a fair quantity of verbatim material has been included; if the interpretation given by those of us who carried out the research is not plausible, the reader is welcome to draw alternative conclusions.

1
Background*

The domain of values, as a topic for empirical study in the social sciences, may be roughly demarcated as that of the beliefs of human beings about what is right, good or desirable, and of their corresponding actions and attitudes. Research into values has taken place mainly within the disciplines of anthropology, sociology and psychology. Appraisal of the field is complex, because both within any one of these disciplines and between them conceptualization has been diverse, and a number of distinct empirical styles have evolved. At present there can be no confidence that two authorities who talk about 'values' are discussing precisely the same range of phenomena; and while there have been several (mutually conflicting) attempts to clarify the concepts and analyse their usage, there has been little serious attempt to explicate what it might mean to 'have values' at the social–psychological level. The situation has become more confused because of the fact that it is now quite common for reference to be made in everyday speech to the 'values' of individuals, groups, classes and cultures; yet it is far from clear what is meant, or what are the theories of action to which tacit reference is being made.

A survey of the whole field indicates that methods of research into values may be loosely classified into two groups. The first consists of those studies in which the researcher takes the stance of an observer, and looks at aspects of 'behaviour' under natural or experimental conditions. Much of the early psychological research into morality, typically concerned with honesty and altruism, was of this kind. The second group consists of attempts to discover people's value-related beliefs: by asking them directly, by listening

*I am grateful to the *Journal of Moral Education* for permission to draw on material published in vol. 6, no. 2 and vol. 7, no. 3.

to their everyday speech, by examining their writings, or obtaining their answers to questionnaires. Research of this type accounts for by far the greatest bulk of work normally subsumed under the topic of values.

This chapter is an attempt to sketch in a small part of this very rich background, indicating some of the reasons why the inquiry reported in this book came to take the form that it did. A brief critique of two major 'research programmes' in the social–psychological study of values will be offered; the characteristics of a different type of approach, whose validation lies in 'realist' philosophy of science, will then be outlined. This has not yet been extensively applied to the study of values, though it holds many possibilities for gaining new insights into this and related topics. To develop research into values in the realist mode does, of course, require an analysis of what it might mean to describe a person as 'having values', since the operational definitions of more highly structured psychological approaches are largely irrelevant. An explicit model of the person as a social being, and with an individual 'essence', is required. This chapter is mainly concerned with tentative solutions to these problems. The treatment given here is cursory; for a more thorough discussion, and for a substantiation of some of the points that are here touched on very lightly, the reader is referred to the items under my name in the Bibliography.

Two Research Programmes Compared

Because of the highly fragmented character of research into values there has not been as yet a significant accumulation of coherent cross-disciplinary knowledge. Many 'one-off' pieces of research have been carried out, some of great ingenuity, particularly within the sociological tradition. Values have also figured peripherally, rather than as the central focus of inquiry, in approaches as disparate as Marxian social analysis, ethnomethodology, 'humanistic psychology', and several forms of psychotherapy. There are, however, two longstanding traditions of research in psychology that have given concentrated attention to values, each working with carefully formulated principles of method. They might very loosely be viewed as paradigms in the Kuhnian sense, though it would perhaps be more accurate to characterize them as 'research programmes' of the kind described by Lakatos (e.g. in Lakatos and Musgrave, 1970). That is to say, each one consists of a cluster of hypotheses and rules of procedure, of which part form a hard and permanent core and others a more flexible surrounding layer. Both programmes have grown and thrived; both have successfully resolved inconsistencies, and survived partial or apparent refutation, emerging the richer as a result of what, in Lakatos's terms, would be termed a series of 'progressive problem shifts'. Characteristic of concurrent and potentially rival programmes, they have a partial overlap of empirical content, and some but not all problems in common. They are thus not strictly commensurable.

The Measurement of Personal Values

The remote origins of this research programme are to be found in the attempts to develop a 'science of value' during the latter part of the nineteenth century. It was only much later, however, that 'value' became an important term in psychology, largely as a result of the work of Thurstone and Allport. Basing their ideas on the interpretative sociology of Spranger, they took the study of values to mean the understanding of a person's dominant mode of being-in-the-world, the concerns around which an individual life was centrally organized. The famous *Study of Values* (Allport *et al.*, 1931), was designed to measure the extent to which a person's orientation was theoretical, economic, aesthetic, social, political or religious.

Allport's initial aim was mainly to use his questionnaire in order to help his students to come to a better understanding of themselves; the purpose was that of ideographic study. However, it soon became clear than an instrument of this kind could also be used nomothetically, in obtaining data from large samples, and in the comparison of an individual's value profile with that of a criterion group. Thus the instrument was of potential use in several applied fields, and the systematic psychological study of values was inaugurated. It is a curious irony that, at the very time that social scientists were beginning to attempt to measure values with self-consciously scientific rigour, the logical positivists were asserting that the whole domain lay beyond the reach of meaningful discussion, and that debate in this field was largely concerned with pseudo-problems.

Although the concept of value survived, empirical work in the social sciences was greatly influenced by positivist philosophy, to the extent that many of the methodological canons initially put forward in relation to the investigation of the physical world were somewhat uncritically transferred to the study of human beings. Intelligence-testing had been the first major field of inquiry to be strongly influenced in this way. Following this a variety of elaborate techniques were developed in the attempt to make the realm of private experience accessible to objective measurement, while meeting positivist criteria. In experiments and surveys the main quest was for statistically significant differences and correlations. Methods of research design were borrowed from botany and allied fields, together with the relevant statistics.

Attempts to measure attributes of persons received new impetus during the Second World War: indeed, a number of the concepts and techniques that became central to social psychology, particularly in the United States, were either initiated or developed to a high level of sophistication during this period and the decade that followed. Methods of personality screening based on psychological tests arose in part from the attempt to exclude from combat those who might break down under its most severe stresses; the measurement of motivation was allied to the selection of suitable persons for promotion; the development of role theory to the need for an impersonal system of command and obedience; the study of socialization to the transformation of civilians into efficient fighting personnel. Research into attitudes, which had been initiated before the war, became a major experimental area; psychological research into values was in many respects its offspring.

It was from such instrumental concerns that some of the familiar research methods have developed, passing via academic social psychology into a variety of related fields, such as marketing, opinion-polling, vocational guidance, personnel selection and educational research. The whole approach either directly implies, or can easily be put to use in, the manipulation of one set of human beings by another. And it operates with an implicit conception of the person which acknowledges only very low levels of intelligence and initiative—a view that reflects the real position of the raw recruit in time of war. For such purposes a positivist approach happened to be ideally suited; it was neither necessary nor desirable to try to understand the world from the standpoint of those upon whom the research was being carried out.

From the early 1950s onwards the systematic study of values began to gain momentum. To a few theorists it appeared, indeed, that insight into values might be the fundamental key to the understanding of human behaviour. Notable landmarks of the period were the *Ways to Live* study by Morris (1956), a vast cross-cultural study of conceptions of the good life; and the work of Kluckhohn and Strodtbeck (1961), in which a theory of value orientations (fusions of descriptive and evaluative beliefs about the world) was developed. It was during the 1960s that the most rapid growth of research into values occurred. Conceptualization, however, was often poor, and the work often showed signs of haste and immaturity. The coming of the computer meant that statistical procedures that had formerly been very laborious could now be carried out with relative ease. The study of values, like several other branches of empirical social science, was enticed by the prospect of large and more complex arrays of quantitative data, and by the variety of techniques available for their subsequent manipulation. Altogether about fifty instruments for the measurement of values have made their appearance in the psychological and sociological literature, of which ten or so are marketed for general use. The 'task' required of the respondent varies from test to test, the most common being rating items on a numerical scale, ranking, and choosing between ready-made answers to set questions.

This body of work, though possessing some degree of methodological unity, is far from consistent in its findings. Deep discrepancies have constantly been appearing, and many of these have never been adequately resolved. In a number of cases instruments that might be expected to cover comparable ground give incompatible measurements; and (more serious from a psychometric standpoint) there is little similarity between the 'factors' extracted from the different tests. The situation appeared to be that of a 'degenerating problem shift' (again to use the terminology of Lakatos) within the research programme, an indication that it might be nearing the end of its useful life.

The measurement of values underwent something of a revival, however, as a result of the work of Rokeach (1973), who was determined to rescue American social psychology from the instrumentalities of such dubious agencies as the advertiser and the salesman, and to reinstate it as a discipline that would illuminate areas of universal human concern. His work on values is based on the assumption that all persons over the age of about eleven possess a 'personal value system', made up of a relatively small number of value elements. These form part of the 'core' of the personality, though the position of elements within the 'system' may vary gradually with time, or as a result of certain kinds of experience in which 'dissonance' occurs. During the ten or so years that his research instrument has been available for general use, it has been put to a variety of purposes. The total of reported studies in which it has been used is still small when compared with research using the instrument devised by Allport, though the variety of contexts in which it has been used may already be greater. The 'measurement of values' research programme appears to have moved again into a progressive phase.

The Analysis of Moral Judgment

This research programme, whose inauguration is normally attributed to Piaget (1932), has a more subtle aim than that of simple 'measurement'. Its concern is to try to understand the way in which human beings interpret their social environment, and in particular the stages and processes by which one kind of outlook is transformed into another. Whereas the 'measurement' approach has tended to deal with values-in-general, it is characteristic of this style of research to mark off morality as a separate domain, and to focus attention specifically on moral judgment.

Piaget's foundation study was carried out with children aged four to twelve. Two of his methods required the participant to make judgments in relation to hypothetical situations, and the third was based on a feature of the children's everyday life—the game of marbles. From this work Piaget did not conclude that there was a single simple sequence in the development of moral thinking. He did suggest, however, that beyond the age of about five or six, two main stages can be distinguished. The first, termed moral realism, involves a view of rules as external, grounded in authority, to be applied rigidly and without regard to circumstances. The second stage is characterized by the ability to take another's point of view; judgment is more flexible, taking motives and circumstances into account. Piaget claimed that a child's moral thinking is generally made up of a mixture of the two stages; he also suggested that both types of moral outlook are liable to persist in adults, even though their qualitative expression is different from that which is found in children. Piaget's work, though open to many criticisms (for example, its unsophisticated treatment of social class and its neglect of the influence of parents), was extremely rich in ideas and insights. It marked the beginning of the cognitive-developmental research programme in the domain of morality. For a number of years this was concerned mainly with the validation, extension and modification of the original work.

The research programme took on a new direction, and gained fresh impetus, with the publication of the work of Kohlberg (1963; see also Kohlberg in Gage, 1963). He had found grounds for dissatisfaction both with the psychodynamic accounts of moral development, and with the psychological study of 'virtue', which seemed to give few indications of personal consistency at the behavioural level. In his initial study, which in some respects resembled Piaget's work, he examined the moral judgment of seventy-five boys in the age-range ten to sixteen years. This was done by presenting them with several stories which posed dilemmas between the following of authority-based laws, rules or conventions, and considerations of human need or benefit. The judgments of the boys were elicited, and were followed by various probing questions. Whereas Piaget had been more concerned with the content of moral judgment, Kohlberg made an analysis of the types of moral reasoning that his subjects employed. From this material he claimed to have found six stages, which formed a genuine developmental sequence, increasing in complexity and scope. These may be divided into three levels: the premoral, the conventional, and the principled. Clearly there is some overlap here with the findings of Piaget. Similar investigations were later made in other cultures (the stories being suitably modified in content, while dealing with the same issues as before), and the same sequence was apparently discovered. Kohlberg has claimed that his scheme has universal validity, on the grounds that it is based on the fundamental principle of justice, which underlies the variety of cultural mores and values.

This research is less sociologically oriented than that of Piaget, while making much stronger links with moral philosophy in the prescriptivist tradition; it is also conceptually more precise, and therefore more susceptible of rigorous empirical scrutiny. As a result of this refashioning, the cognitive–developmental research programme gained in complexity, vigour and richness, encompassing a large number of new empirical and conceptual problems. Among these have been longitudinal studies, testing the scheme with a wider variety of subjects, investigating the conditions under which 'stage-change' occurs, looking at the correlates of the different levels of moral judgment, and attempts at the theoretical validation of the whole scheme (see, for example, Kohlberg in Mischel, 1971). More recently such questions as whether the 'moral atmosphere' of institutions can be assessed, the relation between moral judgment and religious faith, and the philosophical adequacy of Kohlberg's higher stages have been added to the programme. Kohlberg's claims are bold, and are very appealing to researchers and moral educators in pluralistic society; for he appears to resolve the dilemma of those who believe in the autonomy of the moral domain, and yet recognize and respect the diversity of cultures.

There are many criticisms of this work scattered through the literature; perhaps Kohlberg has not yet sufficiently indicated an appreciation of the cumulative weight of the challenges to his position. He has been accused, for example, of implicitly commending a particular view of moral excellence, of confusing content and form, of insufficiently distinguishing cognitive development from moral development, of failing to deal adequately with motives and emotions, of not producing a genuine developmental sequence, of sexist bias, and of offering such sketchy stories in the research interview that they cannot count, for the respondent, as realistic dilemmas. All this, however, need not necessarily be taken as a sign that the research programme is in decline. Perhaps the most serious sign of deterioration is the way in which the weakness of the empirical and theoretical roots of the six-stage scheme appears to be forgotten by those who work within this research programme; the publication of a scoring manual for the moral judgment interview may well lead to the institutionalization of categories that are by no means firmly established, and are not a necessary part of the 'hard core' at all.

Some Common Points of Weakness

It might seem strange that these two traditions of research, the one originating with Allport and the other with Piaget, should have coexisted for over forty years with so few indications of interaction or cross-fertilization. Yet situations of this kind are a common feature of the social sciences, whose subject matter is so rich that it can be validly investigated in a wide variety of ways. In the light of the understanding of scientific practice that has grown out of the debate surrounding Kuhn's analysis of paradigms, and particularly the work of Lakatos, there is a relatively simple explanation. For progress to be made in any science, it is necessary to restrict attention and work within a 'research programme'. It does not appear to be possible to make an empirical study of the natural or the social world while allowing all concepts to be in a state of flux; while having, so to speak, a completely open mind. Thus a few hard-core assumptions have to be fixed, in order to allow the work to go forward; some phenomena, and some' theoretical possibilities, are necessarily excluded. In the case under discussion those who have chosen to 'measure values' have ignored the likelihood that the respondents are in different stages of cognitive development, and therefore both hold values and interpret test material by means of schemata of varying sophistication; the cognitive developmentalists, on the other hand, have made an immense simplification in separating off morality from the broader topic of values (cf. von Wright, 1963). In ways such as these all practising scientists are bound to have their vision channelled and their objectives limited while they are engaged upon their work; this need not be a drawback, provided that they are aware of what their commitment has entailed.

Despite differences in subject matter and empirical style, there are certain features that these two research programmes have in common, and that make them less convincing as major keys to the understanding of morality and values. There is, of course, always a danger in making comments of this kind, in that one may be upbraiding a piece of science for failing to carry out tasks that it was never designed to fulfil. However, adherents of both programmes have made very strong claims about the power of their theories to give fundamental insight into the human condition. In both cases it has been asserted that there has been a radically new understanding of the relationship of belief to behaviour, and in both cases a theoretical scheme has been put forward that is alleged to be applicable to all humanity. It is in the light of such claims that the following criticisms are made.

One major weakness is that neither the psychometricians nor the cognitive developmentalists have a conception of the person that is clear and adequate for their field of inquiry. An examination of the theorizing that has taken place within both research programmes might not suggest such a conclusion. If, however, the matter is judged on the basis of practice—the conception of the person that is necessarily entailed by the research procedures themselves—the position appears to be very different. In the actual conduct of research, where the respondent is subjected in the one case to a ready-made questionnaire, and in the other to a moral judgment task, there is a crucial reduction. This might be justified for some research purposes, particularly in the physiological domain of psychology. It will not suffice, however, for the avowed aims of the research programmes under discussion. In order to deal adequately with either morality or values-in-general, a much more substantial conception of the person is required: as an individual, but also as one who exists in a social and historical context. To say this is not to blame those who work within these research programmes for failing to carry out empirical work that lies beyond their self-appointed limits. But, in so far as they work without an explicit conception of the person as a social being, or draw *ad hoc* on other theories, their hard-core assumptions are inadequate.

A second point of weakness is very closely connected. In the more recent development of both research programmes there has been little serious concern with the life-situation of the respondents, with understanding the actual social world within which they operate, from their own point of view. This might be judged unnecessary for some kinds of research—even, perhaps, for behavioural studies of morality in the old style—but this can hardly be said for research programmes that explicitly set out to grasp, from the 'inside', a person's value-related beliefs and outlook. Both programmes theorize a great deal about social life;

how values are acquired and modified, for example, or the kinds of social experience that promote the development of moral judgment. But they do so without incorporating into the core of their methodology any means for ascertaining how a person's categories of thought are related to day-to-day existence. The cognitive developmentalists have the aim of understanding the person as a moral philosopher, but in the practice of their research they investigate very much on their own ground. It is they who devise the hypothetical dilemmas, and have *a priori* grounds for isolating only the respondent's prescriptive utterance for analysis, bypassing the possibility that very sophisticated discourse, related to the person's actual style of life, might be carried on in other terms.

Perhaps there are lessons to be learned here from the study of general intelligence, to which Kohlberg's work is obliquely related. For it has gradually become clear that it is unrealistic to evaluate competence in the abstract, rather than in relation to the problems that a person is frequently engaged in solving. The 'measurement of values' programme, at least as exemplified in the work of Rokeach, is perhaps closer to everyday life in this respect. Although he hypothesizes the centrality of values to the person by relating them to the dubious concept of 'need', the heterogeneous collection of value items that he uses might be justified in another way. We live in a culture that contains, so to speak, the eroded residues of many theories and codes of ethics: Platonist, Jewish, Roman, Thomist, Puritan, Utilitarian, Marxist, Evolutionary, Freudian and Existentialist. Our social life also carries vestiges of the mores of communities and classes that have now passed out of existence. It seems likely that most people, according to their social experience, come to make use of some of these fragments, though without clear awareness of the fact. It is the relative salience of some of these that an instrument like that of Rokeach might, in favourable circumstances, be assessing. This, however, is only a small step in the direction of understanding the person in a social setting, because the method operates at a level of abstraction that obscures many real and significant distinctions.

When this criticism is pressed a little further we come up against another difficulty with both research programmes. Their theories of social action, implicit in the hard-core assumptions and partially made explicit, are inadequate to the phenomena of everyday life. The value theorist tends to pose the question in such terms as 'how are personal values implemented in action?' Some answers take a model from microeconomic rationalism, within which values are rank-ordered and probable net payoffs maximized; such a view goes back to the early work of Talcott Parsons, and is particularly clearly expounded by A. Kuhn (1966). Others take a more mechanistic and deterministic position; values are either causal agents themselves, operating in the core of the personality, or at least are the way causal agencies become manifest to consciousness (e.g. Rokeach, 1973). Cognitive developmentalists tend to put a parallel question in the form 'how is a person's stage of moral judgment related to moral action?' The weak answer is that the research programme is centrally concerned with categories of thought, because these have greater stability than action, and so can be the more reliably assessed. The strong answer, based on Piaget's work on the genesis of concrete operations, is that thought itself is part of action. In the moral area, it is claimed, to know the good is to do the good, and the greater the extent of a person's knowledge (the higher the stage of moral judgment), the closer will be the congruence between what a person believes and what he does. When it comes to the empirical study of belief and action, however, both research programmes tend to adopt a relatively weak tactic, derived from a more behaviouristic tradition; that is, to study correlations between indicators of values or moral judgment, somewhat crude measures of behaviour in natural or experimental settings and other variables.

Views of this kind gain plausibility when certain kinds of case are assumed to be typical, and are taken as general models for the understanding of social action. The paradigm case for the value theorist is the major (and solitary) decision, in relation to which a person is able to weigh up as many factors as possible, perhaps for convenience expressing some of these as abstract values; that for the cognitive developmentalist is the moral dilemma, whose resolution requires the deployment of the most advanced moral arguments of which a person is capable. By far the greater part of social life, however, is not of this kind. Action has to be generated spontaneously, or very nearly so, in response to rapid appraisals of each situation. It is possible, of course, to introduce qualifications (for example, that only certain values are 'activated' on each occasion, or that a person's moral outlook affects the way situations are perceived) in the attempt to produce a general theory of social action; such attempts would be worthwhile if there were no satisfactory alternative.

To say this is not in any way to deny the importance of the calculated decision or the classic moral dilemma, or the necessity for having a theory about these; it is simply to argue their inadequacy as a basis for more general theories. Whereas for the big decisions and dilemmas it may well be justifiable to treat the person as a separate entity and mainly to look vertically, to the individual mind, for an explanation of the outcome, such simplicity will not suffice for understanding the majority of social life. For this we must also look horizontally, to the context and the circumstances, to gain a proper understanding (cf. Rubinstein, 1977). A view of this kind has long been held, in a general way, by sociologists in the *verstehen* tradition (cf. Outhwaite, 1975); central to the whole programme has been the assumption that thought and action can be rightly understood only by reference to the larger context which gives them their meaning. This view has not, however, until recently been articulated in a detailed theory of action at the social–psychological level.

Arising from this very broad criticism there is a more specific point to consider. Neither research programme has required of its practitioners a serious reflection on what takes place during the conduct of research, when tests are taken, moral judgment interviews conducted or experiments performed. Yet all of this is social action, not in any way exempt from factors of the kind that operate in everyday life, and often having particular constraints in addition. People do not give 'pure' data about themselves, in the sense of objective descriptions of some other person who exists, so to speak, independently of the testing situation (as is implied by psychometricians who wish to correct for 'social desirability' responses); nor do they necessarily manifest the full extent of their competence, if the task is uncongenial or the situation one in which they are ill at ease. This point seems to have been largely overlooked thus far by the cognitive developmentalists. For it is clear that Kohlberg's moral judgment interview contains implicit rules of action; until these are carefully examined the character-istics of some of his data, particularly those obtained from working-class respondents and people in cultures very different from that of the West, remain problematic.

A striking illustration of the whole problem is found in the report by Feather (1975) of his work with the Rokeach value survey. He observed that 'delinquent' boys in an institution apparently valued being clean more than all other modes of conduct, whereas a control group ranked this value last. After considering various possibilities he eventually explains the 'anomaly' by suggesting that this response was given because of the particular social situation of the boys being tested. In making this single admission he has, of course, cast doubt on the validity of all measurements of values in which the characteristics of the testing situation are ignored.

Both research programmes, then, despite their undoubted strengths, have serious drawbacks even in relation to their explicit aims. Much of the work that has passed as a coherent body of fact and theory may have little relevance to the understanding of the conduct of most people in everyday life. Some of it may turn out to have been a kind of fantasy, an emanation from the university campus: valid and coherent on its own terms, but reflecting the life and concerns of academics rather than those upon whom they have carried out the research. 'Values' may indeed function as a major part of the conceptual resources of people in this and similar social classes, who experience an unusual freedom from external constraint, and who are able to exercise a quasi-economic rationality in many of their choices. Perhaps also it is not entirely a coincidence that the stages of moral judgment as outlined by Kohlberg exhibit a remarkable isomorphism with the prevailing type of experience that people have at different points in the social stratification system. In particular, the post-conventional morality of the higher stages looks like a very sensible adaptation for highly mobile, independent and free-thinking people, of whom the academic is a typical example. The complaint might be made that this is a travesty of the whole position, though Kohlberg himself has admitted that a person's stage of moral judgment is an embarrassingly good predictor of occupational success in Western capitalist society. There appear to be issues here that cannot be confronted adequately within either of the research programmes, at least as they stand at present. An approach is required that takes social and historical factors seriously into account, while still being distinctively psychological in its orientation.

Features of a 'Realist' Methodology

Thus far this chapter has been concerned mainly with the way two major research programmes have developed, with particular reference to their scope and claims; in terms of ethical theory, the first has a loose but unacknowledged affinity to the naturalist position, while the second makes strong and explicit links with prescriptivism. If now they are examined in another way—in relation to their methodological pedigrees—a further set of differences comes into focus. The 'measurement of values' tradition, despite repeated professions of aiming to take a phenomenological standpoint, is thoroughly positivist in practice. It remains at the level of regularities in the phenomena (of which the central part consists of scores on psychological tests), and deals in correlations rather than causes. In some cases, of which the work of Rokeach is a clear example, generative processes are hypothesized; but these are a long way removed from the research procedures themselves and, while serving to legitimate the theory, cannot be regarded as integral to the scientific work itself. The cognitive developmental research programme, on the other hand, at least in its more recent manifestations, belongs to the very different tradition of rationalism, which is sometimes traced back via Descartes to Plato, and beyond that to the Pythagoreans. In its ancient form this doctrine held that the ultimate truths are directly known to the mind, without the mediation of the senses. Its more modest contemporary version asserts that scientific abstractions should possess logical coherence. At the frontiers of physics, then, the truths to be sought are mathematical; while in psychology it is sound practice to draw out logically integrated structures from the flux of 'living thought'.

Both of these philosophical traditions, the one characteristically Anglo-Saxon and the other French, have been very fruitful in the development of science, and specifically in developing systematic understanding of the human condition. There is a third type of approach, which matured in the German science of the seventeenth, eighteenth and nineteenth centuries—though it also has an ancient origin, for example in the work of the Greeks of Alexandria. Realism, as this tradition is often termed, has been in abeyance in the philosophy of science during the greater part of this century, under the reign of positivism, but has undergone something of a revival during the last decade or so (e.g. Harré, 1970; Baskhar, 1974). Realists adhere to some version of the distinction between phenomenon and essence; they assume that there are generative processes 'behind' the phenomena, some of which are directly accessible, while others may be handled, at least for a time, by means of plausible analogy. A realist epistemology seems to be particularly applicable to chemistry and the biological sciences.

Although there are major precedents at the sociological level, the extent to which a realist methodology can be actualized in social psychology is still an open question. A research programme with this as its deliberate intent is still in its infancy, working out its necessary hard-core assumptions, and its positive and negative heuristic. It is clear that it will place its primary emphases very differently from much of the social psychology of the last forty years, of which the two research programmes discussed in this chapter are good examples. The whole approach sets out to be non-reductionist: that is, to treat the human being, even for the purposes of science, as a person (Harré and Secord, 1972). Among other things, this means that any models used for the explanation of regularities in the phenomena are to be derived from human rather than inanimate sources. The prime concern is with the understanding of everyday life, rather than with the human being in laboratory conditions; if, however, any form of laboratory is used, all that takes place there is to be regarded as social action, subject to the same kind of constraints as those that apply in everyday life. The realist approach is fundamentally reflexive, in that both the researcher and the researched-upon are viewed as perceptive and active; for all their differences in knowledge and background, neither is in a privileged position.

This methodology addresses itself centrally, rather than obliquely, to the problem of action. The focus of attention is on the maintenance of social life, and on the way individuals perform in collaboration with others. For the purposes of research there are two main components to be studied: actions, by means of which social acts are accomplished, and accounts, by means of which actions are interpreted to others. It is assumed that in the giving of the latter a person draws on the same stock of social knowledge as is available for all performances. The realist research programme set out at first to divide social life into coherent consecutive fragments, paying particular attention to the nature of the rules by which each 'episode' is structured (Harré, in Mischel, 1974), though it has now broadened its scope considerably. It is very well suited for the discursive study of values in everyday life.

One of the main aims in the handling of data is the eliciting of what might be termed 'concrete abstractions'. The rationale of such a procedure is well described by De Waele and Harré (Harré, 1976) in their discussion of the study of personality. Here they draw an analogy between their approach and the method of anatomy, which involves the painstaking examination and subsequent comparison of individual cases. Generalizations emerge, of course, but these are very different from those that are extracted by nomothesis on the basis of naive *a priori* considerations. A main type of end product from such research, as with anatomy, is a series of concrete rather than mathematical abstractions, which serve as a guide to the understanding of the class that they represent. There is, perhaps, a degree of arbitrariness in their construction, and they may have a restricted range of applicability (just as there are limitations in applying the anatomy textbook to particular cases). They do, however, often have much greater illuminatory power than numerical data, from which all qualitative aspects are finally drained away. If this methodology is to be applied to the study of values in everyday life a model of the person is required, along with a description of what 'having values' might mean. It is to these problems that we must now turn.

Resources for Model-Making

The question of how to develop an adequate conception of the human being has seriously vexed the social sciences at least since the time of Descartes. With the rapid proliferation of social research since the Second World War the controversy surrounding such issues has greatly intensified. In psychology there has also been a growing awareness of the dehumanizing tendency of some branches of the discipline, and of the way it has so readily become part of the apparatus of social control. Concern has been expressed to reinstate psychology as a moral science, by means of which the freedom and personal resources of individuals might be increased (e.g. Chein, 1972; Shotter, 1975). Contributors to the debate about the person have differed widely in their understanding of the nature of scientific activity, in their conception of social action and in the extent of their knowledge of relevant research. They have taken a range of positions on the vexed questions of whether it is possible to be 'genuinely scientific' and 'genuinely human' (depending on what 'genuine science' and a 'genuinely human approach' are supposed to be). Constantly it appears that sociologists, psychologists and philosophers have penetrated the same territory, apparently not realizing the extent to which others have already been there under another name. In discussing human thought and action it is almost impossible to avoid making use of models, similes, metaphors or analogies. Even the term 'person', of course, is not exempt, since it originally meant a mask; a theory of social life based on this conception seems to have been widely held in the Europe of the Middle Ages and the Renaissance.* Some models are more or less implicit ('withdrawn behaviour', 'emotional block'); others show their presence more obviously in the jargon of particular explanatory schemes ('repression', 'exchange theory', 'cognitive dissonance'). This fact poses a number of problems for the development of a science of the human being, particularly over the question of the relationship between the model and reality itself. It must also be said that some of the disputes between rival research programmes are not so much about directly empirical questions as about which model of the person is to be preferred.

In the natural sciences there have been two main views about the function of models. For positivists they serve simply as heuristic aids, and that is the end of the matter. Realists, on the other hand, give them a more substantial function. The most useful kind of

---

*See, for example, the discussion by Elliott (1970).

model is one that applies knowledge of a mechanism or quasi-mechanism that is relatively well understood to some area where there is as yet no direct means of understanding how the phenomena are caused. Thus the model provides an analogy which 'stands in' for the actual generative process, until such time as it can be investigated more directly (cf. Harré, 1970). The hope is that two of the classic aims of science—simplification and illumination—will be achieved simultaneously, because an accurate description of causal processes also enables sense to be made from some of the variety and complexity in the phenomena.

In the social sciences, however, the function of models is more problematic. Even an approximate 'fit' between theory and fact is much harder to obtain. In some cases there may well be a dilemma between the two aims of illumination and simplification, because there is no clear reason for supposing that what we can know of the underlying processes will be a great deal simpler than the phenomena themselves. The more one aims at illumination, the closer one is liable to come to the method of the novel, which characteristically describes situations, events and persons in their uniqueness. On the other hand the greater the extent to which a theory deals in generalizations, thus achieving the aim of simplicity, the harder it is to make it fit exactly to specific cases. The wide range of models, metaphors, similes and the like that have been applied to human beings in the attempt to develop scientific theories of their behaviour can be roughly divided into two categories. First, there are those that make use of aspects of the non-human world in order to find some likeness to features of behaviour or the working of the mind; second, there are those that draw directly on human experience. In both cases it is legitimate to talk about 'models', in the sense adopted by realist philosophers of science, because the relatively well understood is used as a means of interpreting phenomena that are still enigmatic. Non-human models serve mainly to simplify, and implicitly regard the person as passive; human models are more varied in their function, and characteristically exhibit the person as active. Whereas non-human models are necessarily reductionist (which may be quite appropriate for some purposes), human models are not; though in highlighting particular human powers or types of activity, other important aspects of human functioning may well be disregarded.

The collection of a list of models of the person is not a new task. Three fairly recent attempts to do this are those of Little (1972), Brewster Smith (1974) and Marshall (1977). The first of these offers a light-hearted discussion of the person as mechanism, humanist, scientist and specialist; the second approaches his subject more seriously, though possibly with less clarity, and deals with 'images of the self' as looking-glass, iceberg, onion, chooser, knower and vacuum; the third wittily demonstrates how there has always been a tendency to make mechanical allegories of mental functioning, the type of which is related to the high technology of each age; thus the mind has successively been a hydrostatic device, a library, a servo-mechanism, a computer, and a holographic system. Little examines the problem of reflexivity in some detail. The treatment given here owes something to these authors, though it extends the scope of their work and attempts to sketch the relevance of the models to the topic of values.

To adopt mechanical models or metaphors does not appear, in general, to entail distinct views about the relationship between values and human beings. Indeed, values need not have a place at all. Thus Watson (1919), in his exposition of behaviourism, gave an analogy of the person as a marine gas engine, complete with carburettor, pump, magneto and valve system; personality was 'reaction mass', and reference to consciousness was eschewed. On the other hand, values have a subsidiary place in some mechanistic schemes. Psychodynamic theory, for example, drawing extensively on the physics and chemistry of the late nineteenth century (cf. Henderson, 1972), viewed the mind as a kind of heat engine; values merely appear as a kind of deposit—a sublimate—from the engine's function. It is more common today to regard the person in the light of theories of information-processing, based on the currently popular technology of the computer. Value propositions are simply one kind of datum to be assimilated along with others; there is no difficulty here, provided that some view of the relationship between fact and value is clearly specified. There are signs that new modes of transmission and storage of information will be based on the method of holography, in which there is no need, as with the computer, to deal with discrete items of information. Theories of mental function based on this technique are already being developed. If values are incorporated into such a project, the old conception that a person's life can take on a characteristic orientation because of the pervasive presence of certain values might well be revived.

Turning now to the second type of model, derived from human existence, there is an abundance of theory suggestive of insight into what it might mean to 'have values'. It is quite common in social psychology, particularly that of the American tradition, to view the person as a 'capitalist', and to draw on the theoretical apparatus of business life (incentives, goals, risk, status, competition, exchange, achievement, etc.) to interpret social action. Values have a legitimate place in such a scheme, their meaning almost merging with that of 'value' in the economic sense. Another dominant metaphor is that which has traditionally been called the 'looking-glass self', though it might more accurately be termed the 'narcissist', the one who is searching for self-images. The first clear articulation of this idea is usually attributed to Cooley, writing just after the turn of the century. In relation to values, it suggests that a person might change principles of conduct from hour to hour, according to the reactions that are attributed to various significant others. One of the more controversial conceptions of the person is as a 'reflector', who, in coping with the objective conditions of existence, reproduces these symbolically in thought. When this idea is interpreted in a purely mechanical sense, of course, the person simply becomes a mirror; consciousness reflects, in an almost literal sense, the material conditions of life. In its human version, however, this metaphor points to the way categories of thought arise from practical activity; consciousness and existence are in a dialectical relationship, each modifying the other. Values emerge from action, as well as giving it direction.

One of the most ancient ways of viewing the person is as an actor, who puts on characteristic garments and performs in roles. The assumption is that there can be standard forms of appropriate behaviour, especially in relation to institutional life. The concept of role would stand out in sharp contrast, for example, to the seventeenth-century bourgeois idea of a 'calling'—a pattern of life (including work) in which a person engaged with conviction and dedication. Role-prescriptions 'contain' values; and in so far as a person follows the prescriptions, whether with conviction or at a distance, he or she may be said to possess values. A further metaphor is that of a 'scientist' (generally of the Popperian kind); the characteristic activity is that of continually putting forward hypotheses, testing them against reality, and modifying them accordingly. Distinctions are made by 'personal constructs', some of which may be evaluative. It is also worth pointing out that the metaphor itself implies certain values, such as detachment, willingness to revise opinions and the boldness to advance hypotheses. Still within the academic domain, the person might be regarded as a 'specialist', the one who develops a project. This highlights the fact that, because of the limitations on human energy and available time, a person's choice to pursue some activities and skills necessarily entails the neglect of others. The metaphor itself carries connotations of diligence, competence and foresight. It is implicit in the work upon which Allport based his pioneering studies of values; for the six-fold typology described earlier in this chapter may be regarded as pointing to six kinds of specialist, whose lives have gained particular colours from the character of their projects. Finally, mention must be made of the idea of the person as the 'one who overcomes' (as found in existentialist philosophy, particularly that of Nietzsche), because this suggests another aspect of 'having values': the taking of responsibility, the willingness to become an 'unfounded foundation of values', in a world that appears to be absurd. To hold values in this sense is to assert one's freedom, and begin an authentic human existence.

This extremely brief survey of some of the metaphors that have been, implicitly or explicitly, incorporated into social–psychological theory and research indicates something of the richness of the conceptual resources available for discussing the person. And it highlights a crucial problem. There are no clear or objective grounds for choosing one metaphor rather than another; each tends to illuminate some aspects of existence, while obscuring the understanding of others. Also, there is no necessary reason for being committed to a single metaphor; we might look instead for several models that have descriptive possibilities, and something corresponding to a mechanism for action-generation, since long-term and short-term meanings are not incompatible. Thus at one level a pattern of action might be an 'escape' or a 'search', lasting perhaps several years; while at another level it might be divided into many relatively short dramatic episodes and analysed in terms of the person as an actor.

To some extent, then, the choice of models and metaphors must be pragmatic, related to the purpose for which a piece of social science is being carried out. If research is sharply focused, and has moved beyond the stage of exploration and accurate description of phenomena to that of explanation, there might be ground for adopting a very restricted model of the person. On the other hand, when the main purpose is that of marshalling information in an assimilable form, it is prudent to develop a research programme with a broader range of conceptual resources, in order to 'catch hold' of more data, and in the hope of obtaining less of a mismatch between observation and the theoretical terms. At present, because of the poor state of our knowledge, if we were to adopt a single dominant metaphor and attempt to build around it a total account of 'having values', we would almost certainly fail to do justice to the available data. To try to understand values from the standpoint of the person as a 'specialist', for example, might be very illuminating, and add a great deal to existing knowledge; but if we were to concentrate on that alone, we might fail to notice transitory phenomena that would be comprehensible if we conceived of the person as a 'narcissist'. It might be fruitful, then, to attempt something more ambitious, and try to put forward a tentative account of what 'having values' means using a more complex conceptual scheme. For this, I suggest, we do not need a fundamentally new set of concepts; the raw materials are ready to hand.

A Differentiated Conception of the Person

Thus far this chapter has given only the barest indications of some of the unitary conceptions of the person that have been adopted in the social sciences, and their potential relevance to 'having values'. Unfortunately, since the 1930s, when Allport was at work as a socially oriented psychologist and Mead as a psychologically oriented sociologist, those who have directed their attention mainly on society, and those who have focused their attention primarily on individuals, have gone their different ways. The former, especially those in the structural–functionalist tradition, have tended to treat values as part of the whole hypothesized socio-cultural system (e.g. Parsons, 1967). Even when assumptions about broad societal consensus are rejected, values are seen as belonging to some smaller group or class. On the other hand, psychologists who have believed that the topic is worthy and capable of investigation have taken it as non-problematic that values 'belong' to individuals. Often their empirical method has been simple, leading to a simple conclusion: to 'have values' is to have made certain responses to a values questionnaire.

If this general diagnosis is approximately correct, it seems unlikely that a single metaphor of the person, or a single theory of social action, will be adequate to the problem of understanding the relationship between values and persons. Here we need an approach that acknowledges the validity of work in both the sociological and psychological traditions; which takes individuality into account, but which recognizes the proximal and distal social contexts in which the person exists. A model which fits these requirements has been put forward by Ruddock (1972), in an essay entitled 'Conditions of Personal Identity'. Although Ruddock has not himself explicitly related the model to the question of 'having values', it can be fruitfully used for this purpose, granted minor modifications and extensions.*

The broad aim of Ruddock's model is to show how work in several social science traditions, including psychodynamic theory,

---

*I acknowledge with gratitude the help that Ralph Ruddock has given in helping me to interpret his ideas, and in commenting on an earlier version of this chapter. The responsibility is mine, however, for any distortions that may have occurred, and for the adaptation of the model to the topic of values.

symbolic interactionism, social anthropology, existentialist psychology and role theory, can be reconciled to give a body of knowledge that approximates to coherence. He is careful to avoid instances where two or more theories simply use rival terminologies to account for the same range of phenomena, but recognizes that there are many cases where alternative theories are actually dealing with different aspects of the person. The purpose is to provide a unified but not tautologous way of describing a variety of human behaviour and experience, of bringing synchronic and diachronic aspects together.

It should be emphasized, however, that this is not a brash attempt at constructing a comprehensive 'science of the person'. I have already argued, on the basis of the theory of research programmes, that such a project is not feasible. In terms of the same theory, it might be said that the model is a synthesis of components from several approaches whose core assumptions are not incompatible. The exposition of Ruddock's work given here is very brief, since it is simply a summary of already published material, and his citations are not repeated. Each of the terms is used in a precise way; there is a danger that meanings might be read into them from other contexts, which are not applicable in this case.

The model is built up around a *self*, which roughly corresponds to the 'I' of symbolic interactionism. This is the inner centre, the 'psychic nucleus', the locus of the sense of continuity that human beings commonly experience. The self may thus be regarded as that which undergoes experience, and as the source of thought and action. Beyond this point a realist social psychology requires no further explanation of the existence of human vitality.

In order to develop a theory of very close relationships (often dyadic), Ruddock uses the concept of *perspective*, drawing on ideas that were first outlined by Buber and later developed into a workable scheme by Laing and his associates. Action in this mode is not rule-bound in a simple sense, but is based on each person making intuitive appraisals of how he or she is being perceived by the other(s). The early relationships of 'normal' childhood are, from the child's point of view, largely of this character, even if at only a rudimentary level. What is sometimes known as the 'self-image' may be regarded, at least in the early years of life, as a distillation of information received by means of perspectives. As a person gains in maturity and becomes able to imagine the standpoint of another, all kind of complexities develop; the interchange of perspectives occurs not only directly, but also at higher-order levels. When these are in correspondence, a relationship is robust and satisfying; but when attributions are inappropriately made the consequences may be dire, and it may appear to those who are involved that they are caught in a trap from which there is no escaping. Behaviour at a lower level of intimacy is handled by the concept of *role*, illustrating the way each person comes to play a number of parts, relating to different groups of people in various social settings. Ruddock visualizes the collection of roles as being like a tree, branching out from a single social definition, such as 'teenager', or 'widow', to the variety of transient styles that a person adopts in interaction with others, taking on such functions as jester, critic or support. Each human being begins to occupy recognizable roles during childhood; the roles tend to proliferate, and perhaps to be sharply demarcated from one another, as life continues.

Most psychological theories recognize that past experience in some way has a cumulative effect upon the person. Using a geological metaphor, it is possible to envisage the laying down of a succession of deposits from earlier relationships at the perspective level, and from performance in previous roles. These might take the form of habits of thought and action, areas of skill and incompetence, particular anxieties, expectations and views about the self. All this is summed up in the term 'personality'. A person's current performance is envisaged as being structured to some extent as a result of these residues from the past; indeed, to have a 'normal' personality may well mean that there are some roles that cannot be sustained at all.

Another component of the model is the *project*. This is derived mainly from existentialist theory and its assertion of responsibility and freedom, but also from Jung's rejection of the deterministic idea that all behaviour is, so to speak, 'pushed' from behind. For there are some kinds of action, and long-term patterns of growth in a human life, that are not encompassed by the more conventional social–psychological concepts. Each person has something to do that is unique; each is developing in relation to some image, perhaps hardly recognized at the conscious level, of a possible future state. The project may show itself in the activities to which a person becomes committed, though these are only part of a larger pattern. The bringing of a project to fruition corresponds roughly to what other theories describe as becoming 'self-actualized' or 'self-realized'; for Jung the appropriate term was 'individuation'.

The last of the concepts in the model is *identity*, which refers to the degree of coherence, of inner completeness, that a person has achieved; also, qualitatively, to the basis on which that coherence is established. In the early stages of life such identity as a person has is largely conferred by others, though later this may be modified by discovery or conscious choice. Following Goffman, Ruddock uses the analogy of a 'holding company' for the various roles; he does not, however, limit the concept of identity to this aspect, since a more profound coherence also involves personality, perspectives and the project. The concept of personal identity incorporates what other theorists might term a generalized self-image, and the complex of associated belief and affect that is known as self-esteem. (A person's self-image may, of course, be fragmented, and there may be more self-esteem in relation to one area of life than in relation to another, in which case the degree of personal identity would be said to be low).

It should be noted that, while a strong personal identity implies consistency, this can be of different kinds. A person whose identity is derived mainly from one or more roles, or from powerful elements in the personality, may well show a rigidity of outlook and behaviour of a kind that is generally regarded as undesirable. If, however, the identity is based primarily in human relationships, a person's life would be expected to be spontaneous, self-directed and even somewhat unpredictable: its consistency would be less immediately evident to the short-term observer.

Such a brief account does not do justice to Ruddock's elaborately articulated scheme, and blurs many of the subtleties of his analysis. Each component is developed from well established theory; the synthesis thus achieved is intended to enable a more rounded understanding of the person than any single conceptual scheme would provide. The model might be regarded as a conflation of the metaphors of narcissist, actor, and specialist, together with an attribution of the corresponding powers; the possibility of authentication, the existentialist conception of 'the one who overcomes', is also envisaged. It is necessary to bear in mind that there is no intention here of crudely dividing the person into parts, in the manner of Watson's marine gas engine; it is the model, rather than the person, that is thus analysed. In a sense the use of a model of this kind amounts to the assertion that we are justified in developing several interrelated schemata rather than one for the description and explanation of social action. This gives greater scope, but brings with it the serious problem of deciding when to apply one set of concepts rather than another.

In the context for which it was devised, this model serves well. It elucidates descriptions of subjective states such as 'feeling ill at ease' or 'disliking oneself', and reflexive sentences such as 'I have to force myself to concentrate'. The scheme illustrates some of the different modes of interpersonal relating, which are classified, in increasing order of intensity, as centring on role, personality-in-role, perspective, and identity; it is recognized that relationships are not necessarily symmetric. The model also carries the implication that different kinds of therapy and counselling may be not so much rivals for the same domain as addressed to different kinds of malaise—Freudian analysis, for example, being mainly concerned with the personality, and Jungian with the project. Perhaps of greater significance is the fact that the model enables social–psychological sense to be made of biographical data, since it integrates synchronic description with theories of long-term and short-term change. It is thus admirably suited to a realist research programme. The kind of scheme that has been proposed for the analysis of relatively short fragments of social action (Harré, in Armistead, 1974), using the categories of situation, persona, arbiter and rule, would then belong to Ruddock's level of personality-in-role; but there would be scope for realist analyses appropriate to other social modes, covering periods of time of different duration.

The scheme is, of course, far from comprehensive. There are some aspects of the person with which it does not attempt to deal. No mention is made of cognitive structures, and there is no clear place for dealing with intra-group and inter-group phenomena as such. Rather than add on further components to handle such aspects of the person, which would make the model unwieldy, it is more fruitful to regard it as the basis for a research programme that cuts across the fields of several others. Thus some of the social interaction believed by Kohlberg and his followers to be significant in moral development belongs to the category of role, some to perspective and some to identity. To have become consolidated at the principled level of moral judgment in Kohlberg's scheme (for example his paradigm case of Martin Luther King) would almost certainly mean having attained a high degree of personal identity; the converse seems to be less plausible. In short, while there may be occasional exact correspondences with other frameworks, the fact cannot be avoided that alternative research programmes are generally not commensurable.

If the model is to be used to illuminate what might be meant when a person is said to 'have values', it requires a little modification. Ruddock has used the term 'role' rather broadly; the major limbs of his 'role-tree' are made, so to speak, of different stuff from the smaller branches. Precision would be gained if the use of the concept of role were confined to situations that are relatively tightly structured, where distinct expectations are placed upon performance; typically these would be in institutions and formally constituted groups—the domain covered by the theory and research of the major exponents of role analysis at the social–psychological level (e.g. Biddle and Thomas, 1966). An important feature is the possibility of distancing the self from the action, and for many kinds of manifestation of what existentialists would call 'bad faith'. There is a strong tendency for this to occur under coercive regimes, where a person may go through the motions of role-performance, thus avoiding retribution for non-conformity, while hoping to maintain a private identity, diminished but intact. The concept also casts light on a peculiarly modern problem; with the increase of mobility it has become possible for a person to perform many roles, conform to many expectations, and in so doing to forfeit a substantial sense of personal identity.

For the understanding of the relation between values and the person, the most notable omission of the model is that it does not allow account to be taken of the way meaning is created, maintained and transmitted within a cultural tradition. The person is successfully located in the objective social system, but the fact of existence in one or more zones where meanings are shared needs clearer articulation. In ready-made theory the term that comes nearest to an effective treatment of this aspect of human life is 'social life-world', as used by contemporary authors such as Berger, Berger, and Kellner (1974). This refers to those socially constructed realities that are commonly taken for granted, virtually as if they were part of the natural order. It is within a social life-world that 'normal' activities are carried out in collaboration with other people; day-to-day life continues more or less smoothly because those involved are constantly drawing on shared assumptions, beliefs and meanings. The origins of this concept are in the phenomenological tradition, notably in the work of Husserl, and later that of Schutz (Kockelman, 1967). Both these authors described a person as possessing a single 'social life-world', suggesting that this is experienced as if it were arranged into different 'fields', some of which are perceived as having greater salience than others. Berger, however, modifies the usage, often applying the term in the plural, and emphasizing a social life-world as the shared possession of a number of people. He shows how one of the most characteristic features of life for the individual in modern industrial society is the 'pluralization of life-worlds'; there is no single framework of meanings within which existence is given significance.

The concept of 'social life-world' as a seventh component in the model provides a backcloth against which the other six take on a new significance. Most people exist in several social life-worlds; action and relationships within any one of these may be at one or more of the levels already described. For example, within the social life-world of work a person is likely to occupy one or more distinct roles, and also to have some relationships at the level of interpersonal perspectives. As the project evolves it will probably require the integration of action across the various social life-worlds. The development of a strong personal identity would seem necessarily to entail a resolution between different systems of meaning that at a first-order level were apparently unrelated or even incompatible.

If such considerations apply to adults, they do so with possibly even greater relevance to adolescents, whose faculties for discerning meaning develop dramatically, at precisely the same time as their social experience is greatly enlarged. The model gains in another way by the introduction of the concept of 'social life-world': it now becomes possible to give an account of the social scientist who makes theories, carries out research or even attempts to develop integrated models of the person, since these activities are themselves legitimated by shared meanings. In other words, the model now becomes fully reflexive.

The adoption of a scheme such as this, which uses several components, keeps a greater number of options open; it invites the social scientist to deploy a variety of conceptual meshes, rather than being prematurely committed to a theory that might not be apposite. This is a sound policy when one is striving mainly to obtain an accurate and critical description of the phenomena; at a later stage it may be possible to use tools of greater precision. Despite an enormous volume of research we are not yet, I believe, at that point in the understanding of values in English adolescent life.

What Does 'Having Values' Mean?

A model such as has been described would have many advantages for the empirical study of values; in particular, it would enable a wealth of data to be assimilated without having to sacrifice the sharp sense of the uniqueness of each person. It might be possible to avoid both the Scylla of gross reduction, as occurs in many psychological research programmes, and the Charybdis of undisciplined ideographic description, in the manner of the novel. As a first step, the model can be used to illustrate some of the ways in which values might be 'attached' to persons.

Values and Social Life-world

Since society is antecedent to the individual, our account must start here. Values become deeply embedded in social processes

during the course of their evolution: the means of providing for
physical necessities, together with the accompanying fabric of laws,
customs, education, medical practice and religious beliefs. In some
cases the incorporation of values has been deliberate; there are
many instances where planned actions have had unexpected
consequences, involving modification of existing values or the
emergence of new ones; also, we have to reckon with many cases
where values have evolved without anyone having made relevant
plans at all. In these and other ways, as people develop characteristic modes of action in relation to the material and social
possibilities that they perceive to be available to them, patterns of
preference and standards for judging persons and situations are
established, gradually becoming part of the 'taken-for-granted
world'. Values are thus a major part of culturally shared outlooks,
attitudes and meanings. In real life it is extremely difficult to
separate beliefs about 'what is' from those about 'what ought to
be', as was clearly recognized by Kluckhohn and Strodtbeck
(1961) in their conception of a 'value-orientation', and is made
explicit by those holding a naturalist view of ethics. Gradually
values are incorporated into both vocabulary and the way
language is used, since this inevitably reflects the central concerns
of a community, and hence its action-guiding principles.

Before a person is born, then, values are already 'there' within a
culture or subculture. They are, so to speak, part of the air that
everyone is breathing. Later, perhaps with the experience of
contradictory systems of meaning, or some traumatic tearing-apart
of personal life, there may be a realization of the way in which
social existence has been fabricated by human beings, and of the
fact that it does not necessarily have to be the way it is. Although it
is difficult for a person who lives within a social life-world
to appreciate its contingent character, and the nature and extent of
the values that are embedded within it, these points may be much
more apparent to an observer who has another framework of
meanings to use as a basis for making comparisons. Culture shock
may be partially explained as a sudden awareness that a previously
taken-for-granted world is a social construction, and the
accompanying sense that no values are securely founded.

Values and Perspectives

The theory of interpersonal perspectives implies that there may be
a highly transient mode in which a person can be said to 'have
values'. In certain kinds of interaction people do not so much
follow preconceived rules in directing their conduct as act in

accordance with the perceptions they have made of others' perceptions of themselves. Action in one 'perspective situation' may well be relatively consistent, and yet be at variance with that that takes place in another. Thus, arising from the variety of interpersonal perspectives and the possibilities and limitations which these provide, the actions of an individual may show a number of patterns which reflect, perhaps in a distorted fashion, the values held by others. Even a child of six or seven years old might appear to 'have values' in this mode. The chameleon-like way in which a person held values at the perspective level might not be evident to the other participant(s) in any perspective relationship; nor would it necessarily be obvious to an observer whose access was incomplete. It is plausible to assume that commonsense psychology, which often uses a form of trait theory and attributes considerable consistency to individuals, is restricted by the fact that systematic knowledge about a person across several sets of interpersonal perspectives very rarely occurs.

Although the concept of perspective has mainly been applied to dyadic situations, and in particular to intimate relationships between the sexes, it is not necessarily limited to such cases. The theory may well be suitable to apply to certain kinds of small group, in which there is great intimacy and no clear structure, where social life is fluid and flexible. The behaviour of the group might appear to express certain values, and the individuals who belong to it could be said to possess those values, at least during those times when the group was physically constituted.

Values and Roles

In many cultural settings it seems to be the case that beyond the age of about five a person comes to occupy distinguishable roles (which may indeed be geographically separated), and begins to feel the pressure of formalized expectations. There are rules or prescriptions for every role, one aspect of which may be discovered by asking the 'role-senders', and another aspect of which is accessible by consulting the perceptions of the person who occupies the role. The prescriptions generally take the form of rules or guidelines for appropriate conduct; these can be logically related to values, in the sense of more general and less situation-specific principles of action. Thus it may be said in a simple way that the person who performs a role according to certain perceived expectations does, in a certain sense, 'have values'; the values 'lie behind' any reference scheme for the guiding of action within the role. In such circumstances it would not so much be a matter of ranking of several relatively abstract values, but simply of making reference to rules of immediate perceived relevance.

The situation is, however, made more complex by the fact that people occupy their roles with different degrees of sincerity and commitment. Under a highly coercive regime it is even possible for the greater part of public life to be a deliberate mask, an act of deception in which no one is deceived. A social scientist under such circumstances, inquiring into values, might get no closer than value-in-role, since the research would almost certainly be viewed with suspicion; what the values meant for the identity of any one individual would remain obscure. A person who occupies a number of roles, and who does not make conscious connections between them, might 'have values' (in this limited sense) that are mutually contradictory. This is especially likely if the roles are themselves situated within different social life-worlds. A person might also be much more conscious of values implicit in one role than in another, or might operate at different levels of abstraction in each case.

Values and Personality

If personality is regarded as consisting mainly of residues from previous experience, then it follows that a person at a particular point in time may 'have values' in relation to what remains from past action at the perspective level, or performance in obsolete roles. Using another terminology, it is possible for a person to have 'internalized' some patterns of reaction to others, or prescriptions for more structured action, and for those to remain operative to some extent even after the conditions that gave rise to them no longer occur. There might also be instances where habits that had been formed, initially as a result of the deliberate implementation of values, continue long after the basis on which they were significant had disappeared. In this kind of way action acquires a colouring from previously held values. When Peters (1974) suggests that to describe a person as 'having character' means that he or she has developed a particular style of rule-following, he is occupying very similar (though more restricted) ground.

This discussion can be taken further, into the territory of classical psychoanalysis. Some of a person's values might, under some circumstances, be part of an elaborate framework for coping with a reality that is too frighteningly unpredictable and spontaneous. Action in the past may perhaps have been 'punished' severely, or the person may have made incorrect inferences from the reactions of others, with the result that some options are, for the time being, closed, and resources for handling present contingencies are limited. Freud's 'anal character'—stingy, grudging, critical and routine-bound—is a relevant example. Even more striking is the notorious and related case of the 'authoritarian personality', with its characteristic ethnocentrism, desire to dominate (or submit), and tendency to attribute moral turpitude to members of an outgroup. It does not necessarily require a full commitment to the mechanics of psychodynamic theory to acknowledge that values may become incorporated into the personality by processes about which a person may have little insight. As Rokeach (1973) has recognized, following the earlier work of Katz, it is possible for values to be transformations of fears or anxieties held at a deeper level, and thus to have an 'ego-defensive' function.

Values and Project

When the person is viewed from the standpoint of existentialism, as an individual thrown into the world and having to make sense of a period of life that is finite but of unknown duration, a different aspect of what it might mean to 'have values' comes into focus. It is possible for a person to envisage some desired future state, albeit vaguely, and to begin to formulate intentions and resolutions accordingly. The evaluative aspect of the project is thus almost coterminous with what other theorists call an aspiration: though Ruddock, following Jung in particular here, recognizes that the project may be largely undertaken on the basis of tacit knowledge, so that there may be instances where a person goes through the greater part of life without awareness of its meaning. Where the project involves a prolonged and considered commitment that runs counter to the prevailing values of society, or at least to one of its dominant social life-worlds (the campaigner for radical social change, perhaps, or the creator of a new style of art), the metaphor of the 'one who overcomes' is applicable; to take responsibility for holding and living by values outside conventional guidelines may prove to be a heavy and lonely task.

Although there is ground for thinking that the concept of the project has its clearest application to the second half of life, when people are, so to speak, within viewing distance of their own death, it may well also have a relevance to adolescence. The commitments and aspirations of youth may be considered as part of the whole project; their meaning for the person may, of course, change in the light of later experiences, and their place in the whole pattern may become apparent only when the project is virtually complete.

Values and Identity

This points to the strongest sense in which we may speak of 'having values', because a person's development may be such that certain kinds of belief are an essential part of his or her being; the abandonment of these would mean a loss of identity, and personal disintegration might well ensue. Here, perhaps, is a partial explanation of martyrdom, and of the willingness of political dissidents under totalitarian regimes to go through extremities of suffering for the sake of cherished principles such as truth or individual freedom. It seems that about the only way to obliterate the values in such cases is by a direct assault upon the identity: by reducing the person to a vegetable state by means of drugs, or by physically destroying connections in the brain.

These, however, are extreme instances. People generally develop a personal identity by means of a synthesis of fragments from the variety of positions and recurrent experiences that are available to them. They find that some frameworks of meaning are more convincing than others; they feel that certain roles are close to being an authentic expression of themselves; there are aspects of their personality that they acknowledge; they accept some 'reflected appraisals' from the perspective level as having verisimilitude; they begin to form a project that expresses the kind of person whom they conceive themselves to be. Thus in discovering or perhaps deliberately choosing an identity a person may well come to hold certain values in a particularly significant way; for those who are cognitively sophisticated, these may even be part of the basis on which integration is achieved.

Each kind of society, or stratum or group within it, poses particular problems for the development of personal identity. In a small community which formed effectively a single social life-world for work, play and domesticity, personal identity and social identity might be virtually the same. In modern industrial society many people are at another extreme: a person's life may be so fragmented, and so little sustained by any one system of meanings, that it is very difficult to find a basis for personal integration. The psychological solution may well be not to have a clear identity—to be 'hollow'—and not to 'have values' in this most profound sense, at all. The problem is less acute for those whose life is relatively flexible, who have some degree of control over the way they work, the choice of place to live and their general style of life; perhaps it is at its most serious for those who are virtually powerless before social forces that they can neither withstand nor comprehend.

Values and Self

Since it is the self that initiates action and undergoes experience, it may be said that it is ultimately the self that 'has values' in relation to all that has been discussed so far. For example, the self may be or may become aware of values embedded in the social life-worlds and in personality; the self may find satisfaction or discomfort in role-performance; the self experiences fulfilment in value-expression, guilt at value-violation, anxiety in value-conflict, enhancement in the harmony of perspectives and in the out-working of a project. Values may be held with varying degrees of proximity to the self; at the identity level there is the greatest intensity, permanence and awareness.

The Purpose and Implications of this Scheme

Since the attempt to make a synthesis of this kind for relating values to persons is still in its early stages I realize that it may have many deficiencies, and certain ambiguities that are yet to be resolved. The unashamedly naive excursions into the theories that form the components of the model have been given for illustrative purposes, and nothing of great importance hangs on the validity of my extremely brief exposition. The scheme is intended to be the basis for description rather than for explanation in terms of cause or process, though it seems likely that it could be refined for such purposes. Probably several alternative integrated models of the person could be developed, serving much the same purpose, using different conceptual components; they would, no doubt, be not strictly commensurable with the scheme outlined here. My purpose, however, has simply been to illustrate how values are woven into the fabric of human life—personal, social, institutional, cultural—in a variety of ways, and to show that instructive distinctions can be made between aspects of a very rich range of phenomena. As such, there is here a vocabulary appropriate to descriptive analysis of values and persons in the realist mode. The model extends the realist research programme somewhat by integrating a number of concepts hitherto kept separate into a single scheme, and by suggesting that action is of several kinds, to which different types of descriptive and explanatory terms might be applicable. In this way sense can be made of one of the most striking impressions that one receives when interviewing a number of people by approximately the same method, while allowing them the fullest possible freedom of expression. It is, simply, how different each person is from all others, and how little of the interpersonal variation relevant to values seems to be captured within either the positivist or the rationalist research programme discussed earlier in this chapter.

The scheme that I have proposed gives a framework for interpretation of data, but initially leaves open many important questions. It is, in effect, an invitation to the social psychologist to be ambitious and to try to understand the person holistically, risking the censure of those who would say that the concepts have an inadequate empirical grounding, or that their range of applicability is not clearly demarcated. If a single point in time is taken, the model draws attention to the fact that each person participates in several modes of social life concurrently, and that the understanding of any one of these requires knowledge of the others. If, on the other hand, change over an interval of time is studied, the model suggests a number of important developmental questions, some of which are not commonly raised by established research programmes in social psychology. We might ask, for example, whether the person has entered any new social life-world, or whether any existing frameworks of meaning have changed in salience; what new 'deposits' have been laid down in the personality; what relationships have advanced to, or receded from, the perspective level; whether there have been any modifications in the bases for personal identity. Ruddock developed his model virtually as a theory of the formation of personal identity, postulating the existence within the person of a 'strong inner drive towards integration'. Here, however, the question of personal consistency is left open; the model is no more than proto-theoretical.

It is worth noting, finally, that the concept of a *person* itself has come to be, in part, an ethical one; it has descriptive meaning, but also perhaps contains some latent imperatives. For to talk of persons is to imply that they should be treated with respect and consideration; that they should not be reduced to the level of an object. Those who participate in experiments and surveys are often designated by some other term ('subject', 'respondent', 'organism'), thus implicitly relieving the social psychologist of certain human obligations. In this inquiry there has been an attempt to work out the practical as well as the theoretical implications of dealing with persons, as the following chapter will show. In fact, had this not been done it is very unlikely that this piece of research could have been carried out at all, because adolescents are extremely sensitive to whether they are being given the status of persons. Where this is not the case, they have their own means of ensuring that nothing is extracted from them against their will.

2
The Design and Conduct of the Research

In the previous chapter reasons have been advanced for developing an approach to the study of values that would be aligned to a realist, rather than to either a rationalist or a positivist, scientific tradition. A possible theoretical position from which to carry out such research was also outlined. These considerations provide some kind of justification for the method of inquiry reported here, following the general practice when an attempt is made to legitimate a new approach. Such accounts, however, have something of the character of sales-talk, and obscure almost as much as they reveal: they are given with a particular audience in mind, and in order to achieve specific ends. The development of innovative research, as it occurs, is far from being the rational outworking of a carefully articulated plan, drawn up after all the relevant literature has been reviewed and all pertinent factors taken into account. It involves opportunism, serendipity and naive experimentation, and in its early stages only a partial awareness of what might be most significant for theory and for method. At least, it is with such a view of science that this piece of research has congruence. For although there have been some common threads running through the whole of it, the completed work looks very different from what was envisaged at the outset.

The main purpose of this chapter, then, is to sketch out the various stages in the progress of this research, drawing on notes and drafts made at the time. This shows, in approximately chronological order, some of the main developments that took place, and the basis for particular decisions about method and design. Even though intended as an alternative to more formal kinds of presentation, it still cannot pass as pure 'natural history'. Many of what at an earlier time were simply clues, intuitions or vague impressions have now become substantial; so like any retrospective account, this chapter is inevitably coloured by later considerations.

In Quest of a Method

The immediate background to this inquiry was the reviewing of a large volume of research concerned with morality and values. Considering the highly structured nature of the bulk of psychological work, it seemed that there was a place for the kind of method that, in dealing with individuals, allowed a person great freedom in talking about value-related themes: a means for qualitative exploration, such as had often been viewed merely as a prelude to the construction of a systematic testing instrument. At the same time, there was a considerable literature devoted to understanding how it might be possible to develop a social science that would be genuinely concerned with persons, that had made very little impact on research into the domain of values.

The pursuit of these and other initial lines of thought gradually crystallized into three closely related problems. The first was the practical one of developing a research method that would remedy some of the defects of existing approaches; it was also my hope that this would be such as to leave those who participated with an increase of insight and personal autonomy, or (if that was too much to expect), that at least they should not have been treated as mere objects, violated, labelled or diminished. The second was that of finding a conception or model of the person that would be able to integrate psychological and sociological approaches, and that would have the potential for explaining the research activity itself as well as the phenomena of everyday life. The third problem was that of giving some account of the relation between values and persons, thus enabling the data generated by the research to be interpreted. It was only slowly that these initial considerations were worked out, to reach a position containing some degree of internal consistency.

The method of research itself emerged as a result of various experiments and explorations over a period of about three months, with the generous collaboration of about twenty boys and girls in the age range that was to be studied. Much of this work was carried out by myself with boys in a small grammar school about to be 'comprehensivized', where I had taught for two terms during the previous year. From that time I already had good contacts with a number of the pupils, my relationship with them being somewhat different from that of a permanent teacher, since it was known that I was not a member of the school establishment. Some of the trials were made with small groups during lesson time, and some were made during the dinner hour. Valuable assistance in carrying out trials with girls was given by a part-time research student, who had the post of a pastoral teacher in a comprehensive school, where she knew some of her pupils very well. In the early stages our exploratory work was often fragmentary, sometimes hurried; much of it was subject to the contingencies of school life, and to the fluctuations of interest and commitment that are only to be expected when one is trying to involve people in a project that is not their own. Later, when the outlines of the method had taken shape, we moved out of the school context with its authoritarian connotations, and abandoned the view that researcher and researched-upon must be of the same sex. The research method was not devised from a distance, but was negotiated at almost every stage. Since it has now become plain that it is one to which many adolescents relate very readily, its development, final form and mode of operation are in themselves part of the phenomena to be interpreted.

A promising starting point for new research appeared to be an ideographic method which might elicit a person's repertoire of value constructs and explore the ways in which they were used. One possibility here was the 'situations grid', a technique devised by Kelly (1955), which had not been subsequently taken up on a scale comparable with some of his other ideas. For Kelly the main purpose of such a method was to enable an adolescent client in psychotherapy to identify the people who might be of help in certain traumatic situations. Among the circumstances envisaged were financial difficulty, making mistakes, loneliness, and trouble with parents. The client was presented with a brief and general description of each type of 'situation' and invited to indicate, out of various possible 'significant others', the one who might be of greatest and of least help, the others being ranked in between. In this way a grid could be built up, as a result of which the person would have worked out what human resources were available for times of emergency. This method at least was aimed at being anchored in the realities of adolescent life; something of relevance to the study of values might grow from it.

In the first trial studies these ideas were developed in two directions. One was to find a list of role-titles that would include the main 'significant others' in the lives of some of today's adolescents. This proved to be harder than anticipated, because it was soon evident that the idea of passive turning to others for help, implicit in Kelly's suggestions, was not judged to be appropriate. A whole range of typical modes of relating to others was described. Some of those who took part conveyed also their sense of the dynamic state of their close relationships: a person who had been judged a vital support a month previously might now not be perceived as significant at all. In this, as in other ways, adolescents were often on shifting sands. The other main aspect to be developed at this stage was the list of 'situations'. My first collection, very much in the spirit of Kelly's work, had contained descriptions of being misunderstood, frustrated, angry, conscious of failure, bored, and faced with an important decision. The underlying image, a crystallization of the stereotypical adolescent as found in commonsense psychology and its more learned extensions, was not acceptable to the participants; their characterization of themselves was more subtle than that of a victim or a rebel. Nevertheless, the underlying idea of representing adolescent life by focusing on incidents that either had particular significance or epitomized some of its main features seemed to be both meaningful and acceptable.

One of the main tasks, then, was to find a set of generalized 'situation descriptions' that was more true to life than the ones that I had initially put forward. Here it seemed more fruitful to deal with the real past than with mere hypothetical suggestions. Accordingly, the participants' part was to recall an incident in their recent experience that corresponded to each of a number of 'situation descriptions', and to write down what had happened, simply to remind themselves. There was a good deal of conversation while writing was in progress; it quickly became evident from the general manner with which they handled the task that they were engaged here in a deeper way than they had been in the preliminary work for the grids. Some of the items were striking an immediate chord with them, corresponding well with their experiences. Because the groups were small, and there had been time for a climate of mutual trust to develop, it was possible to gain a number of insights from the discussion that accompanied the trial studies. Those who took part made many constructive criticisms of what we were asking them to do. Some of these were very general—for example that we had overestimated the significance of school in their lives—while others were detailed— for example that they found a five-point rating scale easier to handle than one with only four points. The character of the 'situation descriptions' was progressively modified with their help. But the observation that had the greatest significance, considering the main aim of the research, was that the discussion of the 'situations' involved them deeply. Here, more than in any part of the trials, it seemed that we were beginning to deal (if indirectly) with values, and in a way that was true to life.

While this phase of development was going on I was still intending to reintegrate the material into some kind of grid test, though the way in which this was going to be possible became increasingly hard to discern. The aspect of the trials that had the most vitality and perceived relevance for the participants was a long way removed from the constraints of grid methodology. So at this point a crucial decision was made: to press forward with the 'situations' aspect of the pilot work, and to leave aside the grids. This involved the risk of moving into a type of research where the guidelines are relatively few, though there were strong grounds for thinking that this was the right way to go. Positively, the 'situations' seemed to provide a natural access to the participants' central concerns, and to be stimulating a kind of personal and expressive narrative that we had not previously encountered from adolescents. Negatively, there was ample cause to be wary of approaches that yielded precise numerical data but failed to represent the character of social life. Although grid methods aim at capturing something of the unique subjective world of each person, they (in common with nomothetic approaches) were weak in this respect. I certainly wished to develop an ideographic method; unlike the advocate of grids, however, I was reluctant to reduce this aspect of their subjective world to mere numbers, believing that for a proper account of values it was vital to understand the social context in which meaning is founded. A more discursive and qualitative approach was required.

From this point forward the task of the pilot studies was more clear-cut. The aim was to produce a list of 'situation descriptions' that would be relevant to values and that would enable participants to give their accounts freely, without the kind of artificiality for which some of them had criticized the tests in which they had first been involved. Work now went ahead rapidly; since detailed chronological order here is unimportant, some main aspects of the subsequent development will merely be summarized.

The first list of 'situation descriptions' had not been judged particularly appropriate, as has already been implied. By the end of the time when I was still expecting to form a link between the 'situations' and the 'significant others' along the lines suggested by Kelly, we had emerged with twelve rather better items, as shown below:

1 A situation in which you were very angry or annoyed. . . .
2 A situation in which you got on really well with people. . . .
3 A situation in which you felt you were powerless or misunderstood. . . .
4 A situation in which you were deceived, or 'had'. . . .
5 A situation in which you were very lonely, or when you felt there was no one to help you. . . .

6 A situation in which you had done something very well. . . .
7 A situation in which you had to make an important decision. . . .
8 A situation in which you 'got away with it', or were not found out. . . .
9 A situation in which you were helpful or kind to someone else. . . .
10 A situation in which you made a serious mistake. . . .
11 A situation in which you felt afterwards that you had done right. . . .
12 A situation in which you were very disappointed. . . .

This list was further modified as a result of the negotiation process. It was suggested, for example, that item 3 contained two different concepts—that the same item overlooked the fact that misunderstandings usually involve both parties; that item 6 expressed success too strongly; and that few would be so bold as to respond to item 9. In the end two items from this list were rejected as unsuitable (nos 4 and 9); five were accepted without modification (nos 2, 7, 8, 10, and 11); five were retained with changes of wording (nos 1, 3, 5, 6 and 12); five new items were introduced. Thus the final version contained fifteen items, with an added flexibility in that the participant would be invited to choose up to ten of these, rather than have to think up something to say about each one. The wording of the actual instrument, as it was used, is shown below:

Below are listed 15 types of situation which most people have been in at some time. Try to think of something that has happened in your life in the last year or two, or perhaps something that keeps on happening, which fits each of the descriptions. Then choose the ten of them which deal with the things that seem to you to be most important, which cover your main interests and concerns, and the different parts of your life. When we meet we will talk together about the situations you have chosen. Try beforehand to remember as clearly as you can what happened, what you and others did, and how you yourself felt and thought. Be as definite as you can. If you like, write a few notes to help you keep the situations in mind.

1 When there was a misunderstanding between you and someone else (or several others). . . .
2 When you got on really well with people. . . .
3 When you had to make an important decision. . . .
4 When you discovered something new about yourself. . . .

5 When you felt angry, annoyed, or resentful. . . .
6 When you did what was expected of you. . . .
7 When your life changed direction in some way. . . .
8 When you felt you had done something well. . . .
9 When you were right on your own, with hardly anyone taking your side. . . .
10 When you 'got away with it', or were not found out. . . .
11 When you made a serious mistake. . . .
12 When you felt afterwards that you had done right. . . .
13 When you were disappointed with yourself. . . .
14 When you had a serious clash or disagreement with another person. . . .
15 When you began to take seriously something that had not mattered much to you before. . . .

While we aimed as far as possible to take into account the suggestions that were made during the trials, three principles guided the final selection of the items, and the details of their wording. First, the 'situations' should have, at least potentially, a relevance to aspects of what is commonly considered to be the domain of values. For example, the first item might give indications of latent value conflict, the second of a congruence of values, the third of a person's use of values in making or justifying decisions, and so on. The items also cover various modalities. Some are active, some passive; some have an individual, some a social reference; some emphasize relatively enduring features, others, growth and change. The second principle was that the 'situations' should be such as to impose the minimum of 'constraint' on the participant. A framework was necessary, but it should be one that did not involve premature attribution of values. Thus each of the 'situations' can be interpreted in a variety of ways, some of which may not involve values at all. Third, the 'situations' should be ones that corresponded with the life-experience of adolescents of both sexes, and from a wide range of social backgrounds: in other words, a boy or girl should be able to look at the schedule, and recognize there the basis for an authentic self-portrait. It was hoped that as a result of the way it was constructed—through negotiation—the instrument itself would encapsulate some of the major concerns of adolescent life. However, because of its lack of specific content, it was deliberately designed to be something of a psychologists' 'projective test'.

This description of how the early list of 'situations' was transformed into the instrument that was actually used has left aside another set of changes that was occurring concurrently, in the way the whole research interaction was envisaged. At first the 'situations' had been intended to serve a subsidiary purpose, that of provoking thought about 'significant others' and the kind of ways their influence might be felt. There was no intention of going into details. Gradually, however, it became clear that there was the basis here for a method that might be sufficient in itself; one that would enable adolescents to talk freely about their experiences and concerns, with the opportunity to give comment, where possible, on their actions. This meant that the whole character of the research, as a meeting between persons, had to be reconsidered.

Initially the interaction had been viewed as a kind of interrogation, rather along the lines suggested in some of the major texts on the methodology of the interview. The researcher would note down the salient features of each 'situation' as it was described, and would follow this with some direct questioning. Any comments that involved or implied values would be followed up with further questions. In practice this did not work well; the whole structure was felt by the participants to be strained and contrived; the persistent questioning, the almost nagging 'why?' seemed to be unacceptable and inhibiting. There were, however, some instances of a very different reaction, where a boy or girl largely bypassed the researcher's imposed structure and offered instead a fluent and sensitive account of experiences corresponding to some of the 'situations'. Statements about the grounds of action, and comments on performance, emerged 'naturally' during the conversation, and were of much greater subtlety than those elicited by the rather heavy-handed interrogation. This pointed towards developing an approach that would be near to a free conversation, in which the participant would be encouraged, but as far as possible not trammelled, by the researcher.*

Around this time another part-time research student, who had had considerable experience with young people, largely in non-school contexts, became involved in the research. Her plan was to use the method in three youth clubs, in order to investigate in a tentative way whether the mode of self-presentation adopted by the participants (largely from lower- or middle- or working-class backgrounds) corresponded with the image presented by more conventional research (for her finished work see Clark, 1976).

---

*From an ethogenic standpoint this might be interpreted as a change in the cues by which the participants could interpret the research encounter. The answer to the question 'Why not ask them?' as a prescription for social inquiry (Harré and Secord, 1972) in this case seems to be because it would lead to a different, and less fruitful, definition of the situation.

Several full trial interviews were conducted, so as to develop competence and discover any further possible difficulties. The details of the method were soon finalized, and were summarized in a document that would be a guide to any others who might carry out this kind of research. The schedule would be given, if possible, to potential participants a day or so in advance. They would be assured of the confidential nature of the interviews, and that no information about them had been or would be obtained from sources other than themselves. Great care would be taken with the seating arrangements, so as to avoid implying interpersonal barriers or direct confrontation. The interview would be tape-recorded. The interaction itself would follow some of the practices of non-directive counselling, keeping interrogation to the minimum. 'Why'-type questions were to be put with caution, and when they were used to explore the ground of a person's action they were to be cast in the form 'Do you know why. . . .?', thus implying that an answer was not necessarily expected. In this way it was hoped that interviews carried out by different researchers would become approximately comparable, while the flexibility and freedom of the method remained.

The method of research that finally emerged was the product of a joint effort, and I acknowledge with gratitude the contribution of the two who worked with me at this stage, especially since their background experience and range of ideas were very different from my own. It must also be said again that great help and encouragement was given by the boys and girls who took part in the trials. My own work was given added impetus by the fact that two of those who took part in pilot interviews (a seventeen-year-old boy and a fifteen-year-old girl) were about as articulate as any whom I have interviewed since. If the first full trials had been very difficult, the conclusion might have been that we were on the wrong track. Later, on the other hand, sufficient skill had been developed for handling situations where *rapport* was harder to generate and sustain.

The research method that evolved in this way has certain features in common with other approaches to persons, whether or not for the purpose of research. In its broad aim it is somewhat similar to *verstehende* sociology (cf. Outhwaite, 1975), since it sets out to understand consciousness in relation to the person's life-situation, and to view existence not as a set of separate phenomena, but as an interconnected whole. In general 'tone', and in the attempt to achieve an empathetic understanding, it is not unlike some methods of psychotherapy, such as that of Rogers (1961) and his followers. The actual mode of conduct of research has something in common with other forms of interview, particularly those that are not tightly structured. Probably the closest affinities here are with the 'critical incident' technique as used, for example, by McPhail *et al.* (1972) in their research into the personal relationships of adolescents.

The method also accords with the way I have characterized values and their relation to persons. It was suggested earlier that 'values' refers to an area of human life where there is sometimes a concordance and sometimes a discrepancy between belief and action. If so, then it would appear that a single method of inquiry in the realist mode could hardly do better than discuss with people some of their characteristic actions and the grounds on which they make their retrospective appraisals, providing them with the opportunity to exhibit what resources they have available for the guidance of action in the future.

The method is ideographic, but only in a limited sense. While it convincingly demonstrates the uniqueness of each person's outlook and social situation, it does not set out to elicit the full repertoire of evaluative constructs of any one individual, or to explore such dimensions as cognitive complexity. It simply collects a very large number of vignettes from adolescent life, in which value issues may be important, described and appraised in the boys' and girls' own terms. Theoretically the assessment of the person in relation to values requires a vastly more thorough type of investigation, though whether such a project would be desirable is another matter. There are, in fact, many practical limitations to this kind of work, especially when the aim is to provide data from a wide range of social backgrounds. In research with adolescents one important issue is that of obtaining willing co-operation; if prolonged and rigorous assessment were attempted this would almost certainly lead the participants to define the situation as one inimical to their interests, and therefore to disclose little about themselves. Thus (as also often occurs in the physical and biological sciences), it may be necessary to obtain data by whatever methods are feasible, and to compensate by as careful and critical an interpretation as one can make.

Research Design

The practicalities of this piece of research were dictated to a considerable extent by the nature of the method itself. Most obviously, there was the fact that it was very slow in use. A single interview might effectively require half a day, allowing the time to establish the basis for a highly personal conversation, to make the tape-recording, and to conclude the encounter in a mutually satisfying way. Work in youth clubs might be restricted by the rather short period that they were open during the evening—in some cases only two hours. Even under optimum conditions, to carry out three full-length interviews in a day would be work well done. Besides the simple time factor, the method was exacting, demanding high levels of concentration and imaginative understanding from the researcher, and in some cases the additional effort of maintaining a difficult interaction. Further constraints were present in the method of processing the data. To go through a one-hour interview thoroughly, making adequate notes and a few verbatim transcriptions, might require three hours or more, and for some purposes it would be necessary to listen to parts of the tapes a number of times. Moreover, the data were not of a kind that could be atomized, transferred to cards and later stored in a computer. It quickly became evident that for the handling of such apparently unstructured material the main apparatus for data-processing would have to be the human mind, attending to the meaning of each person's discourse with the utmost concentration. There are, of course, severe limitations to the load of information that it can carry. These considerations led to the tentative conclusion that this kind of work was necessarily committed to fairly small numbers, at least as compared with the size of sample used in much psychometric work. One researcher might be able to assimilate the data from about sixty to eighty interviews, though it was clearly desirable that the work should be carried out, if possible, by more than one person. With the arrival of further substantial help the plan that finally emerged was that about half of the interviews would be carried out by myself, and the rest divided between the three others. Since they were all women, about half of the total of interviews would have been carried out by a male, and half by a female interviewer. It was also intended that we might each interview about equal numbers of boys and girls. Granted these conditions, the problem was then to find an adequate design.

It is worth pointing out that the very first decision had already been taken before the method itself was developed. This was to carry out a study of values in a novel style among adolescents, some reasons for which were briefly mentioned in the Introduction. Around the time of initiating pilot studies I had also decided that the research would not focus on any of the alleged 'problems' with which adolescence is commonly associated. Crime, delinquency, rebellion against parents, truancy, promiscuity, drug-taking and all the other features that contribute to an adverse stereotype would simply be taken as part of the whole array of data. No distinction between 'normal' and 'abnormal' would be made. Immigrants, who would hardly feature in a significant way in proportion to a total of about 150, would not be included in the study.

At this stage I had not worked out a full theoretical position, but simply had a sense that all was not well with the psychological study of values, and a desire to collect a body of data which there was ample evidence to believe would be rich and revealing. By extrapolation from the conventional wisdom of survey methodology, it seemed advisable to draw on several geographical areas, including both densely populated urban regions and smaller communities. This policy involved a latent hypothesis, of which at the time I was only partially aware: if there were common patterns in the values held by boys and girls in widely disparate areas, these might be related to broad historical and social factors affecting the position of adolescence in society. Had the study concentrated instead on one place, the information might have been far more detailed, and different kinds of pattern might have been discovered. There is certainly scope for this kind of work, using the same method. In the terminology of Marsh, Rosser and Harré (1978), then, these ideas were a compromise between two types of design. On the one hand there is the kind that involves the intensive study of a very few or even one member assumed to be typical of a class; on the other there is the extensive design, which examines characteristics of a larger sample, but with far less regard for detail. This inquiry is clearly intermediate in character, though work that builds upon it is likely to develop in the direction of the intensive design, once the basis for typification is more clear.

It was obviously desirable to make some sort of distribution according to social class, and considering the middle-class bias of a great deal of existing work on values, to ensure that the 'lower' part of the stratification system was properly represented. A common practice in social research is to make a straightforward dichotomy between 'middle-class' and 'working-class'; if the Registrar-General's categories are used, the division occurs between the manual and non-manual sections of category III. In this research, however, such a device might be misleading; for many families that are *'petit-bourgeois'* in character would be technically classified by this system as 'working-class', and one might miss some parts of the working-class altogether. In order to ensure that the Registrar-General's categories IV and V would be represented, I decided to use a three-fold class division. Group A would consist of categories I and II, and so encompass the 'upper–middle-class'; group B would be intermediate, consisting of category III; group C would consist of categories IV and V, the more generally and traditionally 'working-class'. If the participant was living with, and dependent upon, both parents, classification would be based on the father's occupation; in the case of divorce or separation it would be based on the occupation of the parent with whom the participant was living. The information would be gathered during the course of the interview, if possible as part of the conversation; guidance in the interpretation of such ambiguous titles as 'engineer' would be gleaned from other clues, such as the type of house and area in which the participant lived. Data obtained thus might not be particularly reliable, and even if it were, it would be very superficial from the standpoint of a rigorous class analysis. This, however, was the necessary price of the position of trust that the research required; the participants were to be assured that no records or opinions relating to them had been, or would be, consulted.

With relatively small numbers such as those with which research of this type is concerned it is not, of course, correct to speak in strict terms of a 'sampling' procedure. Statistical considerations are not applicable. I was looking, rather, for a set of what might be termed 'limiting' and 'distributive' devices: the former to set a boundary to the study, and the latter to give it an internal structure. The initial intention, then, was to make the 'limiting devices' the age-range 15.0–19.0; residence in England; membership of the indigenous population. The 'distributive devices' were to be sex, age, social class and type of area. I also intended to make note of each participant's educational attainment, but not to use it as a distributive device.

These ideas were largely formed in advance, without taking account of what might happen during the actual conduct of the research. It soon became clear however that, whatever one's aim might be before carrying out a set of interviews in one place, the outcome would always be different from what had been anticipated. Our policy was to regard unforeseen contingencies, not so much as difficulties to be overcome by tighter forms of control, but as additional kinds of evidence. One of the factors with which we had to reckon was that some who had expressed a willingness to participate failed to appear for an interview. On the other hand there were occasions when a person was invited at very short notice, simply because he or she happened to be free at the time. In some instances a person who had not been approached expressed willingness or even eagerness to join in. Whenever this occurred we judged that offer should be accepted; this was one reason why in a few cases we went beyond the intended age limits. Owing to factors such as these, it was very difficult to build up a 'sample' in a systematic way. The human character of the encounters, which it was necessary to preserve at all costs, meant that one could not 'advertise' for participants with particular features of age, social class, sex and background. It was better to be an opportunist at the time, and later to make what we could from the results.

It also became evident during the conduct of the research that the division of territory into 'conurbation' and 'the rest', as found in some of the official population statistics, is very unsatisfactory as a basis for characterizing the area in which a person lives. Some small towns and villages are classified as part of a conurbation, while in reality they are virtually self-contained communities. Many boys and girls were strongly bound, psychologically, to their home areas. Because of this I decided to make the division of territory between 'urban' (referring to densely populated areas with population over about 200,000), and 'the rest', not on the basis of official classification, but the character of the actual locality where the interviews were conducted.

The following criteria were finally adopted for the design.

1 The total 'sample' would be about 150 adolescents, resident in England and of the indigenous population. They should mainly be in the age range 15.0–19.0, the very outside limits of age being 14.0–20.0.
2 There should be an approximately equal division between the sexes.
3 There should be an approximately equal division between 'old' (over 17.0) and 'young' (under 17.0).
4 About half of the 'sample' would be from urban areas, and about half from small town or rural areas.
5 A three-fold class division would be used, with sufficient in each class group to enable comparisons to be made, while bearing in mind that the proportions for the groups A:B:C in the actual population are approximately 2:5:3.
6 The research would be carried out in several regions, widely separated from one another.
7 There should be a basic frame which must be completed for the study to make a minimal claim to have represented the adolescent group according to the 'limiting' and 'distributive' devices initially adopted. In going beyond this frame every attempt would be made not to distort the character of the 'sample' too far in the direction of any one group.

The study was carried out in five urban areas (Guildford, Leeds–Bradford, Liverpool, London and Southampton), and five non-urban areas (Cheshire, Hertfordshire, Somerset, Surrey and West Yorkshire). The structure of the 'sample' is shown in the table 2.1.

Table 2.1

			Basic desired sample*	Actual numbers interviewed		
				'Urban'	'The Rest'	Total
Boys	A	o	6	4	5	9
		y	6	2	6	8
	B	o	15	6	7	13
		y	15	7	10	17
	C	o	9	9	7	16
		y	9	10	7	17
Girls	A	o	6	5	5	10
		y	6	1	8	9
	B	o	15	6	9	15
		y	15	7	8	15
	C	o	9	4	5	9
		y	9	5	10	15
	Total		120	66	87	153

*In every case but one (older boys of group B) the basic requirement has been exceeded. The deficiency of 2 in this cell was not judged to be a serious drawback, especially considering the many difficulties in making allocations at the border between the social class groups.

Making Contact

It was essential for research of this kind, which involved providing the kind of conditions under which participants could be at ease, and the setting up of a situation in which they might feel that they were being treated as equals, to take great care with the general mode of making contact. On the character of this the fruitfulness or otherwise of the subsequent interaction largely depended. It was not possible, however, to follow a single pattern in the initial encounter; youth clubs, for example, which might appear to be ideal ground for carrying out the interviews, have a somewhat restricted clientele—neither the very 'top' nor the very 'bottom' of the social class spectrum are to be found there; nor generally are older girls, or those who are socially very insecure. Some boys and girls were contacted at school. Here care was taken to dissociate the research as far as possible from the 'establishment', and the researcher from the 'authorities' (whose co-operation by non-involvement was generally exemplary). One set of interviews was conducted in a school youth centre, towards the end of the summer term, when many boys and girls had very little to do. The situation was very like that of a youth club, but it was open all through the day. Some of the school-based research took place during the half-term break or the holidays; here the reason for using the school was that this was the only place in the area where privacy could be assured. Other interviews took place at youth clubs, where the atmosphere was generally very informal, though the physical conditions for interviewing were not always easy, because of noise, interruptions or the lack of a suitable private room. It was also necessary, as in a school, not to be too closely associated with the leaders, since they are obliged to some extent to co-operate with the police and the probation service, and often, behind the atmosphere of bonhomie, to maintain what is in effect a two-class society. A further proportion of the interviews was carried out 'privately', in the participant's or a friend's home, or some other convenient location.

The actual contact that led to an interview took one of four forms, which can be termed 'direct', 'mediated' (two types), and 'unsolicited'. The first category refers to those occasions where an interviewer was introduced to one or more potential participants, and then had the opportunity to explain the nature of the research and ask for co-operation. The second refers to cases where a person other than the researcher made the initial overtures. In the majority of instances here the 'mediator' was an adult already in close touch with a group of adolescents, who could do some preliminary work in setting up the research before the arrival of the interviewer and could even, on the basis of existing friendship, invite some 'unlikely' boys and girls to take part; there were also some occasions where one or more of those who had been inter-viewed themselves took the initiative and drew in someone else. The fourth class, here termed 'unsolicited', refers to the few instances in which a person learned about the research and offered to take part without invitation.

In the course of this inquiry, then, three types of location were used, and contact was established in four different ways. A numerical analysis for the whole sample is shown in table 2.2.

The research was thus a long way removed from the highly controlled conditions of the ideal laboratory experiment, but this was necessary for the obtaining of data of this kind. As the research progressed, a general point emerged, which has sig-nificant implications for the evaluation of this kind of work. It

Table 2.2

Location of interview	Place of education	53
	Youth club	62
	Private	38
Mode of contact	Direct	53
	Adult-mediated	85
	Peer-mediated	9
	Unsolicited	6

seems that it is possible to provide conditions such that participation will appeal to almost any sector of the adolescent group. As it happened it was for purely pragmatic reasons that this research was set up in a variety of ways, without a prior theory of the social encounter that would lead to the interviews. It now appears that there was a range of motives for participating, as will be discussed in the following chapter. In view of this it seems unlikely that the method was such that it necessarily excluded certain types of person. Certainly the characteristics of the participants bear no resemblance to the conventional picture of the 'volunteer subject'.* We were to draw boys and girls from a broad spectrum of backgrounds, from the children of managing directors to those of manual labourers and the permanently unemployed. Some had characters that were judged as law-abiding and upright;

---

*Rosenthal and Rosnow (1974), in their book *The Volunteer Subject*, conclude that volunteers in 'behavioural research' are likely to have such characteristics as good education, high social class, desire to seek approval, and sociability. They offer advice to researchers on how to lower the possibility of bias in their samples, which may be summarized as follows: make the appeal interesting and non-threatening; convey the impression that it is 'normal' to volunteer; explain the purpose and importance of the research; offer the volunteers remuneration; let the request for help be made by a person of high status. There are difficulties in accepting these conclusions, since they seem to assume the existence of a general set of conditions; for example that the appeal will be given in public, that the hearers accept the conventional status system, and that the offer of money makes no significant difference to the way the research situation will be defined. There is no consideration of the possibility of varying the conditions under which the request for help is given, so as to avoid the bias arising from the use of a single method. Their findings probably would be applicable to this research if the adolescents had been exclusively recruited by means of a public appeal in a school assembly. In fact this method was not used at all.

others were hostile to conventional authorities such as parents, school and the law. A wide range of academic ability was included, from those going to university with excellent academic qualifications, to some judged 'educationally subnormal'. While a number of participants appeared to be confident and outgoing, there were others who had a reputation for being shy or unsociable, and several who had received some form of psychiatric treatment. It appears then that, without initially being aware of what we were doing by making contact in a variety of ways, the four of us who carried out the empirical work have gone some way towards guarding against the formation of a markedly atypical sample. It is interesting to speculate on what would have happened if what we did haphazardly and at first without awareness had been incorporated into a rational plan. Making contact might have been far more efficient; on the other hand, the artifice might well have been detected, and inhibiting messages conveyed to those whose co-operation we were seeking.

Handling the Data

During the development of the research method the prime focus of attention was on finding an approach that would elicit values, and that would also be acceptable to adolescents themselves. Even after the decision to abandon grid methods and to use a form of interview had been taken, the main concern was to discover how to provide the conditions for a 'natural' and fluent conversation. Contrary to advice given in some of the manuals of research, the principal objective was that of obtaining rich data, while the question of how to process them was largely left aside. It was only after the first few interviews had been carried out that the problem of handling the material, which was clearly going to be vast in volume, was faced. How to do so in a manner consistent with the general tenor of the research only emerged gradually, and as a result of much trial and error. For while there is a considerable literature on the techniques of interviewing, and on the pitfalls associated with the interaction itself, much less has been written about the processing of tape-recorded interviews of a relatively free and unstructured kind. There seems to be a common assumption that interviewing for research mainly involves the asking and answering of questions; if so, the data can presumably be processed in the same general way as that from questionnaires.

For this kind of work there appeared to be two main pitfalls to avoid. One was that of using passages from interviews simply as illustrative material, without any overriding structure or control.

This technique is highly dubious, since it is possible to make almost any point by a careful choice of extracts. The other pitfall was that of being over-mechanical, of failing to interpret remarks in their context, of avoiding empathy or imaginative reconstruction. The suggestion has been made, for example (Banaka, 1974), that interviews be transcribed verbatim, and then be subjected to content analysis. On practical grounds alone such a policy would scarcely be feasible, since 150 interviews would involve between one and two million words. (Presumably the research interviews Banaka envisages are brief.) In any case the underlying assumption of most methods of content analysis, that frequency is related to importance, can hardly be regarded as valid for this kind of research. Meaning and significance are grasped in a very different way: by attending patiently to a person's discourse and intonation, by noting the details that are emphasized and those that are passed over quickly, by supplying imaginatively some parts of the context that were never made explicit. Such an attempt to put oneself into another person's place and to view the world through his or her eyes looks, perhaps, more like the art of the novelist than the practice of a scientist. Nevertheless, it is essential for this kind of work. This need not entail any sacrifice of rigour, though it does involve going far beyond the surface character of the data, where psychometric work generally remains. It appeared, then, that some novel techniques for dealing with the interview material would have to be devised. And throughout it would have to be remembered that the participants were not giving simple information about themselves, subject merely to the limitations of their linguistic ability and their memory. The interviews were social encounters, necessarily sharing many features of interaction in everyday life. The tape-recorded material should not be taken simplistically, at face value, but regarded as disclosures made to one who was to a large extent a stranger.

In order to obtain an initial grasp of the interview content, two methods were used. First, as soon as possible after an interview had taken place, a brief report was filled in; on this a few particulars about the participant, and about the encounter itself, were recorded, together with a brief summary, in a sentence or so, of the interview content related to each of the items chosen. At a convenient time later a more thorough examination of the tape-recording was made. This involved summarizing the narrative parts, transcribing verbatim small fragments of material which seemed particularly relevant to the topic of values, and making notes on any points that might have special significance. The report forms and the full summaries provided the store of data for further use. The material could then be handled in any number of ways. The policy that was finally adopted for this research was to use several methods of data-processing, and to treat the results as cumulative. At the lowest level there were such rather mechanical tasks as examining the patterns of choice of item, and the simple categorization of content item by item. Additional insight could be gained by noting any topics that might have been expected to be discussed by adolescents, but that in fact featured only to a small extent. The most substantial part of the data-processing involved the collection of material related to particular topics, regardless of the item on the interview schedule to which it was initially attached. At this stage large portions of the tape-recordings were re-examined, additional notes were taken, and transcriptions were made of longer passages that could be used for illustration of points for which there was now substantial evidence. On this basis it was then possible to put forward hypotheses concordant with the whole tenor of the data, though not necessarily derived from it by any straightforward process of induction. This was the programme that seemed to be most appropriate to an exploratory study of this kind.*

The 'Reliability' and 'Validity' of Interview Data

It is a commonplace in empirical work in the social sciences that before a test is established as fit for widespread use, it must be demonstrated to have both 'reliability' and 'validity'. The former term refers to such features as internal consistency, the capacity to give the same results with the same sample on different occasions, and independence of the researcher, the location and other attendant circumstances. 'Validity', which is dependent on 're-liability', denotes the extent to which a test produces the information for which it was designed, indicated by such measures as the correlation between the test score and a performance criterion.

The interview presents an essential conflict between these terms as conventionally understood. Suppose, for example, that 're-liability' is taken to be the prime objective: the inference would be to make the interview highly structured, to foresee as many contingencies as possible and prescribe for them in advance. One might envisage a scheme in which provision was made for handling not only verbal responses, but also particular kinds of affect: the extent to which one might attempt to bring the transactions of an

---

*I wish to acknowledge here the excellent help given by Carol Borrill, who handled not only the data from interviews she had conducted, but also that from the other two female interviewers.

interview within rational control is almost infinite. It might include training interviewers to present themselves in certain ways, to use similar gestures and tones of voice, and to make the same kind of evaluations of what takes place moment by moment, together with the appropriate responses. The logical conclusion of such a programme of rationalization would be not to employ a human interviewer at all, but to use a very advanced computer which, presumably, was not only monitoring the respondent's verbal performance, but also obtaining concurrent information on galvanic skin response, blood level of adrenalin, electroencephalographic pattern and so on. But where would such a relentless pursuit of 'reliability' lead? In proportion to its success, 'validity' would decrease. For the main purpose of using an interview in research is that it is believed that people are more likely to make significant disclosures about themselves in an interpersonal encounter than they would in less amicable situations. It is the distinctively human element in the interview that confers its particular authenticity. The more the interviewer is rational, calculating and detached, the less likely the encounter is to be perceived as a friendly transaction, and the more calculated the response will also probably be.

In keeping with a realist methodology, it seemed to be a sounder policy simply to regard the interview as a meeting between persons: perceived by each participant in a particular way, within which behaviour is monitored according to some pattern, and for which an appropriate persona is adopted. What was needed, therefore, was not a technique for establishing 'reliability' and 'validity' (or some judicious compromise between the two, if indeed they are incompatible), but a view of the person that takes account of the particular character of the interview. Cicourel (1964) is a notable advocate of this view. He lists some of the unavoidable features of the interview, which might conventionally be regarded as problems. For instance, there are many factors that differ from one interview to another, such as mutual trust, social distance and the interviewer's control; the interviewee may well feel uneasy and adopt avoidance tactics if questioning is too deep; many of the meanings that are clear to one will be relatively opaque to the other, even when genuine communication is intended. However hard the researcher may try to be systematic and objective, the interview brings with it many features that are common to all interpersonal encounters, as well as some that are peculiar to meetings between strangers. In the light of such considerations there seemed to be ground for scepticism even about the notion of a 'good' interview. A 'poor' interview (which perhaps means that it left the researcher feeling perplexed, discouraged or distressed) might be just as valid as a 'good' one, and might indeed provide important evidence.

Thus, while it may be appropriate to use pragmatic criteria to characterize interviews, and to take precautions against researchers' fantasy, such as making careful inter-interviewer checks in the development of content categories or discussing some of the 'findings' with participants themselves, the conventional notions of 'reliability' and 'validity' may be misleading. What is needed, rather, is an understanding of the interaction itself, linked to a model of the person that enables at least some of the important factors to be taken into account. 'Reliability' and 'validity' would be predicates applicable not so much to the content of the verbal data, as to the framework within which the actual phenomena of the interview were explained. Such a task is attempted in the following chapter.

3
Evidence from Interaction

When the decision to use an interview method was first made, I had little realization of the evidence that might be gained simply from the carrying out of the research, although pointers to that effect were there in some abundance. The data, so I thought, would almost entirely consist of the verbal information about themselves that the participants gave. Much of the literature on interviewing, and the majority of the research that has used the interview, conveys that impression. However, the establishment of contact with the participants, the interviews themselves, the following up of a few cases, and subsequent attempts at validating some of the tentative findings through further discussion together provided a valuable extra dimension to the knowledge gained from the accounts themselves.

It is worth making a comparison here between the type of approach that has been used in this research, and the more disruptive techniques of ethnomethodology, sometimes known (after their main inventor) as 'garfinkeling' (Garfinkel, 1967). A chemical analogy is appropriate. 'Garfinkeling' is like the method of the shock tube, where a chemical system at equilibrium is subjected to a violent perturbation; much can be learned about the behaviour of the system under normal conditions from the reactions that occur during the very short period while the system readjusts itself. A method such as the informal interview with a stranger, which involves a social encounter of a kind for which there is no clear parallel in the everyday lives of the participants, can be likened to taking a set of reactants and putting them into contact with another compound, under novel conditions; the reaction that takes place gives indirect evidence about the nature of the reactants, and hence about their probable behaviour elsewhere. In other words, the study of how the participants conducted themselves during the interview and in the surrounding circumstances, together with the hints they gave about how they interpreted it, reveals something about their expectations and resources for the guidance of action; and so, indirectly, about values in everyday life.

Setting up the Research

The first clues that a potential participant received about the nature of the research were conveyed during the initial invitation, proffered by either a researcher or a 'mediator'. There were indications that the verbal content of the first explanation of what they were being asked to do did not mean very much, and could even be misleading; this was not surprising, considering that the majority had had no experience that was even broadly similar, to which the request for help in the research could be related. Gradually, through trial and error, ways were found of making the introduction more comprehensible; in the terms used by Goffman (1969) this was a matter of carefully deciding not only on the impression to be 'given' (through verbal content), but also on the impression to be 'given off' (through non-verbal signs and symbols). In many cases the apologia for the research came to take approximately the following form:

'Have you ever found that some of the people that you see a great deal, such as teachers, youth club leaders, and even parents, do not know what you are really like? Some of us are going round meeting people in their teens, and getting them to make a tape-recording with us, in which we chat together about some of the things that have happened to you, and about how you think and feel. Gradually we are collecting information from the tapes, and building up a picture of teenage life, as you yourselves see it. Later our findings will be published, so that people can understand more clearly what it is like to be a teenager today.'

In some cases where invitations were made in advance of the interviewer's arrival, a document was sent to the 'mediator' giving guidance, along these general lines, about how to present the research.

An introduction of this kind provided a link between a common adolescent experience and the purposes of our work. (If its tone appears to be over-sympathetic towards the participants, and to contain implied criticism of some of the adults with whom they are frequently in contact, it must be said that there are grounds for believing the general accuracy of its description; it was common, for example, to find associated adults wanting to know what had been discovered about particular boys and girls; and in one case a youth club leader gave indications of feeling seriously threatened by the intimate acquaintance with some of her clientele that one of the researchers had gained.) The necessary details about how the 'chat' would be carried out, the explanation of the confidential nature of the tape-recording and the assurance that no other sources of information about the participants either had been or would be consulted emerged naturally during the discussion when the purpose of the request had been established.

In the first meeting, and throughout the encounters that ensued, no attempt was made to accommodate to the ways of adolescents in matters of dress, manner or self-presentation. We certainly wished to convey clues that would affect their definition of the situation, but unlike some of those directly involved in youth work we made no attempt to imply that we were participants in their 'scene'. We hoped, rather, to make it clear that those who took part would be treated as equals (in so far as the whole setting allowed it), and with respect. This included an acceptance of the fact that in some ways they might want to be 'different'. There is some evidence from the tapes that adolescents are inclined to be suspicious of outsiders who try to be like them and to join in their activities. On the other hand, many boys and girls wish to be treated, in certain respects, as adults and to work with them on an equal footing; we hoped to convey the impression that this would be the case during the research.

It gradually became apparent that a number of further clues were being given inadvertently. Initially, for example, the word 'interview' was used a good deal in introducing the research, the assumption being that it would have connotations from such events as the televised interview, in which the focal person is generally treated as being of some importance. In fact, however, the word was something of a deterrent, because it was more commonly associated with such direct experiences as a cursory and often unhelpful encounter with a careers guidance officer, or the process of selection for a job, an episode that is by no means always happy or successful. In both of these instances the adolescent is treated as relatively inferior, powerless and passive, with only little opportunity for authentic self-expression. Thus the general manner in which the research was characterized (implying respect, equality and the chance for the adolescent to take initiative and be largely in control) was discrepant with the use of the term 'interview'. The replacement of this word by a phrase

such as 'tape-recorded chat' seemed to facilitate a more straightforward definition of the situation.

A typical indication of the delicacy of the introduction was given
on one occasion when I met a group of boys and girls from the
lower academic band at a school, and asked for some to co-operate
in the research. I mentioned that the previous day I had been
doing similar work at a remand centre, meaning to imply 'None of
you need be deterred from taking part, not even if you have been
"in trouble".' The impression that some received, as I discovered
from later conversation, was that the research had some connection with the law. Since several of those present had been involved
in brushes with the police my remark, which was intended as a reassurance, had the opposite effect. On the other hand, surprisingly,
the word 'research' was one with which a number of the less
academic boys and girls could identify, because some of their projects for CSE, involving the collection of data and commenting
upon them, are known by that name. So when it was explained that
we were doing a piece of research, they knew what we were about.

Other clues towards the definition of the situation were given by
tangible sign-vehicles, again to use Goffman's terminology. The
most important of these was probably the tape-recorder. I had
feared that this might be construed as a form of spying, associated
with such events as the Watergate affair, and therefore that it would
be resented. It appears, rather, that the tape-recorder was
generally taken as an indication that the 'chat' was of some
significance, that what the participants said would be taken
seriously. This was probably an encouragement for most, though it
was expressly stated by a few to be daunting, as if more might be
required of them than they were capable of giving. The interview
schedule also seems to have conveyed a distinct impression; a few
were quite willing to talk about themselves, but doubted whether
they could meet the imposed requirements. On the other hand
many boys and girls, on reading it through, seemed to recognize
the outlines of a portrait of themselves, even to the extent of
identifying with the 'situations' in such terms as 'yes, that was the
time when I . . .', as if someone had found out about them in
advance. For some this aroused considerable apprehension, while
for others it implied that the research was genuinely in touch with
their concerns.

In the previous chapter the somewhat haphazard and varied
methods of making contact with participants were described. I
suggested that one outcome of this was that we were not collecting
data from a 'sample' that was strongly biased towards certain
personality types simply as a result of the form of the initial
invitation. The main 'motives' for taking part in the research,

which varied from person to person, were probably the following:

1 curiosity: this would be a new and perhaps interesting experience, a change from a boring routine;
2 appreciation that someone was willing to spend time and take a personal interest in oneself;
3 desire to learn more about oneself;
4 belief that the research interview would be a way of getting practice for other interviews;
5 desire to please the mediator;
6 pressure from others who had taken part;
7 fear of being left out of an experience that others had enjoyed;
8 the 'need' for someone to talk to;
9 perception of the researcher as a potential ally in defence of accepted authority;
10 perception of the researcher as a potential support in defiance of authority;
11 desire to help in social research, along the lines of the initial apologia.

This list is made up from passing impressions, from conversations with participants after their interviews were over, from remarks that were passed back by those who had helped to set up the research, and from a short follow-up questionnaire sent to a small proportion of the whole 'sample'. The 'motives' can be illustrated by the case of four participants, three of whom were interviewed at the same school. The first was with a boy who was in the strange position of having been permanently banned from lessons because of various acts and attitudes of defiance; he was nevertheless required to attend school, where he spent much of his time 'hanging around' or doing odd jobs. His main motives appear to have been escape from boredom, appreciation of company, and looking for support against authority. The second was a girl who was highly respected by the staff, and had been 'nominated' by one of her teachers. She seemed to see that the interview might have instrumental value, and was clearly anxious to please both her teachers and the researcher. The third was a boy who had been invited by some of his own age-group who were a degree less academic and more 'rough' than he, though there was no in-dication of coercion in the cruder sense. His participation may well have arisen from a combination of social pressure and desire not to be excluded. The fourth illustration is provided by the following incident. Just as an interview was coming to an end in an office in a youth club, several boys came in, wanting to know what was going on. When this was explained to them they all wanted to take part. The leader of the group then pushed the others aside, sat down, and demanded to be interviewed, against the outspoken complaints of his friends. For him this was a matter of prestige, and he gave an excellent interview; the possibilities of the situation thus being pre-empted, none of the others returned.

It is also relevant to consider the possible motives for non-participation after a request had been made. This analysis is somewhat more speculative, based as it is on evidence of an even more fragmentary kind. Besides sheer indifference, which did not appear to be common, there were probably four main motives for non-participation:

1 fear of incompetence, of being unable to find enough to say or of not being able to find words adequate to the task of self-description;
2 fear that too much might be revealed; that the discussion would unavoidably move onto painful or shameful ground;
3 a sense that one was not worth interviewing;
4 fear that adults who were closely involved might come (despite the researcher's assurances) to know about the interview content.

Explicit statements of the first three motives are to be found in the comments made by some of those who did in fact take part, despite their fears. We are aware of only one instance of the last 'motive'; this was a boy whose mother was very keen that he should give an interview, and who (under the circumstances) wisely refused.

The reception of the research in different places had a number of divergent features. The main ground of variation appeared to be not the type of institution (school or youth club), but the extent to which a sense of confidence and co-operation between adolescents and adults had developed. In some places we were conscious of having to build up trust against the prevailing climate, whereas in others it seemed to be virtually taken for granted that, if a respected leader was prepared to introduce the researcher, the work was thereby guaranteed. In addition mention must be made of two other effects. The first might be termed 'snowballing', where the first contacts were difficult (one solution being to begin by inviting someone with a reputation as a forceful personality), but where it became progressively easier to invite people as impressions of the research were spread around by those who had taken part. The second might be termed 'fading'; in these cases the research made a strong impact at first, but interest quickly waned.

The difference between the two effects is partially accounted for by the available resources for activity and excitement. In a place of extreme boredom, where boys and girls had almost nothing to do, even participation in social research was something of a landmark; but where social life was already rich and eventful, this was just one diversion among many, bringing quite heavy demands and possibly few rewards.

There were seventeen cases where a person expressed willingness to take part, provided that a friend could be there also. This condition was accepted, since it appeared that there might be no other way in which the participation of certain types of boys and girls could be obtained, even though there was the possibility of a modified form of self-presentation arising from what Goffman would call a 'team'. The distribution, according to the main divisions of the 'sample' (see chapter 2), is shown in table 3.1. It is tempting to infer from this that the 'need' for a companion was greater for those in the younger age range, and for those from working-class backgrounds. At any rate, it seemed that in these cases facing a stranger might pose an almost unbearable threat; these boys and girls wanted someone whom they knew well to be there to reassure them, so to speak, of what they were like, and to help in their performance. Being part of a 'team' was their general way of interacting with strangers, or facing unfamiliar situations.

Table 3.1

Social class group	Age-group	Boys	Girls
A	'Old'		
	'Young'		1
B	'Old'		
	'Young'	2	2
C	'Old'	4	1
	'Young'	2	5

The setting up of this research, then, was an activity subject to many unforeseen contingencies, which might have been regarded as setbacks, but which could also be viewed as sources of evidence. In one place it was hardly possible to go wrong, whereas in another a single casual remark might cause serious problems. It is clear that those who took part were recruited under conditions that were by no means standardized. As it happened, this was probably an advantage.

As researchers, we had a fairly clear idea of what we were about, right from the start; even if our first attempts were clumsy, by the second interview we were already one hundred per cent more experienced in the performing of this novel social act than any of the participants. As the inquiry went forward we progressively gained in knowledge about how to carry out our task, manage our presence acceptably and cope with various contingencies. Those being interviewed, however, were making their first attempts at a performance of this kind. Here they had to rely on fragments of knowledge obtained from other situations construed as similar, from interaction with others whose social distance was comparable to that perceived in relation to the interviewer, and from such sources as television, reading and hearsay. This raises the question of the types of encounter present already in their experience, which might be assumed to have broad similarities to the research interview. What scenario was considered beforehand as appropriate for their conduct?

The following list is based on hints and comments that participants themselves gave:

1 an interview with a careers guidance officer;
2 an interview for a job;
3 a tutorial or private lesson;
4 a meeting with a social worker or probation officer;
5 being 'in trouble' with the police or other authorities;
6 a talk with a parent;
7 acting;
8 seeing a psychiatrist;
9 confession.

There is some ground for thinking that whatever scenario, from these or other sources, was judged to be appropriate beforehand, it was generally abandoned as the interview progressed, when the unusual features of the interaction were recognized. The conversation, having begun (in terms of the model outlined in chapter 1) at the level of 'personality-in-role', went on to that of interpersonal perspectives: here the persons involved are more spontaneous, each making moment-by-moment appraisals of what the other is thinking and feeling, and monitoring performance accordingly. A relevant analogy would be that of an actor who abandons the set part and begins to 'ad lib' in direct response to the audience. Although some evidently (especially younger boys) had little skill in this respect, many participants were surprised at the performance they had achieved.

The Interview Itself

It is probable, then, that the participants came to the interview with widely varying motives, fears and expectations, and a range of provisional definitions in the light of which to guide their conduct. The interview itself can be divided into five main 'episodes', implying that during any one of these something approximating to a single set of tacit rules or general guidelines for conduct was being followed. There is some degree of idealization about the description given here, since a number of the interviews did not follow this pattern precisely, and improvisations were often necessary. Some comments on the more idiosyncratic aspects are given in the next section, where the styles of interaction are discussed.

Initial Conversation

After the first greetings, which were carried out with the minimum of ceremonial, opportunity was given to the participant to gain further evidence about the nature of the interaction that was going to take place. It was our policy as researchers to try to do most of the talking at this stage ourselves; this had the overt (and sincere) purpose of giving more information and reassurance, while also allowing the participant to become familiar with the setting, and to develop some impressions about the person to whom he or she was about to convey very personal information. In telling the participants something about ourselves we were trying to convey the message: 'Since we are asking a lot from you in getting you to talk about yourself, we are willing to do our part and disclose something of ourselves to you.' A further reminder was given at this stage about the confidential nature of the interview, and it was made clear again that no dossiers had been consulted or information about the participant sought out in advance.

During this period there was time for the meaning of other 'sign-vehicles' to be assimilated. The seating, for example, was arranged so as to imply no difference of status between the two persons involved. The chairs were of the same height, without an intervening desk or table, and care was taken over their positioning so as to suggest a friendly but not over-intimate encounter. They were not face-to-face, which implies 'I–thou', but at an angle of about 45°, as if to convey the impression of 'We': two people engaged on subject matter with which they both were concerned. The presence of the tape-recorder, and the fact that the researcher had control of it, could not be avoided. It was possible, however, for most other obvious indicators of status difference to be removed.

Another clue given at this stage was the absence of an official notepad. The meaning of this arises from the fact that the occasions when an adult makes notes on a teenage boy or girl are almost always unpleasant: an encounter with a teacher or doctor, or (more significantly) the police. The observation that no notepad was being used implied that no attempt would be made to 'label' the participants, or to 'take down evidence' against them. Our general practice was simply to have available the same sheet of paper (the interview schedule) as did the participant, and where necessary to write down a few words beside each of the items which were chosen.

Our aim was to convey evidence, through tokens such as these, that would lead to a more reassuring definition of the interview situation, establishing at least three main points. First, negatively, it would not be like those encounters with adults in which a teenager is treated as self-evidently inferior. Second, though informal in tone, it was an occasion on which the participant would be taken seriously. Third, there would be no pressure to make unwilling self-disclosures; the control would be left, as far as possible and desired, in the hands of the person being interviewed. Goffman (1969) points out that social observers are inclined to look for discrepancies between impressions 'given' and those 'given off', using the latter to check the former. There is ground for thinking that adolescents frequently engage in this activity (even if without full awareness of what they are doing), especially in their dealings with strangers. The first episode of the interview was, in effect, a period during which they could use this skill and so have a basis on which to frame their subsequent actions.

Rehearsal

The second stage was to have a preliminary conversation about the material that would be covered in the interview proper, with the tape-recorder off. The participant was invited to say which items had been chosen, and to summarize in a sentence or two what would be the main content of each one. At first there was no conscious rationale for doing this, but simply an intuitive sense that something of the kind was needed to facilitate the actual interview. Retrospectively it seems probable that the function of that episode was two-fold: to enable the further sharpening of tentative definitions of the situation through providing the sketch of a scenario for the tape-recording, and to activate memories of events half-forgotten. Every attempt was made to accept what had been chosen for discussion, and not to imply that some topics were of greater interest than others for the purpose of the research. In a few instances a participant began by choosing only a very few items, but later he went on to add others; where this was so, we were quite willing to work from that starting-point.

The 'rehearsal' was also a means of giving further time for those taking part to become familiar with the whole setting. In many cases this was the occasion for a cup of coffee. With experience it became possible to judge when a participant had gained sufficient information and confidence for a satisfactory recording to be made, the time varying greatly from one person to another. There were even instances where it was plain that this moment had been reached, because the preliminary discussion of an item became transmuted into the full narrative, without any further prompting.

The Tape Recording

After a short and deliberately obvious testing of the tape-recorder (an additional reassurance that the earlier conversation had not been recorded), the interview itself began. The participant selected an item, and began to give an account of what happened, while the interviewer monitored his or her part, as far as possible, according to the guidelines initially agreed. The extent to which intervention was required varied greatly from one person to another; a considerable proportion of the interviews flowed very easily from this point onwards, with the interviewer having to do relatively little, apart from giving indications of intense attention to what was being said.

In some cases there appeared to be a further easing of the atmosphere after about ten minutes, as if the situation had undergone further redefinition, or the participant had discovered that it was one that he or she could handle, despite initial fears. By this stage there was direct evidence about the part that the interviewer was going to play: there would be no embarrassing probes into private territory, but plenty of support if the going became difficult. The significant feature of such interviews is that they became more personal, direct and serious as the encounter progressed, after beginning in a way that was relatively casual or inhibited. Some participants revealed afterwards that they had naturally found themselves talking at a deeper level than they had either intended or anticipated.

Once the conversation was under way, it tended to develop its own natural pace, this varying very much from one person to another. Silences and pauses were acceptable, as long as the participant did not show signs of discomfort. When one item was exhausted or sufficiently explored, the dialogue moved on, at the suggestion of either the participant or the interviewer, who already knew from the 'rehearsal' what might be some of the natural links in the material to be discussed. Although the schedule implied that the interview was to focus on discrete events, the way in which it was most used suggests that the items functioned mainly as guidelines for a coherent self-portrait. It seems probable that an alternative list, used under comparable conditions, would serve almost as well; whereas it is also likely that the same list, taken as the basis for an interview in another type of social–psychological context, would function in a very different way.

There were several occasions when an interview was interrupted unexpectedly, thus providing some additional insights into how the situation was being defined by the participants. Such episodes might be understood as a piece of ethnomethodology in miniature, because an unanticipated disruption sometimes reveals aspects of the assumptions and rules on which a social situation is constructed. Here are two examples, outwardly very different in character, but both pointing in the same direction. The first occurred at a school, where a somewhat unpopular boy from the top social class group was giving a tape-recording. Four much 'rougher' boys, three of whom had already been interviewed, came into the room and asked if they could listen. The participant agreed that they could, evidently regarding it as a challenge to his sincerity; and although it was clearly an ordeal he continued as before, in a style not noticeably different, with the occasional interruption from the visitors. After about ten minutes they went on their way, apparently satisfied with the quality of the account he was giving. The other example occurred at a youth club, where one of the most powerful and unruly of the older boys was being interviewed in the warden's office. He had just been describing his family, and his discovery that he was an adopted child, when the warden came in. The tape-recorder remained on, while the following episode took place.

Warden (apologetically): Hello, excuse me again disturbing. Get a phone number.
Participant (taking microphone in the manner of a news reporter on location): Here we have Brian here. He's doing something very exciting. He's got a yellow shirt on with very smart drainpipe trousers. Course, he's ruined this interview, but—

Interviewer (attempting to take a mediating position, and half-jokingly): We can scrub him off the tape a bit later.
Participant: That Brian bloke. Think I'm going to nut him in a minute if he doesn't get out. He just likes getting in on the action, I think.
(Warden departs).

At this point the flippant and aggressive persona was again laid aside, and the boy continued in the more serious vein which he had previously adopted. These two instances, which are concordant with many other small indications, show how the interview was generally viewed as a special kind of event, more serious than everyday interaction, and with sincerity as its implicit norm.

The Final Question

When the research method was first designed, it was intended that it should end with a direct question. This would involve asking the participant whether he or she was aware of holding any general rules, principles or guidelines for conduct (not linked to specific kinds of situation). Answers here might be values expressed in highly general, and possibly abstract, terms, in the spirit of the approach adopted by psychometricians such as Rokeach (1973). The use of direct questioning, which tended to change the character of the encounter, justifies regarding this part of the interview as a separate episode. The sharpness of the question was mitigated, in keeping with the whole approach, by the assurance that it might not be possible to give a direct answer. The responses could be divided into five categories. First, there were those for whom the question was meaningless; who had, apparently, not even faint clues by which to give the words significance. Second, some gave an answer the content of which indicated that they had been unable to construe the question in a way that corresponded to the interviewer's intent, such as one boy who answered that Chelsea was the best football club in the world. Third, there were those who apparently understood the question but thought that they did not have any principles. Fourth, a small number believed that they did have principles or standards for conduct, but said that they could not express them verbally. The fifth group consisted of those who could answer the question directly.

In view of the very mixed response to this part of the interview, it was not used in all cases during the latter stages of the research. Indeed, it might be regarded as a vestigial remnant from the interrogation-style that was first tried in the pilot work; it was some time, however, before it was recognized as unproductive.

Retrospect

After the interview proper was completed the tape-recorder was switched off; and with it, apparently that particular definition of the situation. Now a more well-established set of rules was generally called into play. The interviewer was to be treated like any other adult with whom one is friendly but not closely involved: with some degree of distance, an appropriate level of reserve, and as an equal. In some instances the 'jokey' style which had been laid aside for the serious business of the interview was once again adopted. Various evaluations of the interview were made during this final episode. It had proved to be enjoyable; the participant had learned a lot, had been surprised at being able to talk for such a long time, was pleased to have been able to give what was wanted, felt that the experience was valuable. One of the most recurrent remarks was that it was 'different': perhaps it is not too far-fetched to suggest that this can be interpreted as meaning that no previous experience provided an adequate basis for characterizing this new situation. Considering the skill with which many boys and girls handled the interview, it is probable that the main resource on which they had to draw was their experience of other interactions at the perspective level, mainly with their peers. The novelty of the situation lay not so much in the style of the dialogue, but in three factors taken in combination: talking freely for a long period, being listened to with attention, and having an adult as the 'audience'. No openly adverse comments were made to the interviewers. The nearest approach to this was an exchange that occurred twice in virtually the same form, in both cases with boys whose manner had appeared 'sulky' during the interview. The interviewer made a disarming remark, along the lines 'I hope it wasn't as bad as you thought it would be', to which there was no reply except a significant silence. Much more characteristic are the following appraisals.

'I think I've said rather more than I, more than I rather wanted to, [Laughter] . . . . more than I would normally, I suppose. I don't know, think about it tomorrow and see what I think then.' [Laughter]

(Girl$_5$, Group A, 17)

'I thought it was about fifteen minutes—quick chat, type of thing, which our careers talks tend to be. But, much more interesting.'

(Boy$_{10}$, Group B(N), 16)

'Different, never done it before. A bit apprehensive about it

at the beginning, but as long as it—helps, you know . . . .
It's good practice to be able to talk to someone.'

(Girl$_1$, Group B(N), 17)

'I think that this is about the first time I've sort of sat down
and discussed myself. I've sat down and discussed other
people, but I've never sort of sat down and discussed myself,
because nobody's really been interested in me as a person. I,
er, they just sort of take you for granted that way, and that's
it. That's the sort of start and finish of the sort of thing.
Never at school, you know, I never even had a discussion
about myself at school. I'm not pulling my school to pieces.
I know it sounds like I am, but I'm not. We used to talk
about other people but never about yourself, you know.
Nobody ever sort of stopped to say "Well, why don't we talk
about you for a change?" We'd talk about somebody else. It
were always about, well, "What, what do you think about so
and so and so and so?" and "How do you think he got on
and so and so?", "Write an essay on so and so". It were
never "Write an essay on yourself", like.'

(Boy$_{11}$, Group B(M), 18)

'I liked talking to you, actually. I've always wanted to do
something like this, you know, sort of talk to someone. Point
is, you can, very rare to find someone you can talk to without
them starting at you, you know. I would never say what I've
just said to you to my Mum.'

(Boy$_{15}$, Group C, 16½)

It would be naive to draw firm inferences from the absence of
openly critical or hostile reactions, since any who viewed the
interview unfavourably would be more likely to express this
elsewhere. Nevertheless, the interviewers were left with a strong
impression that the encounter had generally been given a decidedly
positive evaluation, even by those who had been very nervous
beforehand, or had been in doubt about whether to take part.

Although there was no clear model in adolescent experience
that could provide in advance an adequate set of rules for the
guidance of action in the interview, it was surprising how quickly
a set of criteria for judging performance was developed among
groups from whom some had been interviewed. Among these
were the following.

1 The accounts should not have been trivial in their subject
matter.
2 They should have been authentic narratives of events.

3 The interview should have lasted for some time.

The best evidence here was that provided by the 'mediators', with whom a number of boys and girls discussed what had transpired during the interview. There were other pointers during the interviews themselves. For example, one girl of somewhat 'lower' social background came as the companion of an upper-middle-class girl, intending later to be interviewed herself. Having witnessed the fluent, sensitive and detailed account given by her friend she became discouraged, eventually deciding that she would be incapable of doing what was required. Further evidence is provided by the follow-up questionnaire, about which more will be said at a later point in this chapter.

Styles

From the standpoint of the participants, the request to give a highly personal account of oneself to a stranger with a tape-recorder presented something of a problem—a person whose social life-worlds were entirely different had appeared uninvited, and with only a minimal explanation, making a serious demand. To comply would be to engage in a social act for which there were no clear guidelines, and for the handling of which resources might be inadequate: it might prove impossible to say what was wanted, or too much might be revealed. All the motives that had led some boys and girls not to participate may have been present to some degree among those who were interviewed, perhaps only marginally outweighed by positive considerations. Not surprisingly, the situation was one that provoked anxiety, with the awareness, perhaps, in some cases that something as serious as personal identity was at stake. The 'styles' of interaction may be regarded as the product of the participant's initial and subsequent definitions of the situation and the available resources of personality, deployed in a situation of considerable stress.

The analysis of styles presented surprising difficulties. One reason for this may be that those who carry out social research after having read deeply or been trained in the prevailing methods are far more sensitized to look for aspects of content than for aspects of the interaction itself. Data from interviews are commonly presented without such considerations. Although, intuitively, it was plain that there were great differences between participants in the way they presented themselves, and in the interviewers' own feelings about what had taken place, the constructs by means of which to handle such phenomena were not readily available. In an early attempt to develop a typology of style interviews were characterized as 'coherent self-portrait', 'superior to the schedule', 'changing in tone', 'colourless', 'spate' and 'shambles'. This was far from satisfactory, because each of the types was formed by focusing on one aspect of style, while other significant features were neglected. Here, therefore, the more common method of describing several dimensions along which difference was observed will be adopted; the analysis lacks both purity and rigour, being the result of an attempt to describe impressions of an extremely complex interactive process.

A first and obvious way in which the interviews differed was in the amount of material a boy or girl was able or willing to bring forward. This itself was not directly related to the number of items selected, since there were some participants who chose few items, but spoke at great length, while others chose the maximum of ten items, but had very little to say about them. The shortest interview of all (a 'young' boy in group C from a rural background) was of this latter kind, lasting a mere ten minutes. A small number, all from group A, treated the schedule with a certain superiority, as if to say 'I am certainly prepared to talk to you about myself, but I will do so on my own terms. However, so as to satisfy your nominal requirements I will make links between my account and your schedule.' In such instances the accounts were lengthy, but the number of items chosen were few. Those who had the least to say were either from settled rural backgrounds or from conventional middle-class homes against which they had not rebelled; in such instances boys sometimes were more reticent than girls. On the other hand those who lived in cities often appeared to have a richer resource of material. Differences here may partly have been an artefact of the method itself, which was developed with adolescents in an urban environment. Nevertheless, the interviewers were left with a distinct impression that, even when differences in verbal skill and the perceived relevance of the schedule had been taken into account, boys and girls differed greatly in the intensity and variety of the social experience on which they could draw.

Second, the accounts varied in their fluency and expressiveness. At one extreme there were a few from younger boys that were relatively wooden and colourless, confined mainly to factual material, and markedly lacking in expressive character; the domains of feelings, interpersonal perception and values were avoided, and even opinions were kept, if possible, at a distance from personal life. At the other extreme were those interviews where the participant moved quickly and without apparent strain into an expressive style, as if it were a familiar one, skilfully mixing factual narrative with opinion, declaration of feelings and evaluation. This dimension of difference is not directly related to the question of 'restricted' and 'elaborated' code; some who exhibited characteristic indicators of elaboration were far from being fluent or expressive, while others whose actual language use was to some extent restricted used gestures and intonation to make meanings more explicit.* One of the striking facts about the interviews, taken as a whole, was the extent to which boys and girls were able to use language in candid and direct accounts of themselves; even some who in other contexts had been judged inarticulate—for example one boy who could not read the interview schedule and another who had had no regular schooling since the age of nine because of constant trouble with the law—handled the interview very competently in this respect. A plausible hypothesis is that it is mainly the extent of a person's social experience, rather than intellectual or verbal competence as conventionally judged, that accounts for the major differences in fluency.

Third, there was a considerable degree of variation in the extent to which the participants were active and self-directing in their role. The interview method was designed, in keeping with its underlying view of the person, to place those who took part in a position where they could exhibit some of their resources, with rather less external constraint than is found in most forms of social–psychological research. Some clearly found this situation congenial, took the freedom that they were offered and used it in their characteristic way; it was on this basis that many of those interviewed managed to develop coherent self-portraits out of what superficially looked like a request for descriptions of isolated incidents. Others, however, were unwilling or unable to take an active role; a striking example was that of an eighteen-year-old working-class boy from a rural area who insisted that the interviewer treat the items on the interview schedule as if they were questions, thus deliberately asking to be controlled. A few of the interviews were of the kind that had formerly been characterized as a 'shambles', where the participant did not explicitly abrogate control, but was either unwilling or unable to take it up. Characteristic features of the six in this category (a 'young' girl in group A, a 'young' girl and two 'young' boys in group B, and an 'old' and a 'young' boy in group C) were selecting an item and then being

---

*For an analysis of some of the speech, see Toft and Kitwood (1980). The social class differences (according to currently used measures) are smaller than might have been expected, while regional variation may be more significant than is generally recognized.

unable to identify an experience that corresponded to it; choosing
one topic and then talking about another; going off at a tangent on
to material not related to autobiography; apparently abandoning
the interview and then returning to it. The sense of the situation
being in disarray here was very different from that of being subtly
controlled by a boy or girl who is deliberately using evasive tactics.
It seems likely that those who were very passive or disorganized
did not have the basis for considering themselves the kind of
people who might take or even share control in an interaction of
this kind: at the same time the interview situation just survived
intact, because there was at least some satisfaction in finding a
person who was attentive and accepting.

Fourth, there were differences in the discrepancy between the
style of behaviour adopted during the interview and that which
was followed in 'normal' interaction with peers or adults. Here, of
course, while we had abundant information from carrying out the
interviews, our data about the conduct of the participants in
everyday life were more scanty, coming partly from observations
made before or after the interviews, and partly from unsolicited
evidence about their reputations. The most common type of
discrepancy was when boys or girls who had adopted a confident,
flippant or surly manner before the interview, in the company of
their peers or the 'mediator', changed dramatically in their
behaviour when the interview itself was in progress. One girl, for
example, who had presented herself as very cheerful and outgoing
beforehand, was soon near to tears as she explained how she had
been victimized by her peers, and described her continuing sense
of social isolation. In another case a girl whose friend was present
continued in her bantering manner for some time; eventually the
friend left, at which point the tone of the interview altered and she
began to talk in a serious and highly perceptive way about subjects
that evidently mattered to her deeply. Changes of this kind were
perhaps most striking with working-class boys. The character of a
good deal of their self-presentation is illustrated by the following
extract from a discussion with three Londoners early in the phase
of making contact when (with their knowledge) the tape-recorder
was on. One of them (Gordon) is being amicably mocked by two
older friends for his physical immaturity.

> *Gordon:* A beard by then don't grow that quick. [Laughter]
> Well, beard. [Laughter] A good bit of bum. [Laughter]
> That's whiskers, ain't it? It's just that they're lightweight,
> you know what I mean? Looks like white, but they go
> ginger, don't they? What do you want, a lock of my hair,
> right?

Jim: Yeah, but I can't understand. He got blondish hair, ain't he? Well, what do they call it?
Interviewer: Straw-coloured.
Jim: Straw-coloured, and he's got—
Rod: Who?
Jim: He's got ginger whiskers, ain't he?
Rod: Most people have got, I've got ginger, ginger, ginger pubes. [Roars of laughter]
Interviewer (trying to establish a more serious tone, yet to build on what has been said): Well, most people have got about three, three colours of hair on them anyway.
Gordon: I have—
Rod: What colour's your pubes? Black?
Gordon: Green. [Roars of laughter]

Each of these three, like a number of others, having publicly made a display of being tough and humorous, went on at a later stage (two of them in private) to declare anxious and even melancholy thoughts about themselves. The contrast of tone between this conversation and the discourse of working-class boys in the interview proper will become apparent from extracts in the later chapters.

Fifth, participants appeared to differ in the extent to which they were 'anxious to please'. At one extreme there were a few middle-class boys and girls whose approach to the interview seemed to be dominated by this desire; while willing to be self-directing (if that was required), they were at the same time apparently needing continual reassurance that they were doing the right thing. At the other extreme there were a few working-class boys who seemed to have very little concern to satisfy the interviewer's request, although their participation was voluntary. It is possible here that the interviewers' impressions and the views of the participants may have differed; one researcher later found, for example, that an interview that she had regarded as something of a failure was regarded by the boy concerned as a very significant encounter. Another boy, who publicly exhibited his reluctance to take part, had declared privately to the 'mediator' how much he wanted to do so. Some of those interviewed may simply not have had available a style of interaction with an adult of the kind that they thought a middle-class researcher would judge as suitable. The majority of the interviews, however, were at neither of these extremes. They had much more of the character of meetings between equals, where there was neither deference nor resistance, but a willingness to adopt a degree of openness and friendliness suitable for a meeting with an acceptable stranger.

These five points at least illustrate something of the great variation there was between participants in the way they handled the interview situation, and the difficulty of making broad comments in terms of obvious variables such as age, sex or social class. If a generalization can be made at all, it might be in the terms of the following curious example, involving a sixteen-year-old boy in social class group B(M). He chose seven items, the first six of which were all to do with cars. The 'important decision' was whether to do up an old car; his 'life changed direction' when he began to be interested in cars; 'doing something well' was a major repair he had carried out, and so on. It was only near to the end of the interview that he began to talk seriously about his relationships, and revealed that he had a 'brain-damaged' sister as a result of whose behaviour and reputation he was afraid of being attacked by others. The presence of the sister was also a great source of tension in the home. There was no indication that he had made a deliberate attempt at 'impression management' in the way he had related so many of his choices to cars. It seems much more likely that 'motor enthusiast' was his regular manner of self-presentation among those who knew him well. He continued to adopt this persona in the interview until, almost as if by accident, it slipped, revealing a world of feelings and apprehensions that were generally not disclosed to others, and of which he himself was only partially aware. The changes, which occurred rather dramatically on this occasion near to the end of the interview, are a kind of paradigm of what happened in a large number of cases.

The Follow-Up Questionnaire

As an additional check on reactions to the interview, and the way it had been treated by those who took part, a short questionnaire was sent to seventeen boys and girls, comprising those interviewed in two separate places, in one case by myself and in the other by one of the other interviewers. All three social class groups were represented in this 'subsample'. The participants were invited to give their answers anonymously if they wished, and were urged to be completely candid. Fourteen responses were received. The answers to the first two questions are shown in full; the first eight come from one group, and the remaining six from the other.

Q1. How sincere were you in what you said?
(a) 99.9 per cent—I do believe in God but I do not go to Church (I can't remember whether I said that on the tape). I don't think that matters, though.

(b) What I said in the interview was true.

(c) I think I was as completely sincere as I possibly could be
with a total stranger.

(d) Quite sincere.

(e) I was extremely sincere and truthful.

(f) Totally! I think I surprised myself at how honest and
sincere I was in what I said. I felt relaxed and able to
converse as if you were a friend.

(g) Absolutely sincere.

(h) Completely sincere.

(i) Very sincere.

(j) As sincere as I could be on the spur of the moment.

(k) Absolutely 100 per cent. I didn't feel there was any need
for pretences at all—unlike talking to someone who knows
you and expects a certain reaction.

(l) I was very sincere in what I said and talked about.

(m) There was no point in lying really—as I spoke about things
which are important to me, I think I was sincere. I do try
to be normally!

(n) Totally sincere.

Q2. Did you deliberately *hold back anything that was important,
in relation to the things you chose to talk about?*

(a) No.

(b) There were a few facts which I wouldn't like to tell anybody.

(c) No.

(d) No, I didn't. If you're going to tell someone something it's
not worth telling only half of the truth.

(e) Not really. I believe in speaking my mind.

(f) No.

(g) No.

(h) Not knowingly.

(i) No. Not to any great extent (only held back on minor
trivialities).

(j) No.

(k) No, since everything I talked about was everyday there was
nothing to hide.

(l) I did not hold anything back that was important, relating
to the things I talked about.

(m) No—I picked the subjects deliberately, so that I wouldn't
have anything to hold back. I picked questions where I had
no fear of holding anything back.

(n) Thinking back over what I said, no, nothing deliberate—
but I do think I probably omitted a couple of important
things by mistake.

The subsequent three questions explored reactions to the interview in more detail, and elicited answers that were very similar in tone to those reproduced here, confirming a strongly positive evaluation of the experience, despite nervousness and tension at the beginning. The final question simply invited any other comments; this was left unanswered in the majority of cases, though an 'older' girl from group A, who identified herself in her reply, wrote as follows.

Apart from being helpful to the researchers, I feel, and can only really say for myself, that it was very helpful for me. It was a very good opportunity to talk about what's important to you or just about you to a completely objective person which, I think, is a constructive thing to do in the sense that it helps self-awareness. I also think that the research is very worthwhile as I'm sick of hearing 'What young people think today' from the so-called experts—: perhaps this research will really show what they think etc. as it actually comes from them. Good luck.

The response to the follow-up questionnaire must be treated with caution, since the size of the 'subsample' involved was small. It is also possible that the desire to please might even have been operative when answers were sent anonymously by post. On the other hand, had the interview been viewed cynically, or caused a serious sense of personal violation, it is probable that some would have given expression to their negative reactions, since they could do so without the possibility of recrimination, and at our expense. What is striking is the unanimity in the tone of the replies given to the two different interviewers. It certainly looks as if a general norm of candour did prevail, granted the fact that the participants exercised the freedom of choice of subject matter that was extended to them. It would be bold to claim on this evidence that the criterion implied by Mixon (1972), that all participants treated as similar in an experiment should have defined the situation in the same way, had been fully satisfied. Nevertheless, it seems probable that a broad rule of sincerity and openness was widely followed.

Attempts at 'Validation'

One of the ways in which there was an attempt to 'safeguard against researchers' fantasy' was to have several sessions during which some of the tentative findings of the research were discussed with boys and girls in the adolescent age range. One such meeting was with a boy and a girl who had taken part some months previously; two were with individual 'older' boys in group B, whom I judged from their interviews to have a particularly broad understanding of adolescent life; two further sessions were with a small group of boys and girls who had not been interviewed, but who were interested in the research; there was also one discussion with several girls. The general procedure was for me to raise a topic and put forward what seemed to be emerging from the research, asking for comments. It was made plain that this was not a request for confirmation, but for informed criticism or amplification of our observations.

These sessions were useful in a number of ways. The meeting with the two former participants produced further evidence about reactions to the research, in close agreement with the evidence already brought forward in this chapter, and gave a little further insight into aspects of the interview content. The sessions with the two individual boys were the most valuable in relation to the original aim of obtaining positive 'validation' of findings, especially in the reasons one of them advanced to explain why certain topics were not extensively discussed in the interviews. It became clear, however, that there were severe limitations to any attempt to 'validate' data by this kind of method. Most boys and girls are not themselves experts on the generalities of the life in which they are involved; their knowledge is commonly based on few instances, and their perceptions of the social system are often strictly curtailed. It also seems that when adolescents are asked to make generalizations, as opposed to talking about their actual experience, they have a tendency to relay back in attenuated and distorted form the findings of research of some years back, or stereotypes projected by the media. Although, the 'validation sessions' were thus of limited value in terms of content, the nature of the interaction itself provided useful information. This came particularly from the occasions where more than one person was present.

The interviews themselves had given indication of two dominant forms of self-presentation that are available to a considerable proportion of adolescents, particularly to those in the 'lower' part of the social spectrum. The first, which is one often followed in the presence of alien adult authority figures, is cheerful, casual and somewhat uncaring. It might not be far-fetched to describe this as 'personality-in-role-of-stereotypical-adolescent'. The other is more serious, sensitive, thoughtful, self-critical and concerned about sincerity. The 'validation sessions' showed that there can be circumstances where these two forms begin to merge, or where there can be alternation from one style to another. The one meeting with former participants immediately elicited the more 'serious' style; there was a kind of camaraderie between those who had been interviewed, as if they both knew that the other had an area of life that was generally concealed from view. The two sessions at a comprehensive school, with a group of lower-stream boys and girls who had not been interviewed, were more striking. The beginning of the first of these was in the 'stereotypical adolescent' style, but as it went on and the boys and girls became more involved, it changed character and developed phases in which the 'serious' style became predominant. The atmosphere was curiously similar to that of the discussions with small groups that took place during the development of the research method. During a period of about an hour the circle of chairs, which at first had been well dispersed, came closer and closer, until they were almost touching. The whole situation rapidly disintegrated when the school bell rang and the teacher came into the room. The second session (a week later) was similar, though with so evident a transition near the beginning, as if something of the definition of the previous situation remained.

Finally, something can be learned from the overall attitudes that were shown to the research. Only a very few saw the interview as a 'useful experience', which might be of help in gaining practice for other interviews, or be a means of fostering good relations with the authorities. By far the majority, however, seem to have taken the interview more or less at its face value, without regarding it as instrumental to some other long-term purpose. The challenge that it presented was much more on the interpersonal than the utilitarian level. From the point of view of those carrying out the research, who were wanting co-operation from the participants, and hoping for artlessness in the accounts they gave, this reaction was highly advantageous. In a society whose ruling system of thought is rational and utilitarian in the extreme, it might even be considered refreshing to find such a lack of concern to 'make capital' from a novel source. Alternative interpretations, however, are also possible, as subsequent chapters will make plain.

4

A Survey of the Data

The main aim of this chapter is to provide a broad description of the mass of data contained in the tape-recordings, so that it becomes possible to understand something of the general tenor and dominant emphases of the accounts of themselves that adolescents gave. On this basis, together with a consideration of certain topics that might have been expected to occupy a more significant place than in fact they did, some tentative hypotheses can be put forward about the process by which the accounts were generated. All this then provides a backcloth for the more detailed analysis of certain topics in the subsequent four chapters.

In describing the data it is worth drawing attention to several features of the patterns that emerge: similarities, differences, gradations, and the simple characterization of content. Much of this is amenable to descriptive statistics, and the material can be pressed to yield its due extract of significant differences and correlations. Statistics have not been applied in this way, however, because the units of data are so far from being 'pure' that the whole procedure would merely be obfuscating. Two small preliminary checks have, however, been carried out, because these relate to the degree of reliability involved in the actual presentation of material.

The Total Pattern of Choice of Items

The interest here is simply in the question of which items were chosen, regardless of the nature of the associated material. The distribution of choices for the whole 'sample' of boys and girls is shown diagrammatically in figure 4.1, and the frequencies and rank order places are shown in table 4.1.

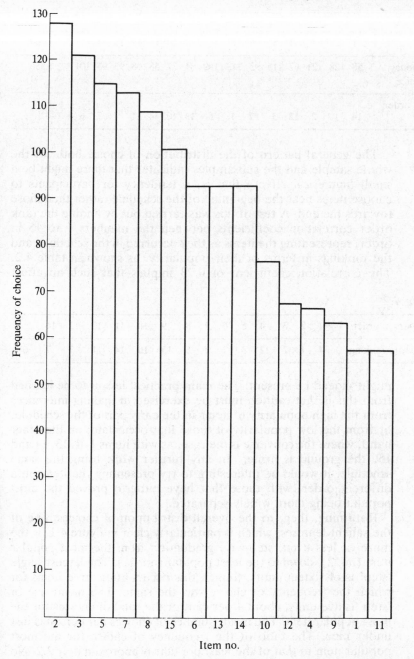

Figure 4.1

Table 4.1

Item	1	2	3	4	5	6	7	8	9	10	11	12	13	14	15	Total
Frequency of choice	58	128	121	67	115	93	113	109	64	77	58	68	93	93	101	1,358
Rank order place	14	1	2	12	3	7	4	5	13	10	14	11	7	7	6	—

The general pattern of the distribution of choice both for the whole sample and the subsamples indicates that there might be a small 'numerical effect': that is, a tendency for participants to choose items near the beginning of the schedule rather than those towards the end. A test of this was carried out by finding the rank order correlation coefficients between the numbers 1 to 15 in order, representing the items as they occurred in the schedule, and the rankings in terms of their popularity, as shown in table 4.2. The correlation coefficient of 0.23 implies that such an effect

Table 4.2

Numbers in order	1	2	3	4	5	6	7	8	9	10	11	12	13	14	15
Popularity ranking	14	1	2	12	3	7	4	5	13	10	14	11	7	7	6

might indeed be present. The main practical lesson to be learned from this is that caution must be exercised in making inferences from the high popularity of items in the early part of the schedule, or from the low popularity of those that occur late; on the other hand, where the converse is the case, as with items 1, 4, 13, 14 and 15, the ground is firmer. In any further work using the same schedule, it would be interesting to try presenting the items in a different order, with those that have hitherto proved the most popular being more widely separated.

Returning, then, to the overall distribution of choices; one of the salient features, which is particularly clear in figure 4.1, is the more or less even, step-wise graduation from the most popular item (no. 2), down to the least popular (no. 11). The largest single 'step' is of sixteen units, though this occurs after three items for which the frequency of choice was the same. The mean size of 'step' is five units, about 4 per cent of the total of choices for the most popular item. The mean number of choices per person is just under nine. The ratio of the frequency of choice for the most popular item to that of the least popular is approximately 2.2. No item has been rejected by a large majority; the most popular was chosen by 84 per cent, and the least popular by 36 per cent. These observations imply that the design of the schedule was sound according to the third of the guidelines discussed in chapter 3: that items should have a perceived correspondence to the participants' life-experience. Had any item been consistently rejected by the whole sample, or by a major subdivision within it, this might have cast doubt on the suitability of the method or the thoroughness of the negotiations that were involved in the early stages of the research. It must be borne in mind, however, that the choice of up to ten items out of fifteen is a narrow one, making the wholesale rejection of particular items relatively unlikely.

Looking at the pattern of choice in more detail, it is instructive to note which items were chosen with the greatest and the least frequency. Some of the results here are perhaps surprising in the light of common stereotypes of adolescence. It might have been expected, for example, that item 1, dealing with misunderstandings, would be chosen by many participants, since there is a common belief that adolescents are liable to perceive themselves as misunderstood, or even have a 'need' to be treated as if they were. No. 1 proved, however, to be last in the order of popularity, equal with item 11. A commonsense view might predict that boys and girls during the teenage years would be very likely to choose item 4, 'When you discovered something new about yourself', whereas under half of the whole sample did so. The five items of greatest popularity (in descending order) were nos. 2, 3, 5, 7 and 8. The first and last of these provide the most obvious opportunity, out of all the material on the schedule, for a strongly positive mode of self-presentation: in relation to people (no. 2, 'When you got on really well with people') and in relation to personal achievement (no. 8, 'When you felt you had done something well'). The failure to choose either of these was rare, being confined to only twelve participants, or 8 per cent of the whole sample. Item 3 is concerned with decision-making, the popularity of which is predictable, though a very wide range of decisions were discussed. Item 5 has to do with different forms of anger, covering rather similar ground to the moderately popular item 14. Item 7 refers to life changing direction, and has some degree of overlap with item 15, which was sixth in order of popularity.

At the other end of the scale, the least popular items (again in descending order) were nos 12, 4, 9, 1 and 11. One of these, no. 12, 'When you felt afterwards that you had done right', has the most evident positive moral connotations of all the items. The others—No. 4, 'When you discovered something new about yourself', no. 9, 'When you were right on your own, with hardly anyone taking your side', no. 1, 'When there was a misunderstanding between you and someone else (or several others)', and no. 11, 'When you made a serious mistake'—in their different ways tend to exhibit the person in lonely or psychologically precarious circumstances; their implied direction is somewhat introspective, and they have a clear potential bearing on self-esteem.

The choice of items was made before a significant amount of discussion had taken place, and while the character of the inter-view situation was still enigmatic. Therefore, if inferences are to be drawn from the way items were selected, these relate mainly to the way the participants would wish themselves to be known by a stranger. Out of a wide range of possible experiences that they could recall, perhaps only some were judged suitable for discussion. The general image diverges sharply from the common view of the adolescent as hostile, uncaring, flippant and irresponsible. The participants, so it seems, preferred rather to be known in this context as those who were sociable, competent, responsible and strong enough to be angry when occasion demanded. Such a self-presentation reveals something of their values, and has an oblique relationship to their conduct in everyday life.

Choice of Item in Relation to Sex, Age and Social Class

In order to examine the way items were chosen within the 'sample', a more detailed analysis was made, keeping the 'dis-tributive devices' of sex, age and social class group but merging the categories of 'urban' and 'the rest'. A correction was applied so as to make the number of participants in each cell the same (a scaling down in seven out of twelve cases).

Table 4.3 shows considerable homogeneity, though a few dif-ferences emerge. For example, item 1 (misunderstandings) was relatively unpopular with those in social class group A, despite the fact that the interview content itself gives little indication that those in this group had fewer experiences that an observer might describe in this way. With item 4 (discovering something new about oneself) it was girls in group C who made relatively few choices. When items 11 (making a serious mistake) and 13 (being disappointed with oneself) are compared, group A made relatively more choices of the latter. The lowest scorers on item 12 (feeling afterwards that one had done right) were girls of group C. Speculative comment might be made on the reasons for differen-ces such as these. It is, however, at a later stage, in the light of the detailed content of the accounts, that the significance of such relatively superficial points becomes apparent.

Table 4.3

	Item		1	2	3	4	5	6	7	8	9	10	11	12	13	14	15	n in each cell (corrected) with original n in brackets
			Number of choices per item															
Boys	A	'Old'	1	9	7	5	7	4	8	8	3	4	1	4	5	8	7	10 (9)
		'Young'	3	10	6	5	10	6	6	5	5	6	1	3	9	5	9	10 (8)
	B	'Old'	6	8	8	4	8	7	8	8	5	8	3	5	8	5	7	10 (13)
		'Young'	2	9	9	3	6	6	8	9	3	6	5	4	6	6	6	10 (17)
	C	'Old'	4	8	7	6	5	6	8	8	4	6	5	5	6	6	6	10 (16)
		'Young'	4	8	8	5	8	6	6	8	6	5	3	4	7	5	9	10 (17)
Girls	A	'Old'	2	9	8	6	8	6	8	7	2	2	2	4	6	8	8	10 (10)
		'Young'	2	8	7	4	10	6	7	4	3	3	4	6	7	7	6	10 (9)
	B	'Old'	5	8	8	5	9	5	7	7	6	3	2	7	8	5	6	10 (15)
		'Young'	6	8	8	2	8	7	8	7	4	7	5	6	5	7	5	10 (15)
	C	'Old'	6	8	9	3	6	6	10	6	2	2	6	2	4	4	7	10 (9)
		'Young'	5	9	8	2	7	7	5	5	3	6	5	3	3	5	6	10 (15)

The Content of the Accounts

A further stage towards obtaining a comprehensive view of the data involves a simple analysis of what was discussed in connection with each item. The broad categorization of subject matter could be made at various levels of abstraction from the specific context, and on a single or multi-dimensional basis. Item 6, for example, 'When you did what was expected of you', could have been handled with some refinement by first making a division between two senses of 'expected' ('required' and 'anticipated'), and then breaking the first category into willing and unwilling conformity; alternatively, or in parallel, the analysis could have been made on the basis of the person or persons to whom an expectation was attributed. In practice, since the main purpose was to exhibit the general tenor of the data without undue elaboration, an intermediate level of abstraction has been used, and multi-dimensional analysis has been avoided. The categories thus produced are far from pure, and in some cases even appear somewhat arbitrary, but have the merit of being closely related to the character of the accounts. Some of them have relatively firm boundaries, such as those derived from item 10, 'When you got away with it, or were not found out'; here it was simply a matter of classifying the various kinds of breach of rule or law. Other categories were more interpermeable, such as those derived from item 7, 'When your life changed direction in some way'; here some cases of moving to another area (category 1) were characterized as also involving changed social circumstances (category 3), whereas there were a few examples of changed social circumstances unaccompanied by a physical move. The categories were developed by two of us in negotiation. Each first made an individual analysis of about half of the interviews; we then jointly worked out a set of categories that appeared to fit all the cases, and re-analysed the material accordingly.

As a check on the robustness of this procedure, an inter-researcher reliability test of the final allocation to agreed categories was carried out with the most popular item (no. 2), and one of the two least popular items (no. 11); in the first case the categories were relatively clear-cut, and in the second they were relatively permeable. The numerical results are shown in tables 4.4 and 4.5; the columns headed 'K' and 'B' refer to the results from the two researchers, for each category. Pearson product–moment correlation coefficients were obtained in each case for the forty-eight pairs of numbers. The actual description of the categories is given later, as part of the survey of all fifteen items.

Table 4.4 Item 2*

Category		1		2		3		4		5		6		7		8	
Researcher		'K'	'B'	'K'	'B'	'K'	'B'	'K'	'B'	'K'	'B'	'K'	'B'	'K'	'B'	'K'	'B'
Boys	A	5	5	5	7	1	0	3	4	2	2	1	1	0	1	4	2
	B	3	5	9	5	0	0	1	1	5	7	2	1	2	4	5	4
	C	2	2	8	7	1	1	3	3	5	4	4	4	6	7	3	3
Girls	A	1	3	5	4	1	2	0	0	4	3	2	3	0	0	3	2
	B	3	3	8	10	0	0	3	1	3	2	3	4	2	2	5	4
	C	2	2	10	10	1	1	3	2	2	5	4	4	0	0	3	2
Total		16	20	45	43	4	4	13	11	21	23	16	17	10	14	23	17

*Correlation coefficient 0.84

The results from this test appear to justify the presentation of the material in the manner that now follows, and the use of the broad content categories as a guide in the study of more detailed topics. In the first stage of the actual analysis the division by age

Table 4.5 Item 11*

Category Researcher	1 'K'	'B'	2 'K'	'B'	3 'K'	'B'	4 'K'	'B'	5 'K'	'B'	6 'K'	'B'	7 'K'	'B'	8 'K'	'B'
Boys A	0	0	0	0	0	0	0	0	2	2	0	0	0	0	0	0
B	1	1	1	1	2	2	3	2	4	4	0	0	2	2	1	1
C	3	2	1	1	0	0	3	1	6	6	1	1	0	0	2	2
Girls A	0	0	3	1	1	1	1	1	1	1	0	0	2	2	0	0
B	0	1	2	2	1	1	3	2	6	4	0	0	0	1	0	0
C	1	2	2	1	2	2	2	0	2	2	2	2	2	2	3	1
Total	5	6	9	6	6	6	12	6	21	19	3	3	6	7	6	4

*Correlation coefficient: 0.94

into the two main groups was maintained; here, however, for the sake of simplicity, the age groups have been fused. Illustrations from each category are given, in approximately the same degree of detail as that used in the interview summaries (see chapter 2).

Item 1: When there was a misunderstanding between you and someone else (or several others)

Categories
1 'Misunderstandings' arising out of carelessness or neglect; e.g., a boy made a piece of carpentry, failed to put it in a safe place, and his friend accidentally broke it; this led to an argument between them.
2 Disagreements of various kinds, which were not 'misunderstandings' in the generally accepted meaning of the term; e.g., a boy found that he tended to have arguments with his father over factual issues, such as which is the richest country in the world.
3 Difficult situations (mostly among peers) arising from the spreading of rumours, the making of accusations or victimization; e.g., a girl was socially isolated and attacked by a group of other girls, probably because they were jealous of her athletic success.
4 Misunderstandings occurring because the participant's behaviour, words or intentions had been mis-perceived by others; e.g., a girl made remarks about her best friend to a third person, who then spread them around in a distorted form; this brought difficulties between the girl and her friend.
5 Cases of 'false accusation'; e.g., a girl's parents claimed after

she had returned home late that she had not told them where she was going for the evening. She believed, however, that she had told them.

Table 4.6 Item 1

Categories		1	2	3	4	5	Total
Boys	A	0	0	0	3	1	4
	B	0	8	0	3	0	11
	C	2	7	0	2	1	12
Girls	A	0	0	0	3	1	4
	B	0	6	1	7	2	16
	C	0	5	2	5	2	14
Total		2	26	3	23	7	61

Item 2 When you got on really well with people

Categories
1 People in general, excluding peers; e.g., a boy had been trying to understand people, to apply some psychology in working out why they behave as they do, and so to have good social relations.
2 Peers, talked about in a general way; e.g., a boy went on a weekend organized by his youth club, during which he met black teenagers for the first time, and found how much he liked them.
3 Boys or girls specifically mentioned as being younger than the participant; e.g., a boy had joined a drama group, and found that he was the oldest member of it; he was surprised and pleased to find that he got on well with younger 'kids', since he usually associated with people older than himself.
4 A specific friend of the opposite sex; e.g., a boy had been going out with a girl for about nine months; they enjoyed many things together; the relationship ended because she moved from the area.
5 A specific friend of the same sex; e.g., a girl had a close friendship with another girl of the same age; they developed deep mutual understanding, and could share each other's problems.
6 People, other than peers, in a full-time or part-time job; e.g., a girl who did not get on well with her mother became very friendly at work with a woman of her mother's age.
7 Older people in a context other than work; e.g., a girl found

that she struck up a friendship with a German friend of her father's; she talked to him when no one else did, and helped to look after his five-year-old child.

8 A mixed age group, such as a family, a play scheme or a sports club; e.g., a girl went on holiday abroad, and found that she formed very close bonds with the members of the family with whom she was staying, despite difficulties in language.

Table 4.7 Item 2

Category		1	2	3	4	5	6	7	8	*Total*
Boys	A	5	6	1	4	2	1	1	3	23
	B	4	7	0	1	6	2	3	5	28
	C	2	8	1	3	5	4	7	3	33
Girls	A	2	5	2	0	4	3	0	3	19
	B	3	9	0	2	3	4	2	5	28
	C	2	10	1	3	4	4	0	3	27
Total		18	45	5	13	24	18	13	22	158

Item 3 When you had to make an important decision

Categories

1 Decisions relating in some way to career or occupation, including the decision whether or not to stay on at school; e.g., a boy was offered three jobs at the same time; he consulted with his father, and eventually chose one of them, largely on grounds of convenience of travel.

2 Academic decisions, mainly to do with the choice of subjects for study at school, but also including any affecting attitudes to academic work; e.g., a girl was put into the lower band, which she believed to be unjustified: she worked hard, and obtained promotion.

3 A choice between schools; e.g., a boy had the opportunity either to go to a grammar school, which would involve a long bus journey and being cut off from local friends, or to go to the comprehensive school in his own neighbourhood; he chose the latter.

4 Major decisions concerning family life, the majority related to parental divorce or separation; e.g., a boy's parents were in process of separating, the mother going back to her mother; he had to decide whether to go with her or to stay in the house with his father, who had previously done little to help him.

5 Decisions affecting leisure activities, holidays, spending of money or a part-time job; e.g., a boy had to choose between giving a lot of his time to setting up the equipment for running a disco, and then being in demand in his locality, or taking the time to do his homework properly for O levels.
6 Decisions concerning a friend of the opposite sex, e.g., a girl had to decide whether to give up a boyfriend, whom she liked, but who was also taking out other girls without telling her.
7 Decisions concerning relationships other than with someone of the opposite sex; e.g., a boy had been advised by his mother to stop associating with another boy of about his age, and had to decide whether to follow her advice.
8 Decisions affecting geographical movement; e.g., a girl's father would probably have to leave the area soon; she would have to choose whether to go with her parents or stay in the locality, where she had many friends.
9 'Decisions are everyday things'; e.g., a boy said that this was an 'everyday question'; he made decisions every day of his life—at work, at home—and had never made any important decisions.
10 Other decisions of various kinds; e.g., a girl had to decide whether or not to have a certain operation.

Table 4.8 Item 3

Category		1	2	3	4	5	6	7	8	9	10	Total
Boys	A	5	2	3	1	0	1	0	0	0	0	12
	B	10	3	1	5	4	2	0	0	0	2	27
	C	13	3	2	1	1	0	2	1	2	1	26
Girls	A	9	0	2	0	2	1	0	1	0	0	15
	B	9	6	2	3	2	4	0	2	0	0	28
	C	10	2	0	1	3	2	0	0	1	2	21
Total		56	16	10	11	12	10	2	4	3	5	129

Item 4 When you discovered something new about yourself

Categories
1 The development of interests, opinions and beliefs, or the rediscovery of old ones; e.g., a girl had a growing interest in music, both instrumental and vocal; she had joined the local church choir, and was generally involved in village life.

2 The discovery of interpersonal skills or qualities; e.g., a girl used to think of herself as shy, and had few friends; later, through the help of another girl and a boyfriend, she found that she could be sociable and converse easily.
3 The discovery of skills and competence of other kinds; e.g., a boy who had seemed to be unable to do anything well at school found out afterwards, particularly through having a job, that there were many practical things that he could do.
4 Becoming aware of personal failings or weaknesses, experiences that led to a lowering of self-esteem; e.g., a girl was told by a group of her friends that she was vain, and came to the realization that they were right.

Table 4.9 Item 4

Category		1	2	3	4	Total
Boys	A	3	1	3	2	9
	B	4	3	4	0	11
	C	7	5	8	2	22
Girls	A	5	1	5	3	14
	B	3	6	3	2	14
	C	3	2	0	1	6
Total		25	18	23	10	76

Item 5 When you felt angry, annoyed or resentful

Categories
1 Damage to the participant's self-esteem, as a result of being slighted or undervalued in some way; e.g., a boy had decided to try to get into the Grenadier Guards, following his brother; another boy was very scornful of his decision.
2 Wilful or accidental damage to property, possessions or the person; e.g., a boy's sister broke a model that he had made and given as a present to his mother.
3 'Unjust' or unwanted intrusion, restriction or demands from parents' e.g., a girl's parents decided to move house, because they found the area noisy and had trouble with the neighbours; she resented this, as her social life was disrupted.
4 Anger or frustration that was mainly directed towards the self; e.g., a boy had taken up smoking a number of years previously, and later found that although he wanted to give it up, he could not.

5 Unwanted intrusion or demands from others (excluding parents); acts of injustice or deception; e.g., a boy who was working in a part-time job in a supermarket found that others in the workplace demanded more than his fair share of work from him.

6 The disruption of a relationship by someone else; e.g., a girl was very angry with another girl who took her boyfriend from her.

7 Anger arising from differences of values or outlook, not included in other categories; e.g., a girl found that she became very angry with people who were negative and apathetic about life, in contrast to her own approach, which she thought was positive and enthusiastic.

Table 4.10 Item 5

Category		1	2	3	4	5	6	7	Total
Boys	A	4	4	3	0	0	6	3	20
	B	7	5	5	0	4	3	1	25
	C	9	3	2	2	3	5	2	26
Girls	A	2	1	5	2	2	1	2	15
	B	12	1	4	0	4	5	3	29
	C	3	3	0	0	4	5	3	18
Total		37	17	19	4	17	25	14	133

Item 6 When you did what was expected of you

Categories
(1–6 are concerned with 'expected' in the main sense of 'required', whereas 7–8 are concerned with 'expected' in the main sense of 'anticipated')

1 Conformity to wishes of parents against the participant's wishes or values; e.g., a girl agreed to become a Sunday school teacher, not because she wanted to, but because she thought that this would please her parents.

2 Conformity to wishes of parents, but not against the participant's wishes or values; e.g., a girl gave a lot of help at home, shopping and looking after a younger child while her mother was having a baby.

3 Conformity to school discipline or norms; e.g., a girl who had a good singing voice was expected to join the county youth choir; she was told it was for the 'good of the school'.

4 Conformity to the expectations of peers; e.g., a girl was

invited to a party by another girl, whom she did not like; she went, because her boyfriend wanted her to go.

5 Conformity at work; e.g., a boy had a part-time job in a butcher's shop, which involved some unpleasant tasks; he was prepared to do what was required of him.

6 Conformity in other contexts than those mentioned in 1–5; e.g., a boy helped to stop a fight in a youth club, in which one of his friends was involved.

7 Success in school work; e.g., a boy passed ten O levels, seven with grade A; this, however, was no surprise, or particular cause for elation.

8 Fulfilment of others' anticipations in some other area; e.g., a boy was currently having a lot of athletic success, which was expected on the basis of his current form.

Table 4.11 Item 6

Category		1	2	3	4	5	6	7	8	Total
Boys	A	2	5	1	1	0	0	0	0	9
	B	2	7	3	1	1	4	3	2	23
	C	3	6	1	0	6	6	2	1	25
Girls	A	1	4	3	0	0	1	2	0	11
	B	2	3	2	1	1	0	4	1	14
	C	2	4	2	2	0	1	0	1	12
Total		12	29	12	5	8	12	11	5	94

Item 7 When your life changed direction in some way

Categories

1 Moving house; e.g., a boy's family moved out from London to a more rural area; the atmosphere of the place and reactions of people were very different.

2 Changed family circumstances; e.g., a boy's father died; as a result his loyalty to his mother, and his sense of responsibility, were enhanced.

3 Changed social circumstances; e.g., a girl from a very affluent home joined a youth club, and there met many new people; she joined in with a group aged about fifteen to twenty-four, who went out drinking together.

4 Getting or changing a job; e.g., a boy found that his life had changed when he started working; he was treated with greater respect, and felt much more adult.

5 Taking up or abandoning some interest or leisure-time

activity; e.g., a girl who had shown considerable musical talent decided to give up her music and take up art instead.

6 A change in outlook, character, or philosophy of life; e.g., after an unpleasant incident with some of her peers a girl decided that she must rely much less on her parents, take her own decisions and generally grow up.

7 A change resulting from becoming involved with a person of the opposite sex; e.g., a girl had recently 'finished' with her first serious boyfriend, with whom she had gone out for several months; as a result of this relationship she felt she had grown up, and become more confident.

Table 4.12 Item 7

Category		1	2	3	4	5	6	7	Total
Boys	A	6	2	3	0	3	3	1	18
	B	6	5	4	2	6	6	0	29
	C	4	4	3	7	2	6	0	26
Girls	A	3	2	4	1	2	4	1	17
	B	9	1	3	3	1	10	1	28
	C	3	4	3	1	1	5	1	18
Total		31	18	20	14	15	34	4	136

Item 8 When you felt you had done something well

Categories

1 Success in school work (academic); e.g., a girl who had initially been put in the CSE group for English went on to do better than many who had been put in the O level group.

2 Success in school work (non-academic); e.g., a boy made a Christmas cake, including the full icing technique; his mother thought it was very good.

3 Doing well in a job; taking responsibility, developing competence, etc.; e.g., a boy had part-time employment with an auctioneer and estate agent; he learned many things about the work, and had been invited to join the firm after leaving school.

4 Getting a job; e.g., a boy felt that he had done well in getting a job as soon as he left school, since it meant that he did not have to sign on, like many of his friends.

5 Some form of achievement in leisure-time pursuits; e.g., a

boy was a member of a 'band'; it gave a performance that
was greatly appreciated by those present.
6 Success in sport; e.g., a boy learned the skills of gliding
   through the Air Training Corps.
7 Giving practical help to others; e.g., a boy who was unemployed helped to decorate a flat for one of the resident
   helpers at a youth club.
8 Giving help in relationships; e.g., a girl helped to arrange a
   reconciliation between a boy and girl who had (needlessly)
   broken off their friendship.
9 A change of life-style; e.g., a girl who had been on drugs
   and had an accidental overdose stopped taking them and
   ended her association with her drug-taking friends.
10 Unfulfilled expectation of doing well; e.g., a girl had worked
   very hard for her exams, and thought she had passed; when
   she was given her results she found that she had failed.

Table 4.13 Item 8

Category		1	2	3	4	5	6	7	8	9	10	Total
Boys	A	2	2	1	0	5	2	3	0	0	1	16
	B	2	4	4	0	11	2	1	0	1	1	26
	C	5	1	5	1	4	6	6	1	0	0	29
Girls	A	5	0	0	1	1	0	2	0	0	0	9
	B	8	2	1	1	8	0	1	3	0	1	25
	C	4	1	0	0	3	0	0	2	1	0	11
Total		26	10	11	3	32	10	13	6	2	3	116

*Item 9 When you were right on your own, with hardly anyone
taking your side*

Categories
1 Relatively trivial difference on matters of fact, taste, or
   opinion; e.g., a girl was the only one in the family to have seen
   mice in their new house, and found it hard to convince the
   others that her report was true.
2 Differences over serious issues related to beliefs or values;
   e.g., a girl found that she always disagreed with her friends
   on issues such as abortion and marriage, and felt alone
   against them.
3 Taking some form of action against the norms or patterns of
   conduct of others; e.g., a girl took a stand against a group of
   others who were victimizing another girl.

4 Cases in which blame was unjustly attributed or apportioned to the participant; e.g., there was a fire at school, and a boy who had a reputation as a trouble-maker was assumed to have been involved, until a teacher listened carefully to his side of the story.

5 Experiences of feeling 'different' or isolated; e.g., after a girl had moved to another district she continued to attend her old school; but she found that she had become a stranger, and her former friends would have little more to do with her.

6 Active hostility or victimization by peers; e.g., a boy found that he was constantly being mocked, picked on, and 'pushed around' by others at work.

Table 4.14 Item 9

Category		1	2	3	4	5	6	Total
Boys	A	2	2	0	0	3	0	7
	B	1	3	3	3	3	1	14
	C	2	3	0	4	7	3	19
Girls	A	1	1	1	1	3	0	7
	B	0	4	5	0	6	1	16
	C	1	1	2	1	4	2	11
Total		7	14	11	9	26	7	74

Item 10 When you 'got away with it', or were not found out

Categories

1 Vandalism of various kinds; e.g., a girl and her friends threw the lights from a roadworks into a nearby canal.

2 Shoplifting and other forms of non-violent theft; e.g., a girl became involved with a group of teenagers who used to steal from a big store, sell the proceeds, and use the money to obtain drugs.

3 Drinking under age; e.g., a girl described how she would frequently go to pubs, though very much under age; sometimes she had got drunk, and been thrown out.

4 Other more serious forms of crime; e.g., a boy and his friend carried out a 'mugging', using an overcoat to smother their victim.

5 Violation of a social value; e.g., a boy made a mistake in woodwork at school; instead of repairing his own piece of wood he surreptitiously took the corresponding piece from the work of a boy who was away.

6 Truanting, or breach of school discipline; e.g., a girl had been through a phase of going to school, registering, and then walking out; a teacher had been 'picking on' her.
7 Violation of parental restrictions; e.g., a boy arranged that his girlfriend should come and sleep with him, while his parents were away on holiday.

Table 4.15 Item 10

Category		1	2	3	4	5	6	7	Total
Boys	A	0	2	1	2	2	3	0	10
	B	3	4	2	2	3	3	3	20
	C	3	5	1	6	2	1	1	19
Girls	A	0	0	0	0	1	2	2	5
	B	0	3	0	1	2	6	4	16
	C	1	0	1	1	1	6	1	11
Total		7	14	5	12	11	21	11	81

Item 11 When you made a serious mistake

Categories
1 Breaking the law, or other regulations or imposed rules; e.g., a boy went off with a friend in a car that he had stolen; they were caught by the police and taken to court.
2 Violation of a personally held value; e.g., a boy felt that he had been over-hasty in criticizing one of his teachers who had unjustly picked on him as a culprit.
3 Imprudent educational choices; e.g., a boy had started out on a certain A level course, basing his choice largely on his performance in O level, but then found that he was not interested in what he was studying, and decided to change subjects.
4 Failure to use opportunities at school; e.g., a girl had truanted over a considerable period, and later came to realize that this was a mistake, as she would get a bad reference on leaving school.
5 Mistakes arising from carelessness, over-confidence, lack of forethought, some of these causing injury or damage; e.g., a girl and her boyfriend had spent an evening at her home when her parents were out; they were drinking, and made a lot of mess; her parents were very angry when they returned.
6 Involvement with people or activities judged at a later stage to have been undesirable; e.g., a girl had started smoking in

order to 'keep in' with others, and then became a very heavy
smoker; she found that she was unable to give up the habit,
even though she had been warned by a doctor that it was
injuring her health.
7 The unwise or unnecessary breaking of a relationship; e.g., a
boy ended his friendship with a girl because he had thought
that she lived too far away, but afterwards regretted what he
had done.
8 Imprudent choices or decisions not covered by any of 1–7;
e.g., a girl had been a bully, but later came to realize, on
grounds of expediency, that this was a mistake.

Table 4.16 Item 11

Category		1	2	3	4	5	6	7	8	Total
Boys	A	0	0	0	0	2	0	0	0	2
	B	1	1	2	3	4	0	2	1	14
	C	3	1	0	2	6	1	0	2	15
Girls	A	0	3	1	1	1	0	2	0	8
	B	1	2	1	3	5	0	1	0	13
	C	2	2	2	1	2	2	2	2	15
Total		7	9	6	10	20	3	7	5	67

Item 12 When you felt afterwards that you had done right

Categories
1 Decisions related to the future, especially career; educational
decisions related to the future; e.g., a girl felt she had done
right to stay on at school beyond the leaving age in order to
try to obtain some O levels, since jobs were scarce.
2 Decisions concerning relationships, mainly among peers; e.g.,
a girl decided to end her friendship with a boy with whom she
had been going out for two years; he was from a different
social background, and was too 'serious' about their
association.
3 Conformity to institutional rules or norms; e.g., a boy who
had a job in a supermarket reported a person whom he saw
stealing.
4 Conformity to the wishes, requests or restrictions of parents;
e.g., a boy was sent by his mother to the launderette, which
he was very reluctant to do, since he regarded it as a woman's
work.

5 Decisions and dilemmas closely related to personally held values; e.g., a boy's brother's marriage had broken down; the boy was asked to say whether he was willing for his parents to look after the child from this marriage; although he realized the disruption it would be likely to bring at home, he said that he was willing for the child to be taken.
6 Decisions affecting a leisure-time activity or part-time job; e.g., a boy had become friendly with a man who knew about drumming; he also took up drumming, and became part of a 'band'.
7 Decisions made while responsible for others; e.g., a boy was supervising a group of young scouts on a walk; the weather turned bad, so he decided to return to camp, and brought them all back safely.

Table 4.17 Item 12

Category		1	2	3	4	5	6	7	*Total*
Boys	A	1	0	0	1	2	2	0	6
	B	2	3	2	0	4	2	1	14
	C	3	1	0	1	3	4	1	13
Girls	A	2	4	1	2	2	6	0	17
	B	6	6	2	1	7	0	0	22
	C	0	3	0	0	3	1	0	7
Total		14	17	5	5	21	15	2	79

Item 13 When you were disappointed with yourself

Categories
1 Lack of success in school work; e.g., a girl who was doing well at school in most respects was repeatedly failing in O level maths.
2 Poor performance in leisure-time activities, including sport; e.g., a boy who was in the junior county badminton team played badly in a school match; he knew he could have done much better, considering the standard of his play.
3 Inadequate 'behaviour'; e.g., a girl was disappointed with herself because she had not stood up to someone who was 'pushing her around' at work.
4 Failure to obtain a specific goal; e.g., a boy who thought he would easily obtain a certain job arrived late for the interview, and was later told that he had not been given the post.

5 Failure in communicating with others; e.g., a boy found that
he was unable to communicate to others the feelings of
elation he derived from listening to rock music.

Table 4.18 Item 13

Category		1	2	3	4	5	Total
Boys	A	4	5	5	1	1	16
	B	5	4	8	2	2	21
	C	6	7	10	2	0	25
Girls	A	8	2	4	1	0	15
	B	14	0	7	3	0	24
	C	3	0	5	0	1	9
Total		40	18	39	9	4	110

*Item 14 When you had a serious clash or disagreement with
another person*

Categories
1 Arising from the slighting of the participant's character; e.g.,
a girl's employer in her part-time job, whom she thought
incompetent, implied that *she* was incompetent, and a row
ensued.
2 Physical attack or provocation; e.g., a boy found that obscene
words had been written on his briefcase; he removed them,
and the act was repeated.
3 Discrepancies in belief or values (excluding parents); e.g., a
boy had 'given up the struggle' with physics, and this led to a
confrontation with the teacher, who thought his approach was
frivolous.
4 Disagreement with one or both parents over matters of belief
or values; e.g., a girl clashed repeatedly with her mother, who
constantly urged her to do her school work and consider the
future, and who disliked her style in clothes and shoes.
5 Unfair distribution of privileges, duties or responsibilities;
e.g., a girl's mother tended to give extra privileges to her
younger sister, and to allow her brother to escape without
making a fair contribution to the housework.
6 Struggle for status or power among peers; e.g., a boy whose
brother had provoked him decided to stand up to him,
although the brother was stronger; this led to an improvement
in their relationship.

7 Unwanted intrusion, interference or demands; e.g., a girl was
living with her grandmother, who was over-curious and over-
anxious about her activities; one evening when she had
returned from the pub the grandmother wanted to smell her
breath, and a serious clash ensued.

Table 4.19 Item 14

Category		1	2	3	4	5	6	7	Total
Boys	A	0	1	6	4	0	2	1	14
	B	2	0	1	5	0	7	1	16
	C	3	0	6	4	0	7	2	22
Girls	A	1	0	5	6	2	3	2	19
	B	5	3	5	8	1	3	1	26
	C	5	2	1	2	0	4	3	17
Total		16	6	24	29	3	26	10	114

*Item 15 When you began to take seriously something that had
not mattered much to you before*

Categories
1 The future, a career, getting qualified; e.g., a girl who had
previously treated most of her life as a 'laugh' had begun to
take the future seriously, and consider a possible career.
2 Academic work; e.g., a boy who had been very slack in his
school work had begun to take it more seriously, realizing the
importance of passing exams and getting a job.
3 Leisure-time activity; e.g., a girl had started to take lessons
in ballroom dancing; she liked the grace in the movements,
and the thought that it required; she had previously thought it
was only for 'creeps and pansies'.
4 Ideas, politics, etc., relatively remote from everyday life; e.g.,
a boy had begun to think about current affairs, and what the
political parties stand for; he was in favour of socialism and
democracy.
5 Beliefs and commitments of a more personal nature; e.g., a
boy had come to take Christianity seriously; he was trying to
express his faith in everything he did, by being responsible
and loving.
6 Money; e.g., a boy found that when he left school his life
changed in many ways; he earned a good wage, and had to
think about the problems of how to spend it.

7 Relationships; e.g., one member of a girl's group of friends committed suicide; they were all very shocked and upset, and realized how important relationships with each other were.

Table 4.20 Item 15

Category		1	2	3	4	5	6	7	Total
Boys	A	2	3	1	5	5	0	3	19
	B	4	3	4	1	4	1	1	18
	C	5	2	3	1	5	3	3	22
Girls	A	6	0	1	1	2	1	2	13
	B	4	1	1	0	3	0	7	16
	C	2	2	1	0	6	0	4	15
Total		23	11	11	8	25	5	20	103

Some Significant Omissions

In the early stages of the research the general tenor of the accounts, of which the previous section gives a small indication, produced certain surprises. The four of us who carried out the interviews came to them with particular expectations, derived in part from everyday observation, images projected by the media, and knowledge of some of the scholarly literature. We found that certain themes were emphasized more than had been anticipated, such as domesticity, relationships, reputations, personal achievement and affiliation with the adult world. There were other topics which we might have expected to occupy a considerable place in candid adolescent autobiography, but which in fact were scarcely mentioned. Four of these are particularly noteworthy for any attempt to understand the place of values in adolescent life. The question of these apparent absences was discussed in one of the 'validation sessions', with a boy aged eighteen in the upper part of social class group B living on a council estate, who appeared to have exceptionally broad social experience. A few extracts from his comments are included; in three instances he was largely in agreement with the tentative generalizations that were put to him, and in the fourth he provided a valuable additional insight on the topic as he understood it.

One of the most obvious omissions was the discussion of the content either of television programmes or of pop music. Superficially this might seem to be surprising, considering the enormous sale of records to the teenage market, and the well documented evidence (e.g. Fogelman, 1976) that adolescents spend a considerable part of their leisure time watching television. Television did receive the occasional brief reference, for example as the immediate precipitant of a family quarrel, or as an occupation to fill in time when there was nothing much else to do. There was virtually no indication, however, of boys and girls attributing learning, growth of understanding, interest, concern or satisfaction to its influence. The situation is rather similar with pop music. It was mentioned in passing, and it was clear that some of those interviewed had a well differentiated knowledge of its many forms and phases; but the greater part of its significance, as it appears from the interviews, was as a valid topic of conversation, as a basis for friendship groups and for rivalry between them, or as a ground for meeting with other people. This general point is the more striking in the light of the frequency with which music itself was mentioned. Among the activities connected with it that were discussed at some length were membership of a 'band', composing lyrics, playing before an audience, running a disco, and the social satisfaction of going to rock concerts. In all such instances the person was actively involved: in doing, making, creating, organizing or meeting, rather than in passively listening or responding. Even the life of the 'camp follower' of a teenage music group— typically the girl friend of a male performer—was portrayed as relatively boring. Thus both television and pop music generally seemed to form part of the 'background noise' against which more dramatic episodes were enacted. For most adolescents they appear to have become pervasive but not outstandingly significant parts of the taken-for-granted world, in much the same way that the British Empire or the harvest festival were in the youth of their grandparents.*

'Television does form such a, such a central thing. I mean, everybody watches telly. Maybe it's because television doesn't have the same effect because there's so much of it, and people watch it, just turn on the box and that's it. You know, there's, there's not that much on television now that really strikes you.'

'Maybe it's just that so much television is watched that it doesn't make an impact on people these days. And, I mean, television is supposed to be such a media that changes, that gives people their—morals or whatever is considered. But— maybe people just don't take notice of television. They'll watch it, but there's nothing—really there . . . . It's strange,

---

*The conventions adopted throughout this book in the presentation of verbatim extracts are summarized in the Appendix.

it's a real time-waster, television. I mean—I could go home and just, um, if the television's on I, I could sit there, and you'd get nothing out of it, but you just watch a comedy or you'd, you'd watch a, um—a, a series that is funny or something on, and you wouldn't really get anything out of it. It's, it's a real time-waster. It takes a lot of time, but it doesn't seem to give anything.'

A second 'significant absence' is a concern with the realm of ideas as a domain of intrinsic importance, rather than as a means to some not-too-distant end. Adolescence is sometimes portrayed, particularly by writers in the psychoanalytic tradition, as a period when some persons will show an intense interest in the affairs of the intellect, an eager searching for a philosophy by which to live, and for ideals in the light of which to strive for a better world. That kind of image is not confirmed by this research. Much more striking was a general lack of concern about or involvement in ideas as such, even among those who were academically very successful. For example, with item 15 ideas as such account for a mere 8 out of 103 categorized choices concerned with 'taking something seriously'. This general picture is reinforced in the way attitudes to school were presented. There was an overwhelmingly negative portrayal of the educational process, even by some of those who were well able to use it for their own ends. However, appreciation of the non-academic aspects of schooling was quite often expressed: it provided, for example, an opportunity for being creative in a practical or artistic way, for meeting and making friends, for outings and travel abroad. Some teachers were clearly included within the category of persons, and liked and respected as such. But about the world of the intellect, taken as valuable in itself, there was an almost total silence. Throughout the whole range of social class covered there was hardly any indication of commitment to school as a source of significant learning, or of concern with truth and understanding as these are academically viewed.

Three types of exception to this picture must be mentioned, though they do not modify it greatly. A few participants made reference to politics as an area of concern, the main emphasis being on socialist thinking. Some also spoke about their religious involvement; of those who expressed an active commitment, it was mainly a way of living and relating to persons, rather than fundamental issues of truth, that apparently attracted them. There were also a few boys who had a well developed knowledge either in practical mechanics or electronics, arising from their leisure-time pursuits; here too their concern was far more with efficacy than fundamental theoretical insight. In all these cases such involvement in the realm of ideas as they did have arose from their practical activity, rather than book-learning. The picture of widespread apathy about the more 'pure' academic realm is scarcely qualified by such instances.

'I know a friend of mine was, um, quite a strong communist and—quite an extreme in that. But other than that I can't think of, I can't think of hardly any people with political aspirations. Um, the reason for that I, I don't know. It, it's probably a lot due to, to—mainly the political state we're in now, and—maybe the complexity of politics I think has gone way above people's heads. I mean I, I would find it very hard to delve into politics, and you need, I think you need a lot of background to understand politics. And people aren't being taught it nowadays. Parents don't teach it to their kids. They, they might, they might, erm,—follow the way that their parents vote, but I don't think that there's any reason behind it, because people don't know about parties or differences. I mean I don't know, I know more or less nothing about politics, and—it, it's a general, it's a general thing, I'm sure. So many people aren't bothered, because they, they don't see anything in it, I'm sure.'

'A friend of mine who'd, well, we were in the same sort of group, into drugs. And it's always going for a higher and more ecstatic feeling when you get into drugs, and, er, especialy when you, if you get into LSD. And, er—I know, I, because I have, and I regret it now, but it's an experience that maybe is useful to me now, because my friend is still going through it, some of them. And one of them has, had got into a state where he found that he could get a, a better high in religion, in a religion, in a way of living, than on LSD. And so he's giving up drugs too, for, the experience in this weird religion that he wanted to get into. So I think there's a very big correlation between religious, the experience —factor in religious, and drugs. I think people are out for the experience.'

A third absence is frequent and direct reference to sexuality as a source of significance. One of the most commonly held stereotypes of adolescence is that this is a period of intense preoccupation with the physical aspects of sex.* The biological evidence about the

---

*The comments made here are, however, compatible with the findings of Schofield (1968), who also used an interview method of research.

early onset of puberty is well-established, and the stereotype has received confirmation from figures showing an increase in the frequency of adolescent pregnancy and venereal disease. In the accounts there were a number of allusions to sexual experience, made almost casually in passing, and there were three instances where this was made the explicit basis for the choice of an item from the interview schedule; two of these were concerned with how arrangements were made for a boy and girl to sleep together, and the third was a girl's description of the awakening of sexual desire. Ward (1976) observed similarly that working-class adolescent girls made few references to sex when interviewed, and suggests that the reason for this was that active sexuality has become so much a part of the taken-for-granted world that it is not outstandingly important. Although that may be a partial explanation, it does not seem to be adequate to account for the observations made in this research. There is some ground for thinking (see chapter 6) that many younger adolescents do not have the social skill to form intimate relationships with the opposite sex; and despite the lowering of inhibitions generally, it is still probable that sexuality is a domain of life too personal for some to discuss with a stranger.

'I think—erm, in teen-teens you start, you really start to begin, you start to learn how relationships work, and how to form relationships and who to form relationships with and what to do and—and maybe sex doesn't come into it so much, because you're on such a low level, erm, early teens especially. I mean, I know that, that I didn't really start to have any boy–girl relationships until seventeen maybe, seventeen and a half maybe even . . . . and maybe it cuts across a different level. But I mean, obviously I can, I can remember at school special people that stood out because they were a lot more mature, and mainly because of sexual relationships, whereas the wide range of people—I know, um, hadn't had sexual relationships, and therefore were on the, the learning level, so much, that they were just growing up and finding relationships important, yes, but not necessarily finding sex in a relationship.'

'Maybe they talk about it a lot. Er, I don't necessarily think they do it a lot. It's, it's a strange thing, I think it was a lot talked about in the, the circles I was in, the friends earlier on, yet, erm, there wasn't much of that kind of relationship going on. There weren't many even boy–girl relationships at the time.'

'Trouble was, I tended to know a lot of extreme people as well, which, which means you always get, you get the extremes. And whereas you, you know you tend to find, you may, you might know someone who was really deeply into intimate sexual relationships with about anybody, and people that are really closed. But I can say there's only isolated people in extreme circumstances that you'd know like that.'

Fourth, there is little evidence in this research that would support the idea that a 'search for identity' is a major feature of adolescence, at least up to the age of about eighteen. Erikson (1968), for example, suggests as part of his eight-fold scheme that the development of a personal identity (a consistent basis for the organization of experience) is the characteristic 'task' of this stage of life. This topic will be discussed in some detail in chapter 8. Suffice to say here that there were very few boys and girls in whose accounts such a concern was clearly evident. There were indications that some wished to adopt a distinctive personal style in specific contexts; that, however, is a very different matter from developing an inner integration.

'Rather than sitting at the back of the group, I remember myself clearly wondering, you know, "Where, where do I stand out?", you know, "Where, where is it that they know it's me there and not someone else?", you know. Whereas someone else does something you have your own, your own way of doing things. And I think very much I tried to, tried to find what was my way of doing things, and what was the identity I had on myself.'

'Maybe, maybe it's only speaking from myself, but I felt always that I wanted to stand out as an individual, and not be the same as the next person. Um, maybe a lot of people maybe do sit back and take things as they come along and fit in. I think maybe you fit in a lot with your values, but, but as standing out as a person, as an individual—I, I know espec-well, lots and lots of people that have, have tried to stand out, and in their way maybe they have gone to extremes, and they're extremely mad or completely crazy, or up about some things, and they do really stupid things, I think forming an identity for themself, a difference. I wouldn't say that, that most people aren't trying to have an identity, because every-one wants to be individual. Everyone wants themselves as a, a separate from, rather than the next person, to show them-selves up as being different.'

'I've known many, many people outside that group and—I, not sure, I mean, looking at some of my closest friends, maybe they don't—necessarily strive for an individ- , well they strive for an individuality. Well, I think everyone wants to be individual rather than just, just a, just part of a mass. And I know myself I found myself very clearly, erm, trying to be an individual, trying to be different from the people around me. Er, I mean, I, I got, well most of my friends I think tend to do that. It doesn't happen so much with girls, I've noticed. Erm—I think they, some of them do, but a lot of them tend, maybe I can't really see it because I can only see it from my point of view, from the male side. But girls don't seem to try and stand out so much. Some of them do, very much, but most seem to be on, on a sort of level with themselves.'

Some Hypotheses About Self-Presentation in the Interview

In the light of the evidence from interaction presented in the previous chapter, together with this cursory review of the tape-recorded data, it is now possible to attempt a characterization of the process by which the accounts were generated. Clearly in autobiographical narrative we are not dealing with straightforward factual description; the relative emphases given in accounts may not correspond closely with the pattern of events in everyday life. Helling (in Harré, 1976a) suggests that such material may be regarded as a mixture of three main elements: personal history, relatively stable aspects of the self-image, and self-presentation adjusted to the circumstances of utterance. The interviews that were carried out for this research seem to fit that general analysis well, though there is the added complexity that the participant was invited to make a deliberate and limited selection out of a vast range of possible material. Granted the following of a general rule of candour and detail in the actual narrative, evidence for which has been given in chapter 3, there appear to have been certain factors guiding the choice of an item from the schedule, or the bringing forward of a topic for discussion during the process of the interaction. Among them are the following.

1 The participant had undergone and could recall a relevant experience. This probably is the main explanation of the absence of choices by class A girls of the first two (criminal) categories of 'getting away with it' (item 10), or the greater number of choices by boys of item 7, category 5, describing 'life changing direction' as a result of interests or leisure-time activities.

2 The experience was judged sufficiently significant to be worthy of inclusion in the account. It is interesting to note, for example, that girls did not refer to success in sport as 'doing something well' (item 8, category 6), and that 'decisions concerning relationships, mainly among peers' (item 12, category 2) were referred to far more by girls than by boys.

3 The experience stood out in some way against a general background of expectations, either in a positive or a negative sense. There was, for example, no category of 'getting on well' with parents, although there was clear evidence that many adolescents had good relationships with their parents; on the other hand there were two categories of 'getting on well' with older people (item 8, categories 6 and 7) outside the home.

4 The subject-matter was such that it could be handled in the presence of a stranger. This probably accounts in part for the initial reluctance of a few to discuss traumatic family situations, and the relatively small number of direct references to sex. Detailed descriptions of crime, however, did not suffer from this constraint. Being 'right on your own' in relatively trivial matters (item 9, category 1) was also, clearly, very safe material.

5 The topic had a connection with what the participant thought the researcher expected or hoped to hear. It is possible, for instance, that the large number of references to negligence, disappointment or lack of success in academic performance (item 11, category 4, and item 13, category 1), is partly explicable in this way.

6 The account of the experience could be presented in a manner consistent with the general image the participant hoped to convey. Thus the first of the categories from item 2, 'getting on really well with people', was so general that it virtually amounted to the participant saying that he or she was a sociable kind of person; on the other hand the relatively small number of choices of the items concerned with 'discovering something new' (item 4) and 'being disappointed with yourself' (item 13) by girls of group C may well be because the material brought forward would in some cases have been too damaging.

Factors such as these do not necessarily work in harmony with each other. Positively, some participants may have settled for the discussion of experiences that they knew they could handle openly and safely in the presence of a stranger, but that were not of outstanding personal significance; or they may have chosen topics that they thought would fit in with the interviewer's expectations, but that were not fully consistent with their desired self-presentation. Negatively, some topics may have been omitted which an observer might have judged to be significant, but which the participant had come to take for granted; others, perhaps, were too delicate to discuss in such circumstances, or would have promoted a disagreeable image. This is not to suggest, however, that conscious considerations of this kind were always, or even commonly, employed. Following the 'realist' methodology in dealing with episodes whose character is enigmatic (cf. chapter 1), phenomena are being explained by saying that it is 'as if' a certain generative process were operating. In this case several processes, not necessarily concordant with each other, have been postulated.

Clearly, then, the explanation of the pattern of choice for any one item, or a single category within it, is usually complex, requiring reference to more than one of the six factors that have been discussed. It would, therefore, be a misguided strategy to draw simple inferences from quantified similarities and differences in the data, categorized at this or a more detailed level. Fortunately in this type of research there is no need to handle the material in such a relatively 'mechanical' way, because the close texture of the accounts is so revealing. The substantial method of data-processing here was that of paying close attention to the accounts, determining what cases could be treated as being similar in certain respects, and going on to elucidate the relevant characteristics. The patterns that emerged in this way were very different from those that would have resulted from a detailed numerical analysis, followed by speculative comments on the causes of significant similarities and differences. However, although the method thus goes far beyond a 'positivist' strategy, the findings were required to be consistent with the general tenor, and specific features, of the quantified data.

It might be said that this is a highly fallible kind of procedure. It is possible that connections have been inferred when in reality there were none, and that important patterns were overlooked because of the inefficiency of the researchers or the inadequacy of the evidence. In other words, that feature common to all scientific work (to which several contemporary philosophers have drawn attention)—empirical under-determination—is present to an outstanding degree in research of this kind. At least there is the advantage that here it is brought out into the open; whereas in many other kinds of research similar features are also present, but are latent and unacknowledged.

5
Relationships in the Family

The start of adolescence is generally taken to be the onset of puberty, with the accompanying changes in physical size and bodily function. From a social–psychological point of view adolescence arrives when boys and girls achieve near-total independence from adults in certain areas of their lives; their projects begin to take on distinctive form; they move into social life-worlds which are evidently not childish and whose control, at least in an immediate sense, is in their own hands. Although this is the case, it is necessary to begin a study of values by seeing adolescents as members of their families, and especially to examine their views about relationships with their parents. For it is against the background of home life, and in a constant interaction with it, that their autonomous life develops.

Before the age of about five most children live in what might be regarded as a single social life-world, whose meanings are provided by the home. In the years that follow a second zone of meaning, that of school, becomes increasingly clearly demarcated; there begin to be large social class differences in the extent to which the meanings within these two social life-worlds are compatible. Around the age of twelve or thirteen a wider range of opportunities becomes available, and many boys and girls begin to find the main loci of their concerns outside the family. The significance of some adolescent activities is partially opaque to their parents, especially if the age gap is considerable. As a result a certain tension develops; this tends to be more acute in middle-class homes, where mutual incomprehension may be deeper, restrictions more extensive and social influence attempts by parents more pervasive and prolonged. From the adolescent's point of view, home often acquires an ambivalent character. On the one hand it is valued as a place of physical provision and (in many cases) of relative stability; a continued loyalty is definitely fitting. On the other hand, some degree of independence from it must be achieved. Adolescence is thus a period of moving away from parents, both physically and psychologically. There are clear values relating to this transition.

Adolescents and Their Parents: Some Comments on the Data

As was suggested in chapter 4, the process by which items were chosen from the interview schedule and by which accounts were given was far from simple. It appears that episodes were often selected for description because they stood out in some way against general background expectations. This may well have been particularly the case with accounts of family life, which is a pervasive and sometimes relatively featureless part of the taken-for-granted world. There was no category of 'getting on well' with parents in connection with item 2, whereas parents often figured in narratives concerned with conflict. Thus item 5 yielded a category of 'unjust or unwanted intrusion, restriction, or demands from parents', and item 14 'disagreement with one or both parents over matters of belief or value', as well as two other categories in which parents were included. The most positive general characterization of family life at this degree of detail was in item 6, category 2: 'conformity to parents, but not against the participant's wishes or values'. Item 12, category 4, was similar in tone, dealing with 'conformity to the wishes, requests or restrictions of parents'. It would be highly naive, however, to make positivistic inferences from such observations, and to conclude that adolescents generally see their relationships with their parents in a negative light. The detailed texture of the accounts shows something of the background against which specific choices of episodes dealing with family life were made.

On close examination it appears that the accounts given by older and younger participants often differed in character. The main issues here were the extent to which boys and girls gave evidence of understanding the implications of their actions on family life; and their ability to envisage the point of view of others—hence the reasons for their parents' actions in relation to them. Among those in the 'older' age-range three main groups could be distinguished. First, there were those who stated or implied that they had always had, and were still having, tolerably good relationships with their parents, and who were able to point to factors that enabled this to be the case. Second, there were those who had been through a period of rebellion, which had more or less ceased as they grew older. Those in the third group characterized themselves as still being in conflict with their parents, a state that had existed since the beginning of adolescence; nevertheless, they could talk about the situation with detachment, including taking their parents' point of view. 'Younger' participants could be divided into two groups: those whose accounts suggested that family relationships were relatively harmonious, and those who described varying degrees of mutual incomprehension, and their continual struggle against what they perceived as unreasonable parental demands. Using judgments based on the whole tenor of the accounts, the rough categorization shown in tables 5.1 and 5.2 was obtained. Participants living with one parent faced circumstances too different for them to be a valid part of this analysis, but cases of adoption or remarriage after the death of one parent were included. The distinction between 'younger' and 'older' was made

Table 5.1 'Older' adolescents

	Boys Middle-class	Working-class	Girls Middle-class	Working-class
Group 1 'Good relation-ships throughout'	6	6	5	9
Group 2 'Conflict, but now past'	3	2	4	4
Group 3 'Continued conflict'	6	7	6	2

Table 5.2 'Younger' adolescents

	Boys Middle-class	Working-class	Girls Middle-class	Working-class
Group 1 'Generally good relationships'	6	6	2	7
Group 2 'Conflict'	4	4	8	3

on the ground of apparent insight, as previously outlined, rather than on strict chronology, though the point of the transition was around the age of sixteen. In cases where harmony with one parent and conflict with another was described, the judgment was based on the characterization of the relationship with the parent who apparently had the greater significance. The numbers have been corrected so that the total for each sex and social class in the 'older' group is fifteen, and in the 'younger' group is ten; i.e. a completely even distribution would mean five in each cell.

There are many difficulties in making inferences from data of this kind. Ideas of what constituted 'tolerably good relationships' may have varied. Some participants did not talk at all about their families, and so are not represented in the tables. It was possible that some of these simply took their homes for granted, without seeing a clear connection between events there and the more dramatic type of episode suggested by the interview schedule; on the other hand circumstantial evidence implied that there were a few who found their family life too painful or too shameful to discuss with a stranger. The exclusion of cases of divorce or separation means that some of the most traumatic situations are not featured at all. Nevertheless, it is against a pattern of this kind that the material discussed in this chapter must be assessed. The tables show that any stereotype of contemporary adolescents as being typically in revolt against their parents is incorrect; and there is at least an indication that middle-class girls are the group for whom an experience of conflict with parents is most frequent.

For younger adolescents the characteristic form in which the question of relationships with parents presents itself is not so much what they ought to do, as how they ought to be treated. To use the geological metaphor to which reference was made in chapter 1, this is a deposit in the personality from the kind of relationships that predominated during childhood. The whole issue tends to become more significant during the teenage period because a major part of the project of most boys and girls is to achieve some measure of psychological independence. At the same time, as they begin to 'move out' into adolescent social life, and perhaps also into the world of work, they may well take on new roles in relation to their parents, the prescriptions for which are mainly laid down by their own peers; associated with this, parental advice and admonitions, at least in certain areas, become less credible. Nevertheless, most adolescents realize that they must remain in communication with their parents, since there are many issues where negotiation is necessary, and others where help is still required. Also, there is generally an acceptance of certain obligations, such as giving practical help in the home. Although there are many variations, particularly in relation to sex and social class position, this is a general framework for understanding values concerned with relationships in the family.

The material then, is organized around three main topics: independence, communication, and co-operation. The chapter concludes with a brief discussion of homes in which there has been a major disruption such as divorce, prolonged illness, or death, dealing mainly with the ways in which values discussed earlier tend to be modified under those conditions. The details of 'family dynamics' are scarcely touched, since this requires more precise and prolonged study than the method used in this inquiry allowed.

The Movement Towards Independence

Around the age of twelve or thirteen many boys and girls begin to find that it is almost a necessity for them to achieve a greater degree of independence from parents than they had before. The most obvious point at which divergent opinions become evident is the restrictions that parents place on the social life of their children: what kinds of activity are permitted, and for how long. Superficially the matter appears to be simple. The adolescent wishes to do something of which the parents disapprove; in most cases a compromise is reached, but occasionally the result is an act of defiance. Debates or disagreements of this kind have an almost symbolic quality; they are tests of the extent to which a more general freedom has been achieved. Thus there are several issues that lie behind the apparently simple matter of restrictions. In relation to parents, these include the adolescent's freedom to think independently, to make decisions and judgments and to become the kind of person he or she wishes to be. In relation to peers, it is important for a boy or girl to be able to exhibit control over movements in and out of family life. It must also be said that the fact that arguments occur, and are generally resolved, implies a tacit acknowledgment that parental authority is recognized as valid. The expectations that adolescents have of their parents, and indeed of their family as a whole, change as they become older, especially as their ability to understand the viewpoint of others increases. There is a movement through a series of compromises, in a continuing dialectical process, until finally a boy or girl attains the status of an adult. Within this general pattern there is great variation between adolescents in their views about the legitimate scope of parental authority, about what constitutes an appropriate degree of freedom at a particular age, and the extent to which they wish to show to others that they are in control. At first it is mainly a matter of debate over restrictions in specific circumstances, which may not necessarily appear to be related. Later, perhaps, it becomes apparent to the person involved that the underlying issues in many cases were the same.

The position of the sexes in the movement towards independence is markedly different, and also depends very much on social class position. In relation to the obvious matter of restrictions, the two main issues for middle-class boys appear to be satisfying their parents that they are doing sufficient school work, and convincing them that in their activities they will not come to physical harm. Several boys from group A described how they either had been assaulted late at night, or were afraid that this might occur; two described how they had not told their parents after being attacked, for fear that further restrictions might ensue. In contrast to this, boys from working-class backgrounds attribute to their parents two main types of concern about their activities: that they should not come to physical harm through their own recklessness, and that they should not 'get into trouble'.*

'Before I was eighteen [sarcastically], "Mummy and Daddy" said you had to be back home by such and such a time, which I thought was, er, completely stupid. Because at seventeen I assumed that, er, one would be allowed to go out to parties, at least to get back rather late, if not stay the night. But—er, it didn't really work. In something like—ten days before my eighteenth birthday I was going off to a party, and I said I didn't know what time I'll be back. "I want you back at half past eleven." So I thought—"No, no, no, ... it's going to take me ages to get back." They said, "No, half past eleven." So I said—Following morning I got back home about eight o'clock in the morning. [Sarcastically] "Mummy and Daddy" had 'phoned the police—saying, er, asking if they could find out where I was. Nobody knew where I was. They were new, completely new friends of mine. And, er, that started a great family row.—Shall I go into gruesome details? . . . . Um—I got back—well I actually got back at about seven o'clock. Mum and Dad were still in bed and I did my paper round, which I have to do every morning. At eight o'clock I got back to the house, and Mum and Dad were downstairs in the kitchen—And, um—"Where were you last night?" "Er, I

---

*The conventions adopted in the presentation of verbatim extracts are summarized in the appendix.

didn't have time to get home so I thought I'd spend the night there." "I told you, you ought to be back at half past eleven. Complete disobedience." "It's only ten days until my eighteenth birthday, and then you said I could stay out the night at, at a party." "That makes no difference at all"—and, er, screaming at each other for a week. Then something like —I was eighteen in another ten days, I went to another party and stayed all night and they didn't say a word. [Laughter] I think it's so stupid. I mean, they're, they've got their built-in principles, which I can understand perfectly. Having such a tight, fixed er—but they also let me go down, they also didn't really object to me going down to the pub before I was eighteen.

'No matter what my Mum does, I mean, I just do what I like anyway, I suppose. It's partly my fault because I can't accept how they feel.'

(Boy$_{14}$, Group A, 18)

'My father starts shouting and moaning . . . . We was talking about houses—and I was telling him about some certain houses what you could park by, and he was saying that you couldn't. And then there was a row about it and—then we got on to cars and that. And he reckoned that I was going to kill myself on, in, cars, because I had been so mad. And— then it turned into a bigger row, so in the end he walked out.'

(Boy$_{17}$, Group C, 16)

'Me and his brother and him went up to my front door and went to go in. And the first thing my Dad says to me, "You've been in trouble with the police again." So I said, said "Yeah". He didn't say nothing after that, he just punched me straight in the face . . . . He just took me in the front room and gave me a severe beating.

'You thought you was sort of old enough to go out, and you wanted to go out and enjoy yourself. But most of the other people, you know, didn't go home until, say, eleven o'clock, or half past eleven. This is when you were about thirteen, fourteen, and so you wanted to stay out as well, because you didn't want to sort of go home early. Used to think "Why do I have to be in by nine o'clock?" and I used to be in by about ten o'clock. And you could never really go out and enjoy yourself with your friends, and that. They always used to stay out later, and it never really used to get going until later in the night, as you probably know—And they, you know, used to say "Be home by nine o'clock" and this. In a way made me resent my parents. I didn't want to, I didn't want to have to come in. I didn't want to have to do anything. I wanted to do what I wanted.'

(Boy$_{28}$, Group C, 17)

Girls, however, especially those from middle-class homes, seem to have the additional problem of convincing their parents that they will not have an opportunity to engage in sexual activity. Thus all-night parties, trips to the country in cars and spending long periods alone with a boyfriend are often proscribed, especially for younger girls.

'It's just, you know, restricting you, is what really annoys me, when your parents restrict you against something and you can't see anything wrong with it. Or—let's say, you can see what would be wrong with it, but it's not going to be. [Laughter] You know, one of those things, you know, like a party they don't think is innocent, and that kind of thing, and going in people's cars and, um—it gets me cross because I've got to make decisions myself, and I've got to do them some-time, and I think I'm quite up to making them myself—and they can't deny it, really.

'It got to the stage once that, um, I was asked to go to another town in a bloke's car and, you know, with some other boys and girls, all friends, and I said "Yes" straight away. I didn't expect they'd say "No". Of course my mother said "No", because she doesn't know the blokes, and went on about the car and everything, and whether we could drive. So I felt—I can't face saying that I can't go. It's so stupid and petty and, um, so I went without her knowledge. It got to the situation where I thought, well, "She's going to find out any-way. There's no way she's not going to um—not find out." So I told her—I couldn't face the fact that if I want to do something I've got either—to do it and face the punishment, or give up. I don't get away with much.'

(Girl$_{15}$, Group A, 16)

'Yes, I think it's much more difficult being a girl. You can get yourself into situations. [Laughter] I think my parents have got their reasons for being worried. They do trust me to a great extent, they know I'm not going to do anything stupid.'

(Girl$_{17}$, Group A, 18)

'My mate says to me—"Come, come and meet my bloke"

. . . . So I said "All right then". She said, like—there'd be another boy there. I said. "All right then". So she's told her Mum that she's coming out with me to a party at my home.

'I had to be in at half past ten. All the way from where we went is a long way—so I come up, I panicked. We got home. I ended up getting home at ten to twelve. Well I got in and my Dad had a car at the time. Well, they knew where my mate lived, so they'd gone up my mate's house, and were having a big discussion. I 'phoned up my mate's home to let my mate, like, my Mum and Dad know I was home.

'He come in, my Dad, dragged me out. "Where have you been?" So I thought "Well if I tell him how far I gone he'll kill me." "Gone to town Dad, I went to town" . . . . "Oh yeah," he said, "What's all this lying to your mate's Mum, telling your mate's Mum that I was, she was coming to a party with us?" So I said "Well, that was because she couldn't come out otherwise." Oh, my Dad hit me, and he's never hit me so hard in all—I mean he's hit me, but the way he hit me that night, I thought he was going to kill me. My mum had to pull him off me. He said "Me and your Mum has been worried sick about you, absolutely worried sick." Oh, it was terrible. So—I couldn't go out for about a month.

'For about six months after that my Mum wouldn't believe anything I told her, but she used to check up everywhere I was going out and everything. I felt like a criminal. Used to come in, used to go "I'm going to a disco tonight". "Where is it?" "Who are you going with?" "Oh, well, I'm going with—" "Well, we'll have to sort that out. I don't know if you can go. You'd better ask your father. We'll come and collect you", or something like that. And I felt like a criminal for about six months. I felt just like I was—I was a criminal, and they was checking up on me every five minutes. I was frightened to say, lie, or tell anything . . . . I spoiled their trust in me for about—six months, and then I gradually worked their trust round again. And I've never done anything really to break their trust—again. But, I mean, admittedly I still lie, because I think—I think everybody lies to their Mum and Dad. Even my Mum admits that she lies to her Mum and Dad, and my Dad admits that he lies to his Mum and Dad. So to a certain extent my Mum and Dad expect you to lie or, or know when you're going to lie, or know—you're lying, if you know what I mean. Though they don't turn and say "You're lying", they know you're lying. But I think that's only because when they was young they did the same thing.'

(Girl$_2$, Group C, 17½)

The whole matter is given a further colouring by what appear to the adolescents involved to be considerations of justice: there should be an equal degree of restriction for members of a family when they are of the same age, and the kind of rules that are made for one person should correspond with those that are made by the parents of his or her friends. It is not simply a matter of justice, however; if people in equivalent positions are given the same degree of freedom, status is not threatened, and the impression of being in control can be preserved.

'I asked my mother could I stay out for half an hour later than when I came in. And she said no, wasn't old enough. And I said "Well, my sister stays out longer. Why can't I?" I said, "She did when she was only fifteen, she stayed out later." My mum said "Well, you're younger, you got to stay in." I just said "Well I'm not." And I stayed out late, and when I got in I got a good hiding. And we started arguing . . . . started arguing, and then I just said to her "Well I don't agree with you. Why can't I stay up the same le- time as she could?" And she just said "Because you can't. You're not old enough, and you're not capable enough."

'I agree with the way she says I'm not old enough to stay out of a night with a lad, and all that, but I don't agree with the way she says I can't come in the same time as what my sister was when she was my age.'

(Girl₄, Group B(N), 15)

'My mother, I used to get on with her for a while. And then she'll say "Right, in at ten o'clock", that sort of thing. Sixteen year old and to be in at ten. For her at sixteen, you know, it's nowt. But for kids like us it's summat, you know—what's the point of being sixteen if you can't do owt, when you're sixteen?

'I got on smart with my elder brother. He's been away quite a couple of times. Been to borstal, detention centre, but only time that, you know, he never used to—lay it on my mother. He never used to be at home. My mother didn't bother then, ... so much about not coming in, doing nowt. But with me, seeing that I'm the youngest, she wants, she thought I were still a kid. But when my older brother was sixteen he was, you know, nearly a man as far as she were concerned. But with me I was still a kid.'

(Boy₁, Group B(M), 16)

The process of becoming independent, symbolized in particular by the negotiations and compromises involved in the matter of parental restrictions, goes through various stages. Objectively, and obliquely related to the legal position of adolescents, both sixteen and eighteen years old appear to be milestones, marking points at which more freedom should be given. Where appropriate concessions are not made, boys and girls may well take what they consider to be their right; with each year of movement towards adulthood their power becomes greater and that of their parents less.

There are major social class differences in the achieving of adult status. The clearest case is that of a working-class boy, who leaves school at sixteen and is successful in finding employment. If he is still living at home he begins to have a position comparable with that of his father; he too is a breadwinner, and a contributor to the family wellbeing.

'Not in such as their attitude towards me has changed. They, they're, how shall I put it? They think the same of me just as if I was fourteen to sixteen, but oh—I'm giving them money, so every time I come home from work it's "How did you get on, eh?", "Have a good day?" "Have a—sit down", sort of thing. I'm not expected to do any of the work at home any more, whereas I used to have to do washing up and wiping up, but I do it out of my own—I feel like I ought to do it, and I do it. But they don't expect it of me any more.

'They don't worry about me any more when I go out at night, you know. They worry, they think a lot of me and worry about it, but—it's difficult to describe it. It was a sudden change.'

(Boy$_{18}$, Group B(M), 16)

'Now I've left school—well, my parents are all right—they allow you freedom, which I didn't think I was going to get. But they, they, they said from the beginning "As soon as you've left school and you're in a good job and you're settled, you're all right." Then they sort of let me go.'

(Boy$_{28}$, Group C, 17)

This research gave no strong indication of a corresponding clear change of status for girls who leave school at sixteen, although several talked at considerable length about their jobs. They are generally expected to make a contribution to household work during the time that they are at school, and if they go on to paid employment this does not exonerate them from their contribution in the home. In other words there is a continuity in home life, between the roles of schoolgirl, daughter-who-goes-out-to-work, wife, and wife-who-goes-out-to-work. While some girls resent this, there was scarcely a hint of a belief among those who were interviewed that it might be within their power to bring about a change in this state of affairs.

'I'm not, I'm not a very important figure. Um, when, when I said I wished to stay on at school I think my Dad were resentful, because he wants me to go out to work—and bring in the money. So—I don't think my Dad would ever put trust in me . . . . they lack confidence in me.

'About a month ago my stepmother left us, for about three weeks. So I was, I had to do all our work then. And um—it wasn't as if it was—an extra thing on top of my school work. It was just the natural thing . . . . And um—didn't appreciate it at all. Um—when I, when I wanted to er, stay on at school my Dad said I had to go to, go to work and all. So I've got two part-time jobs. And, er—and if I say something like—well, "I'm working at school" and all, my Dad'll say "Well, it's only one day a week, isn't it?" And he doesn't appreciate the fact that I'm trying to study and all. So—I don't think I'm very important at all—in the home.

(Girl₁, Group C, 17)

Those from upper-middle-class backgrounds, who generally stay on at school beyond the age of sixteen, and in many cases face the prospect of further or higher education, also do not have clear indicators of a change of status with regard to their parents. A great deal depends on the process of negotiation, through which they try to obtain for themselves that degree of independence that they judge to be their right.

'It's more equal sided now . . . . They still say "Don't be late back", but I do what I like . . . . I think they thought, they felt they were still responsible for me. That was, until I was eighteen they were still legally responsible for my actions. And therefore . . . . I can't understand because, er . . . . because it's not so much the responsibility, I would have thought. It's more of, er, love . . . . which they should be more concerned about.'

(Boy₁₄, Group A, 18)

'When I was fourteen they was obviously more strict—to erm, erm, to some degree. They were, you know, they were

always on about er, not going out during the week, got my
work to do, and, and, er "Oh, you're not seeing that girl
again", and—this and that. And they were you know, they,
they didn't sort of regard me as an individual in my own
right. They regarded me more as, more as a child, you know,
and er, something that they owned.

'My parents now are, er, er, probably up to the age of, er,
fourteen when I started to rebel they, they're sort of, um, I
don't know, how can you say it, they—adapt to me, I
suppose. Is that the right word? They er, they go along, they
don't, they, they tell me to do what I feel like doing, or, as
long as it's not, say, you know, totally out of the question.
But if I like to do what I want to do for when I leave home,
which is very soon, which is—when I go to university I should
be able to take care of myself, instead of having to rely on
my parents. That's the main thing. I get on, I get on very well
with them, you know. I couldn't, I couldn't really ask for
better parents . . . . They still obviously show that they care
by saying, if I'm out at parties they'll tell me "Oh, I'll come
and pick you up at— ", you know. They'll come and pick me
up, or they'll always ask me what time I'll be in . . . . But er,
overall it's, it's a good relationship.'

(Boy$_2$, Group A, 17)

'When they change their attitude to you, you change your
attitude to them and—um—it's like you've come to the end
of a long struggle and you haven't come out on top,
but you've come out—and really it's, um—just um—and
thinking back on it—I probably wasn't very adult a year ago,
though I probably thought I was at the time—I thought it
was very unfair I wasn't allowed to do this and that and—
treated in whatever way, um. But—reflecting on it, it
probably wasn't at all unfair.

'The fact that I couldn't see other people's point of view—
because, even though you might not feel that you're being
selfish at the time, whatever instant it may be, in fact, you do
only see it from your own point of view, or I did—And you
can't understand why other people did, and um—and you
can't understand why other people don't share the same view
and say "Yes, go ahead".

'Yeah, I mean, battles about anything um . . . . well I'd say
bedtimes [Laughter], you know what I mean, or, well just
anything. But anyway now I mean . . . . the battles of, say,
school, or say being in at whatever time or going to bed by
. . . . or, I mean, it doesn't exist now. But, um . . . . well

that's not only because of me it doesn't exist, um I
mean it doesn't exist because I'm older um . . . . say Mum,
who, well she, I mean, didn't, inflict isn't the word, but she
said "OK, you must be in by a certain time." In fact, I mean,
when I think back, I mean very reasonable, no question about
it, very reasonable.
    'In fact, I didn't have many battles to fight . . . . but um, I
just created them . . . . it didn't seem futile at the time at all.
I mean, it seemed like the most important thing happening in
the world.'

(Girl₁₇, Group A, 17)

Those who are at school are necessarily dependent on their
parents in certain respects. Having to look to parents for money
does, of course, diminish the extent to which they can actively
assert their freedom. Thus obtaining a part-time job, besides its
obvious financial importance, facilitates the movement towards
independence; this may be regarded as having equivalent symbolic
character, in some respects, to 'going out to work' for boys who
leave school at sixteen. Since girls tend to be more tied by parental
restrictions, and to be expected to participate in a traditional
'woman's role' at home, it is possible that having a part-time job
has a particular significance for their relationship with their
parents.

'My parents didn't think my having a Saturday job was a
great idea, because of A levels. Very few of my friends had
jobs. My parents tried to say "Oh, you don't have to have a
job, rely on us. You've got enough to do at school." But, um
—I found, you know, you got fed up with having to ask your
father for money. "Can I do this, Can I do that?" And I
found one, and I was quite happy. My brother worked at the
same place as well. We worked in a shop, didn't enjoy it
much, but, um . . . . I like the financial independence. It's
very important. Before it was OK having your pocket money.
You weren't really worried, you know, about doing much.
But, once you started wanting to go out with your friends and
—actually do something without—When you have to ask for
the money they tend to ask you what you're going to do with
it. [Laughter] It's nice to be free without questions.'

(Girl₁₉, Group A, 18)

'It was a very important decision whether I was going to sort
of, depend on my Mum and Dad, have them still support me,
and no independence. I thought "I've got to start some-

where", and I found that the wage that I get is adequate, you know, for the week, and it does give me more chance to go out. Like beforehand, I, I couldn't have very much money to spend, and I couldn't be able to go out, you know. I'd always stay in, have no money to really sort of—to spend. And er, so now at this stage . . . . I've got some money where I can sort of, do what I like and um, not depend on my mother and father.'

(Girl$_{15}$, Group B(N), 16)

The move towards independence that most adolescents make between the ages of about thirteen and eighteen has its effect on the personality. Boys, and to some extent girls also, from working-class backgrounds are generally allowed a considerable degree of autonomy; they become used to standing on their own feet, and betray little sign of *angst* at the prospect of taking the role of an adult. Middle-class adolescents, on the other hand, generally face a wider range of choices, and their future is more open; having been protected by parents in many important matters, they often show a certain indecision, and even voice their apprehensions at the prospect of taking an adult role.

'I think this teacher was saying—implying that I should—do modern languages at university, which I think was still in my mind at that time.

'He said that I should carry on with the English, which, which, I think, having a grounding in English literature has actually helped me in the French and German, which didn't start quite so early. I did take his advice. It would have been quite hard to—do otherwise, actually. Probably interview with the second master who is, is rather formidable.

'Some time ago, I can't remember exactly how long, perhaps a year, I thought "Well I'm not fussy if I don't even go to university at all." But—oh well, I suppose, even though I say it myself I am—I think perhaps one of the more—the cleverer ones at this school, so I ought to at least try. Then I thought that, well, "I'm not fussy about which university I go to. Er, I'm not fussy if it isn't Oxford. In fact if it's not Oxford, all the better, because perhaps it's a sort of protest against the system"—After the, er, sixth form conference at Sussex which I went to I was really taken with Sussex. I thought that, perhaps, well "Sussex is really great. I'd like to go there; piss Oxford. It also means that, er—I wouldn't have to take an exam to get into Oxford."

'For some reason I, well I don't know—perhaps it was

right, I let myself be persuaded that Oxford—was—better. It probably is, I don't know.'

(Boy₁, Group A, 18)

'You have to break away from your parents . . . . it's been quite gradual, um, only in the last couple of years . . . . It was on deciding what I'm going to do after this that you realize that they are not going to be there, and you're going to have to face reality, and it's going to happen one day [Laughter]—You do quite often find that you're having to— um—you know, people do rely on you, they expect things from you—I find this hard at the moment, as my mother's in hospital, and you realize that your parents aren't sort of in-vincible. You're going to have to stand in for them sometimes —and they expect something from you back—you know. You plan your own life and try not to make mistakes. I still find it very difficult, you know, to imagine leaving home and having a flat or anything. And you have to make all your own major decisions, quite daunting—You make so few decisions that, you know, that when it comes to the first one you're frightened of making a mistake.'

(Girl₁₉, Group A, 18)

'I feel that I've been—not sheltered, but I haven't really had to make any decisions myself yet, um—The time will come, you know, when I leave school. I haven't really been exposed to anything that I've really got to make up my mind about that's really seemed important, you know. I really haven't to um—it's all been done for me, I'd say, you know.'

(Girl₇, Group A, 16)

In contrast to the main picture conveyed in this section, there appears to be a small proportion of (mainly middle-class) boys and girls for whom the desired increase of freedom is very little. The social life-world of home remains the most credible in their experience, and they do not 'move out' to a significant extent into the company of peers.

'I tend to much—prefer to be at home after school time . . . . It's just that I—I suppose I just don't, er—erm—I suppose I'm not too keen on the whole class coming round when I'm —like during the summer holidays. It's just that I, I've—I prefer to be at home during home time. Because we go out quite a lot in any case, so there's not much point, because usually we're away . . . . er, to see various relations, not far away

from here. We also go and visit quite a few places like, erm,
zoos etcetera, mainly because I have two young sisters. And, er,
there's my Mum and Dad always used to take me out—when
I was their age. We all, we all just go together.'

(Boy$_{10}$, Group B(N), 16)

The great majority, however, are far from asserting a true
personal autonomy, as the following chapter will show. It is
generally a matter of becoming free from restrictions of an open
and explicit kind, and entering a social world where there are
strong normative expectations, no less powerful because their
presence is hidden and implicit.

Communication

The movement towards independence from parents has been
characterized at an earlier point in this chapter as a dialectical
process, in which both parties are constantly involved: each
making concessions here and there, sometimes succeeding and
sometimes failing to understand one another's point of view.
There are many homes where relationships are generally harmonious; on the other hand, as tables 5.1 and 5.2 imply, the
proportion in which adolescents experience serious problems of
communication may be of the order of 50 per cent. The accounts
suggest that two main levels are involved. In terms of the model
outlined in chapter 1 these may be described as that of personality-
in-role, and that of interpersonal perspectives. The first category
covers explicit attempts by parents to influence their offspring,
and the second the way adolescents believe that they are perceived.

Communication at the Level of Personality-in-Role

For many upper-middle-class adolescents the area where positive
parental influence and advice is most clearly acceptable is that
which relates to their career, and hence also some of their major
decisions concerned with education. This point will be taken up
further in chapter 8. Suffice to say here that the accounts gave
scarcely a hint that such action was regarded as illegitimate, where
the boy or girl concerned was also seriously trying to resolve the
problem of the long-term future; the interests of the parties are
generally aligned. On the other hand parental intervention into
the 'private' life of their offspring (their leisure-time activities,
relationships, clothes, spending, the extent and organization of
their school work, and whether they should be concerned about a
career), is perceived as trespassing beyond the legitimate
boundary of the parental role.

'Me and my Mum don't get on very well at all anyway. And—she's very stubborn, and she's never, er, you know, she's never wrong. I know I, you know, she always says I think I'm never wrong. But I think sometimes she—you know, she thinks she's never wrong. Whenever we're having tea or anything, she'll always come up and say something about my school work, or I haven't done this, I haven't done that. And she really goes on about it, and she makes a scene about everything, you know. She carries on, and when Dad gets home she brings it up again and everything. And, and one day she really just, oh dear, she carried on about school work, and "You'll never get anywhere if you don't do your work", and "You haven't made your bed yet, have you?" and really, you know, shouting at me and everything. So I just walked out the house. And I—er, went down to a friend's house and I stayed out till about eleven o'clock. I was going to stay out all night, but I, I didn't have the guts. I sort of sneaked back about eleven o'clock, and she didn't speak to me that, that night, and she never mentioned it again.'

(Girl$_7$, Group A, 16)

'My parents kind of think that there's a universal wrong and a universal right, and their wrong should apply to me, and their right should be the same to me, you see. But I can't really see it that way. And, you know about, just stuff like going into pubs and drinking, this sort of thing. —But—you see, to them it's all, all wrong, but I don't, you can't really put labels on things and say, because you mean, well in a way I kind of think that you can, because I, I kind of think there is a right and there is a wrong—I mean and there's certain —things that should apply to everybody. But you can't say that one thing that's right for one person is right for another. But —maybe there is a, a universal, things, but it's hard to see it really in that way.

'I was going out with this boy, you see, and I just went round to his flat. They didn't like that, you see, because they immediately conjured up all these immoral pictures and everything. But, I mean, and that was what it, it was about really. So from there you get on to sex morals, and this sort of thing. And they seem, well to my mind they seem to think that that's the biggest immoral thing, you know, kind of, sex before marriage, where you can't, you can't say that, I mean, kind of say to them "Oh what about stuff like honesty, and tolerance?" this sort of thing, that are far more important.

'They kind of say that, you know, well they go about the economic every Sunday dinner time. My Dad goes on about [Laughter] the economic situation [Laughter] of the country and everything. And they kind of think "Oh, this is because the country's morally going down the drain" and everything, and "They've got to get back to God" and this sort of—It's not as easy as this, because I mean, it is a belief and you can't—you can't be dogmatic about it.

'They think they've got the right and wrong. They think that they know what it is. Perhaps, perhaps they do—But, the way they go on about books and stuff like—um—because I've read *Lady Chatterley's Lover*, you see. And they didn't like this [Laughter], because I left it hanging around just as their friends came round. [Laughter]

'To them it was yes or no to it, kind of thing, you know, right or wrong. Not as simple as that—but we—well it is to them. You see I can't, I'm not, see, it's right for them, but it's not right for somebody else. So I mean, their being right about it, fine, because it is right for them.'

(Girl₃, Group A, 18½)

'My home life was strict—um—yeah, because my father was strict, and, er, especially about work. See, my elder sister, she's about twenty-two now, she went to Oxford, which is one problem you see [Laughter], because, um—she, she went to, to, erm, a grammar school, and then she, she went on to Oxford. And she did, she did well there. She only passed out last year. And—therefore I mean she, she's the eldest. Next, my brother younger than that was expected to do something like that and he didn't, and he did pretty badly and he only went to a polytechnic. And then the brother after that, um, the one just above me, um, dropped out of school completely and got a job now. And there was al-always a pressure, throughout all of each one of our home life, of work and school, and it was very strong. And that's mainly the reason that I gave up home life, and then I wanted to get out and get into, into enjoying myself outside home, because there wasn't any enjoyment at home. It was a strict pattern that you got in to. I used to avoid my father most of the time, even in the house. And—it wasn't too hard, because I could keep in my room all the time—and, er, do the things I wanted to. And even, under that strict pattern, be-because I think it was because it was so strict, I didn't even want to work.

'There was a real tension at home. And you were expected —to fit into whatever my Dad said. So whatever his values were were your values, because you were told them. And that was it, and that was right, according to him.'

(Boy$_4$, Group B(N), 18)

In working-class homes parental intervention is more tied to specific occasions, and general influence is less pervasive. Some of the disparity in the character of accounts from those at different ends of the social class system may perhaps be attributed to variation in linguistic style, since members of the middle-class have a greater tendency to adopt a generalizing mode; it is unlikely, though, that this is a full explanation. There are often smaller differences in age between working-class parents and their adolescent children; there are more relatives in the locality who fill the gap between generations. A wider range of social activities is available, especially for fathers and sons, which can be shared without a sense of strain. Parental restrictions are often made on largely prudential grounds, as was illustrated in relation to nocturnal activities. There are more instances in which adolescents are allowed to make decisions without interference. The consequence seems to be that in families where relationships are generally good, working-class boys and girls are more likely than their middle-class counterparts to turn to one or both parents for advice, including matters relating to their private lives.

'I went on the pill about three months ago. I was still under sixteen at the time. So I never told my Mum, because I didn't know what her reaction would be. Then when I turned sixteen, last month, well my Mum's—my brother's girlfriend, the doctor put her on the pill because she was underweight, to make her put on weight . . . . So I go up to my Mum and said "Mum, can I go on the pill?" and, um—"Why?" So, well [Laughter], "You know"—So, well, she told me, you know, what I shouldn't do and what I must be careful about and all that, and, um, said "Go to the doctor". So I pretended I went to the doctor and um, I had my pills from, you know, the time before. So I told her I had them, told her what the doctor told me about a month ago. [Laughter] So she never did find out about me and Alan before—but she don't mind now . . . . like that I feel ever so—you know, but I normally tell Mum mostly everything.'

(Girl$_{15}$, Group B(M), 16)

'I want to get married early. I want my, I want to be young when my kids are young. I don't know why, but I've got this fixation, I don't want my kids to be young and myself old,

that's one thing I don't want. I mean, I was lucky. My Dad
was—my Dad not old, he's young and fit and runs a team.
And I enjoy my, I find that I get on better with my parents
that way, whereas if they were, they were middle-aged, and
over middle-aged, they wouldn't come out, and they wouldn't
kick a ball about with me. They wouldn't be able to er . . . .
take part in my social activities you know, or go camping with
me, or enjoy a holiday. I mean, when I go on holiday they
wouldn't come into a river or a sea, swimming with me,
whereas my parents do. I want my kids to enjoy their, their
younger parts of their days, you know.'

(Boy₁₅, Group B(M), 17)

'My parents left the decision about my job entirely up to me.
They said, you know, "Your life, you might as well choose
now."

'Yeah, they think, when you go out to work, obviously
you're going into the big bad world, in which case they feel,
my Mum especially, any problems I get, should be able to
sort out for myself. I mean, if I have a problem I can't, then
all well and I'll go either to my Mum or my Dad. But, er, so
far I haven't had to. And she feels that my brother, he did it
when he first went out to work, you know. He went through
and sorted out all his problems, and that sort of thing. She
thought I'm easily, um . . . . I have the ability just as well as
him to do it, in which case, you know, she didn't really
bother. I mean, when I told her I was taking this job rather
than the other job where I'd be getting more money she said
"Well, it's up to you. If you think you can manage on that
money," she said, "then fair enough", she said, "Once you
start you're going to have to manage on that money."'

(Boy₂₂, Group C, 17)

Communication at the Level of Interpersonal Perspectives

This mode is more subtle, being concerned not so much with direct
attempts to exercise influence on action as with conveying
messages to adolescents about the kind of people they are believed
to be. In other words, attributions of traits of character, or of
consistent patterns of action, are involved. Here the social class
differences are even more marked. Boys and girls from middle-
class homes where there is disharmony often describe their parents
as mis-perceiving them in some way: the issues include whether
they are reliable, responsible, considerate, truthful, hard-working,
pure, well-mannered, wholesome and intelligent. Comments in

this vein are rare from adolescents from the 'lower' working class. It might be suggested that this is simply a matter of difference in role-taking ability; that, however, does not seem to be an adequate explanation, since a consideration of the actual circumstances of existence suggests that it is unlikely that working-class adolescents (girls especially) generally lack skill in comprehending interpersonal perspectives. It is more probable that failures of communication at this level are in fact more frequent for middle-class adolescents. Some of the social life-worlds in which they participate outside the home may be virtually incomprehensible to their parents; they often appear to be living by values that are incompatible with their long-term advantage; they may have the sense that their parents, used to the experience of ownership, wish in some sense to own them; they may also believe that parental views and attitudes are corrupt, old-fashioned or unintelligent, especially if the age-gap is wide.

'I got taken over by the, it was sort of, my life completely—I used to get back from school, didn't get time to eat, just have to rush off and rehearse. And when the rehearsal was finished, after we'd go down the pub and get as drunk as possible—it was just unhealthy. Getting back at one o'clock, and then getting up at eight o'clock to go to school, or rather not getting up. Now I've grown up basically—I still abuse myself to a certain degree, still drink too much and do silly things, get into fights all the time—and I get into trouble at school a lot, but—my attitude to things is a lot different now—um—Sort of, I won't stay up all night because I know I'll feel ill for two days. And, er—um—try and keep fit, you know, playing football and things. And, um, I'm more responsible now.—It's all relative, I mean, I think I'm more responsible, but my parents think I'm totally irresponsible. I doubt they, they've noticed any change in me. I mean, I don't have anything to do with them really.—They see me so little. They obviously think I'm pretty messed up and everything, but they worry, and I do get very depressed sometimes. I can't be bothered to sit down and talk to them.'

(Boy$_{15}$, Group A, 17)

'My parents both have been brought up in fairly middle-class ways. And they almost resent the new kind of attitude to people.
    'At school these old ways didn't seem to be working . . . .
and, er, as my attitude was changed, so I tried to convince my parents to change. Er, little things like, er, kids playing in the

streets outside. They get very annoyed with this . . . . and, er, they, they're still back in the British Empire days, "Rule Britannia", and, er, "Englishman's home is his castle" . . . . and I could see some of their point of view because, er, there are little kids playing on bicycles who don't even live on the estate, and so the parents can't be caring where they are.

'I said they were a hundred years out of date . . . . Er, my father almost had an obsession with it, ke-keeping little kids out, from out, coming inside, outside our window. So he couldn't see it. Oh, I told him he was mental, he should go and see a psychiatrist, because of his views.'

(Boy$_7$, Group A, 17)

'My parents say what people to go around with and what behaviour to make—like they don't like me hanging around town. Obviously that's natural, and it's up to me whether I hang around town or not, and what kind of trouble I'm going to get into while I am hanging around town. But um—they—they say rude things about, you know, about me and that, all call names if I hang around town, a slut. It really annoys me, um—that they um—whatever I do is my decision. They shouldn't try and rule my life. And, um, friends I want to go around with, whether they approve or not, boys and that, I mean, I shouldn't have to be thinking "Well, I hope my Mum's not seeing me with him". Well I don't, but I'm sure if she did see me with some of the people I go around with, um, she wouldn't like the idea, um. I mean, she made comments about them when I didn't tell her I was going around with, no, but—I've just got to decide for myself. Everyone's got to get into a scrape sometime or other, I mean, that's what life's all about, isn't it? Experience and all that. And, um, she just, um, wants to try and decide that I grow up respectable, and talk nicely and have conversations with people. It's just not on. You've got to decide yourself. If I decide later that's what I want that's fine, but they won't. This is the free-est time of your life, isn't it? You're supposed to be free from all responsibilities, but with them there telling me not to go into pubs, because they connect pubs with trying to pick people up—you meet people in pubs, you know, it's a place to go and meet people. But if I met someone in a pub it'd be "You picked them up in a pub", you know. It's the way they can translate what was completely harmless into something quite horrible. They can make it sound horrible.—They are trying to do this to knock me to my senses.

'I tried to have a very intellectual conversation with my

Dad once. And I got so cross because I thought we were
having this really clever conversation, and we were talking on
and on, and I was arguing away. I can't remember what it
was about now. And then he went out and said to my Mum
"It's like talking to a brick wall." And I was so cross that
after that I just gave up. I just um—making a comment like
that when I was really thinking of what I was saying, and
saying what I thought was important to me . . . . it's just—
obviously that he just couldn't understand a single thing that I
was saying. And I'd, I'd reasoned and understood some of the
points that he'd made. Not all of them . . . . that he couldn't
accept any of the things that I'd said. Just shows the generation
gap and that, you know, couldn't do it. Just got to take them
as they are and they can take you as you are, or stuff it,
kind of thing.

'And they'd like me to be "very good", you know, really
"good". Talk to their friends and be nice, and go out once
every month when they've completely vetted the situation
first. But, um—they try and mould your character, and they
don't realize that it's already formed.'

(Girl$_{15}$, Group A, 16)

There is a particular kind of disharmony of interpersonal
perspectives which seems mainly to occur between boys and their
fathers in working-class families. The immediate occasion for an
argument, or even coming to blows, is a disagreement over some
factual issue, not necessarily related to personal life. Underlying
this the issue appears to be one of rivalry in knowledge and
intelligence: to be 'ignorant' (which is to be lacking in both) is a
disgrace. Since there were no corresponding accounts from girls it
is plausible to infer that 'ignorance', in this sense, is judged to be a
more serious deficit in the male sex.

'My Dad says something like, er—sort of, like, war things,
like "America's supposed to be the richest country in the
world", and—or Russia, like, and who's got the most nuclear
warheads, and all this type of thing. This has been going on a
couple of weeks as it goes. Every time something crops up
about war on the telly or on the news or anything, you know,
he starts off, you know.

'I argue that Russia's the biggest, and he says that America
is, because—er Russia like, they, they've not joined up with
any country. They're on their own, like, you know. Although
they, they've got Poland and that, what belongs to them, and

East Germany and that, but they're on their own, ain't they?
They're communist, they're on their own. Because and you've
got America, you've got NATO is it? You got England just
recently joined that not long ago. Then you got all the other
countries joining it. Now if America were so strong they
wouldn't need them, would they, really? I mean when you
come to think of it, if they're so strong they wouldn't need it,
you know. Russia don't need it, you know what I mean?
That's why I argue that it's the biggest country. We have a lot
of arguments, and I never think I'm wrong, all right? I
know I'm wrong sometimes. And my Dad ends up, like, sort
of having a dig at me, like, going to clout me or something—
And, er, like . . . . and he says, er, "I'm thirty-five, I'm thirty
years older than you, and you're trying to tell me how the
country's run and all this lot, when I've been living in it twice
as long as you." But thing with my Dad, like, he doesn't
watch much news. He always reads the daily paper, some.
Page three, that's all he gets to. But he always erm, reads the
paper, but he doesn't watch much news on telly.'

(Boy$_{11}$, Group C, 15)

This far this chapter has not made clear distinctions between
parents. This is a great over-simplification, because it is quite
common for an adolescent to have better relationships with one
rather than the other, particularly at the level of interpersonal
perspectives. In some cases boys are able to communicate more
effectively with their fathers than their mothers, the bond with the
former arising from their maleness; there are also instances where
a girl has a relationship with her father vaguely analogous to that
of a lover. In relation to values a particularly important type of
family is that in which the father's culture is working-class and the
mother's petit-bourgeois; here it is almost inevitable that an
adolescent will fail to achieve mutually satisfying perspectives with
one parent.

'Sort of pretty scared after the fire at school, I suppose.
Frightened of getting expelled, and I think, I don't know what
my Mum would have said, neither . . . . I couldn't care, not
at all. But Mum, don't know what she would have said again,
you know—My Dad wouldn't say nothing, because he was
expelled when he was thirteen. Anyway my Mum, sort of, she
was worried . . . . My Dad don't say nothing when I told him
I got to go to court. He laughed at me and that. Called me an
idiot, said it was my own fault. My Mum, you know, she's, go
mad.

'I always seem to get on all right with my Dad. It's just my Mum, I can never get on with her—You know, if I start saying things at home, like "I'm knocking off some bird tonight", she goes mad, you know. If I say it to my Dad, he goes "You lucky little sod", you know, "Well bring one home for me", things like that. My Mum starts going mad at him, you know.'

(Boy$_{15}$, Group C, 16½)

Conversely, of course, if an adolescent in this kind of family (especially a boy) develops harmonious perspectives with the mother, communication with the father will probably break down.

If this section has conveyed a predominantly negative tone, it must be remembered that the nature of the research method was such that it tended to highlight episodes in which background expectations were not fulfilled. Accounts of effective communication and general harmony tended to be less vivid than those dealing with specific instances of conflict. They were probably much harder to give, because there would be relatively little to say.

'So far my Dad has never let me down, and that's quite incredible, as I'm sixteen . . . . and in all the years I've known him he's never let me down, and this I value very highly . . . . And I'd do anything for him, and he knows it. And I'd put myself out for him as he'd put himself out for me.'

(Boy$_{15}$, Group B(M), 16)

'We, we always try and work something out, and we try not to row anyway, and if we do it just sort of blows over. If there was some, such a small thing it doesn't really matter to anyone's life . . . . I think we agree, more or less, because I think we're able to discuss things, as a family . . . . they always, they always try and help me, and I always try and help them.'

(Girl$_3$, Group B(N), 19)

'She really does mean a lot. I mean my Mum, my Mum's, I mean, I don't know, if anything was to happen to my Dad, I'd miss my Dad obviously. But my Mum, I mean, like, you can always find another Dad, but you can never find another Mum. Because, I mean, your Mum, I mean, you were part of, of your Mum, and you was, you know, from birth you was with your Mum. And I think I'd really, I wouldn't know what to do without her. Even now, I mean, your Mum there, always your Mum. And if you're ever in any trouble, you can always go to your Mum, you know, and tell her. Whether it worries her or not [Laughter] is a different thing, but your Mum's always there to look after you.

'My Mum and Dad really do, I mean my Mum and Dad care about me. I mean, like, my Dad will say to me "Where are you going?" and I have to ask my Dad everywhere I go. I mean, I am seventeen, and I have to tell him where I go. But, I mean, he only asks me because he worries. But I never used to see that when I was younger, you know. I used to think "Oh no, I've got to be in by half past ten, because he'll only moan at me." But I mean, now that I'm older I can see the reasons.'

(Girl$_{18}$, Group C, 17)

Co-operation

Despite the somewhat negative tone of the previous two sections, there is a widespread recognition among adolescents that active and positive co-operation with parents, in certain specific areas, is justified. The most obvious example is that of giving assistance in the day-to-day running of the home; like the assertion of freedom against parental restrictions, this sometimes appears to take on a symbolic significance, as an indicator of the extent to which, from the adolescent's point of view, a more general sense of harmony exists. One of the categories derived from item 8 (doing something well) concerned giving practical help of some kind, much of which was related to home; about half of the cases were from boys of group C. Item 6, as has already been pointed out, had a large category of willing conformity to parents. In addition to such direct references, the accounts contained a number of descriptions of anger with parents, siblings or friends, at the violation of values related to co-operation. Girls generally give more help than boys, though their accounts suggest that what they do provides rather less ground for satisfaction, and that the threshold for resentment on specific occasions is often low. Co-operation in the home is largely a consequence of their role-position.

It appears that help tends to be given more grudgingly in affluent homes. Here there is less sheer necessity, and in some cases a degree of organization that has the appearance of managerial control; occasionally boys and girls in this kind of situation have the sense of being used as a form of cheap labour.

'My father is very keen on, you know, keeping his lawn well-
trimmed . . . . and with his arthritis he isn't—his legs are
particularly bad, and so it's difficult for him himself to cut it.
And he, er, he often used to ask my sister and myself to, um,
do the chore for him. We've got quite a big lawn, and he
used to like it cutting about twice a week. And I often used
to, well, you know, when he asked, me, he expected me to
say "Yes, of course I will". And I used to, oh [Laughter],
sort of sulk, I suppose, and not want to do it all the time, you
know.
    'I don't, I don't particularly like the task. But, er I suppose
when I stop and really think about it, you know—I should
have been more willing.'

(Girl$_2$, Group A, 18)

'I'm always expected—I think in our family I'm always
expected to do chores. Either doing sewing or, you know,
housework . . . . I'm always expected to be in the kitchen
cooking or something like that, with my mother . . . . I think
it's because I've always enjoyed cooking I just do it. Because
when my sister does it she tells everybody she's done it! . . . .
I don't mind doing it. Like my brother's always doing painting
around the house, and doing the rubbish, taking the rubbish
out—You just expect them to do it, I don't do it . . . . Yeah,
they all chip in. We're all given our own jobs . . . . We're all
expected to keep our bedrooms tidy.'

(Girl$_{10}$, Group A, 16)

'My parents, they, sort of, were giving me a lot of things—
and I was not er, not really very good to them, sort of thing.
I thought, "Now if they wanted me they should give me what
I want", sort of thing, and don't have to give anything to
them—Well it just carried on like that for a while, and I
thought "Well, if I'm better they won't keep shouting at me
and arguing at me, and things like that". So I started being a
bit better and that. Taking cups of tea to them in bed, sort of,
being like I should have been in the first place, not thinking
that I deserve everything . . . . so I thought I'd be a bit better
to them. And then they stopped arguing with me and started
treating me more, as more as a grown-up instead of a child
sort of, more mature . . . . They treated me more as an adult
and I treated them more as I should have done in the first
place. And we get on much better now, a better relationship
than it was before.'

(Boy$_{11}$, Group A, 15)

In contrast to this the value set on co-operation reaches its most positive expression in certain working-class homes. Where both parents are employed adolescents may be prepared to take on heavy and even disagreeable commitments, realizing that running the home is a shared responsibility.

'My mum and dad, they go to work full-time every day, both of them . . . . They work all week . . . . come in about five o'clock, and I know they're both tired. And I like, you know, having things done for them, have the tea and tidy the house. So that she can just sit down and relax for a while, while we have our tea. And I, I'm always tidying . . . . I hate seeing, you know, places untidy.'

(Girl$_4$, Group B(M), 15)

'My Mum always does the washing on Sundays—you know, for school on the first day of the week. And, er, she said "Oh, the washing machine's broke down". And my Dad's a bit of an electrician, you know, but he couldn't fix it. It needed a fan belt. So he said "Oh, you'll have to go to the launderette." And I have a younger sister, you know, I think she's eleven at the moment, she was about ten then. I said, "Well, why can't she go?" you know, "It's a girl's job." He says "She's a bit young to go to the launderette," he says, "You get going." I said, you know, "Oh it's always me who has to go." And he said "You either go or you get to bed for the rest of the day." So I said "Oh, I'll go." So I went, and erm—I got to the launderette. And I just felt angry, you know, because I was the only boy in the launderette at the time. They were all women or girls. Getting funny looks at me, and I felt terrible. When I got home I said to my Mum "Why do I have to go to the launderette!", you know, "I'm the only boy there and felt terrible." Well, um, later on I thought, well—"I was right to go. You know, it was my job, you know, in that type of situation." But, er, I've never had to go since.'

(Boy$_{12}$, Group C, 14½)

The value is qualified in two main ways. First, the demands made should be perceived as just, in relation to the pressures that parents themselves have to face; second, what is required of one member of the family is equivalent to what is required from others. Girls are sometimes resentful against their brothers because of the relatively light demands that are often made of them; and some of the most violent quarrels between sisters, especially in working-class homes, have a dispute about house-work as their immediate precipitant.

'My parents both had jobs and—I was sort of chief cook and bottle-washer. I, it annoyed me and aggravated me, and an awful lot of little things like this. And my brother and sister-in-law came to live with us. I didn't like that at the time because then, erm—well my sister-in-law, although I like her very much, she domineers in the house. She was, it was "David do this", and, "David do that", and she'd know that David would do it. And it annoyed me, and I couldn't sort of —stay at home and shout and scream because this wasn't me. So I used to go out on the streets and, well, I'd just do something, well anything that came into my head at the time, through sheer anger, although I must admit I was always very disgusted and ashamed about it later, as I am now.

'Er, the last thing I think I can remember doing was a neighbour who'd just had his car, er, well, not a car, a large van, with his name printed on it. He was a contract-worker, and he'd done some work at our house. And somehow I just linked him with our home at the time, because he was there so much. And I used a big tin of black paint, and I smeared it all over his car, and I thought "Well, that serves you right", and it was just like paying off—I felt it was one sort of debt that I'd paid.'

(Boy$_1$, Group B(N), 17)

'Sometimes my Mum depends on me too much. You know, when my sister goes out my Mum depends on me to stay in of a night, and mind the kids while she goes out. And she enjoys herself, I can't. Some places we agree with one another, and some places we don't.

'My Mum says I have to give a he- help in with the family, and keep my eye on all the kids and that. If anyone picks on them I should help. I do.

'I'm late for school and all that. She depends on me to stay with them. That makes me late for school then. And I get in trouble. Like, my sister's out of work, she should do it, but she won't. So I get stuck with it.

'Well about two weeks ago our Janet, she went down to Social Security and left me with the kids, with my niece and with my sister there—And I just left the place, because I couldn't get tidied with them all being in it. So when my sister came in she started, "Why isn't this place cleaned?", and I said "Well, what do you think I am?" "I suppose you should clean this place." I said, "You've got no right to tell me what to do"; said, "You're not that older than me." You know, she thinks because she goes out and my Mum's at work, I've got to start working in the house—and tidying up, doing dishes, tea, everything else. I just tell her "Well, I'm not what you think I am to clean up and all that. So that's my mother's place", I said, "Maybe I have to give a hand, but her place mainly." My sister just expects me to do everything when she goes out. Just leave it for her when she comes back.

'My Mum finishes quite early, so—all right to come in and still do a bit of work. And she's been saying she's been given this job to fit in to feeding, with her housework. But she just doesn't. Just stay there and leave it all to us, or sometimes just to me.'

(Girl$_4$, Group B(N), 15)

Occasionally the co-operation between parents and adolescents reaches a much deeper level than that of role. It is as if those involved begin to share, at least to some extent, a common project. The evidence (which is only fragmentary in this respect) suggests that this is relatively uncommon among members of the middle class, the main exception being that of a boy who has already decided to follow his father's occupation, and is working with him. The most striking examples come from working-class boys and their fathers.

'Actually my Dad is the sort of person that—he doesn't say a lot. I mean, when he wants to say something, he'll say it. But if he's, sort of, got nothing really important to tell you, he doesn't. The only time that I find we get on really well together is if we're working together. Like on—we've got a caravanette, and we've only just got it, and I started working on that, trying to make it look a bit different to everyone else's transit caravanette. So, I couldn't really do a lot of it myself, because it was quite a bit of hard work to do, and of course I had to get my Dad to help me, because my brother's never in and he just turns his back on that sort of thing. Because he feels um, once he's done, sort of, five days at work, the weekend is his.—When my Dad was giving me a hand I found a lot, a lot about him that I didn't really know about. I always thought that he was the sort of person who didn't laugh at jokes, that sort of thing. I found that when we were working together he had, you know, a really good sense of humour. He was telling me jokes he'd heard at work, that sort of thing. And I'd never really thought it was possible for him to be able to do that sort of thing. And I've really been

finding out what a dad's for. Whereas before I didn't really
think of him as a dad, I just thought of him as someone
there.—And now I really think—actually I think of him
more as a sort of older brother, rather than as a dad,
although you know, he's old enough to be my grandad. I
found, you know, he wasn't like a dad. He was just like
someone from work, you know, that I would just sort of talk
to about anything, you know. There was a bird walking up
the road. I say "That's quite nice", you know, and he'd turn-
around and say "Where?", you know, look around the side of
the van. I'd think to myself "Crikey me", you know. I found
that I was getting on with him a lot better when we were
working together than when we were just, sort of, indoors
watching the telly, something like that. Whereas, as I say, he
doesn't say a lot. He's very quiet. I'd never really had a lot of
respect for my Dad. Like when I was skiving and got caught,
and he'd give me a good bollocking, like, I didn't really take
much notice of it. Whereas now, if, if he's got something to
say to me, and he says it, and even though it's bad against me
perhaps, I take notice of it. And I think to myself "I'll try
and put that right", whereas before I couldn't care a damn
about it. And, er—it's much better, as I say. Now everything
just about going right—sort of, after I've known him for
seventeen years. It's just like knowing him, for a sort of, a
month, that sort of thing, you know. I've been with him sort
of seventeen years, but I've only really known him a month,
that sort of thing. It's good. It's like not having a dad for
seventeen years and suddenly he walks back into your life
—and you get to know him in just a month.'

(Boy$_{22}$, Group C, 17)

Although girls probably spend far more time and energy than
boys in giving help to their parents at home, there is little
indication that their actions take the form of purposefully initiated
projects, in a way comparable to what occurs in some cases with
boys. Co-operation is generally of a more mundane kind, and
when willingly given is little more than a routine response to the
conditions of existence as these are perceived.

Conflict in the Home

The evidence brought forward in this chapter is sufficient to under-
mine any crude stereotype of a pervasive clash of values between
parents and their adolescent children. There are many sources of

conflict, such as difficult physical or financial circumstances, personality differences, destructive patterns of interaction among several members of a family, and relationships outside the home; in any particular instance it would be simplistic to hypothesize a single cause. There are, however, certain types of conflict between adolescents and their parents that can be directly related to values. In keeping with the discussion in the previous three sections, the following appear to be some of the major issues:

1 disagreement over the extent or nature of parental restrictions; violation of the value set on independence;
2 restrictions (applied inconsistently) between members of a family when of the same age or status;
3 interference or influence attempts perceived as illegitimate;
4 disharmony at the level of interpersonal perspectives;
5 disharmony arising from differences of outlook between parents;
6 excessive demands for help within the home: violation of the value set on co-operation;
7 unequal distribution of demands made on members of a family when of the same age or status.

Cast in these very general terms, these points apply widely, both between the sexes and throughout the range of social class. As has been shown, however, there are marked differences in detailed content, in the range of application and in the kind of circumstances under which a value is perceived to have been violated. Arising from persistent or extreme conflict, there are certain types of act of defiance that are judged to be legitimate as forms of protest and as assertions of power. Some of these, in ascending order of seriousness, are: arguing, rudeness, engaging in behaviour of which parents are known to disapprove (but which is not forbidden), openly disobeying parental restrictions, disappearing for a few hours, 'using the home like a hotel', going away for a short period, and leaving home more or less permanently. Although an act of defiance may appear to be spontaneous, some degree of advance calculation is necessary. For example, those who wish to go on to further or higher education have to face the prospect of several years of dependence upon their parents beyond the age of sixteen; if their behaviour is too provocative they will make their own future uncomfortable, and the more extreme forms of defiance are barely realistic.

Family Disruption

This far this chapter has dealt mainly with values held by adolescents from homes where there had been no serious trauma. Such evidence taken alone, however, might be misleading, because about one-third of those who were interviewed were from families that had experienced major disruptions of some kind. The largest category here was parental divorce or separation; in addition there were cases where one parent was dead, where crises had arisen because of serious or prolonged illness, and where family life had been seriously affected by the presence of a retarded or handicapped child.

The interviews provided a great deal of material on these topics, which would probably merit a detailed study in its own right. In relation to a general study of values, however, accounts of family disruption have a particular significance; for they show the presence of certain kinds of expectation or assumption which might otherwise have remained in the background; as in the case of the 'garfinkel', it is sometimes the case that the dramatic tearing apart of a social life-world reveals the values in accordance with which it normally coheres. This brief discussion, therefore, is confined to showing how certain aspects of the picture already given in this chapter are emphasized or amplified by accounts of family life that did not pursue its 'normal' course.

Parental divorce or separation generally brings many problems to adolescents, especially if they are relatively unable to take both their father's and mother's standpoints, and even more if they mainly see the situation with reference to themselves. There is often a feeling of division of loyalty, and a sense of guilt in having to choose between parents. In addition there may be a fear of being rejected by both, and thus having no base of love and acceptance from which to move out into the world.

'My parents were divorced—quite, when I was quite young. But never stopped, and it's still going on now. I—then my mother,. because I'm the eldest my mother tells me everything that's going on, produces evidence about this and that and the other. And my father does the same. It's the evidence, it's from the High Court. I think it's exactly, you know, contradictory, what my mother's got and my father's got. And it got to the state I really believed whatever my father said, or I did —and I thought "My Mum, God, she's going on again." I got to the stage where I didn't know who the hell to believe any more. I only left home two, I left my parents for two years. I thought that would straighten them out. They'd know what

I'm annoyed about. And . . . . I couldn't take much more. I'd
been through the, you know, the whole screaming and
shouting thing, and the occasional fight. And, God—and it was
just getting too much of a strain, you know, going in and
know you'd have to talk about the same things.'

(Girl$_{13}$, Group A, 19)

'My Nanna started just shouting at me, sort of, saying why
did I want to stay—with my Dad instead of coming with her
and my Mum. Because she doesn't like—my Dad's parents,
and, er, she doesn't like the idea of us—staying with my
Dad, and around his parents. Because, you see, she doesn't
like them at all.—I know he never did nothing for—me and
my brother really, and my Nanna has. She's done all—times
for me, and things like that.

'I was just fed up. Why should we have to make a decision
anyway, who we have to live with? Or why couldn't we live
with both our parents—at, at that time?

'I said "Why, why did they have to start arguing in the first
place, and leave each other?" I didn't understand why they
were arguing—and fighting in the first place. In the end I
just, I just got up and ran out.

'They were all there in our house, and my Mum was—
packing some of her things, and my Nanna and Grandad were
there, and, they were all saying "You can come and live with
us if you want to", and all, all this. And my Dad—we didn't
know who was really going to stay in the house, who would
have the house anyway, if they did get divorced. So we said,
we just decided to stay in the house, and whoever—had the
house, we'd stay with . . . . and so we said we'd stay there.
And my Dad—was staying there.'

(Boy$_6$, Group B(N), 15)

'Mum and Dad, when I walked out on them—my Mum and
Dad are divorced and, er, what is it, I don't know how to put
it, you, er—my Mum's getting married, my Dad's getting
married. And now they, they always—they want you, but
they only want you when it's convenient for them. Otherwise
they don't want to know you, sort of, yet they do, but—on,
er, how can I put it? Um—they do and they don't sort of
thing. They want to, want to go out and—they say "I'm
going somewhere." They disagree, they think I'm still a baby,
you know, and everything, and that's what—I had this big
disagreement with them, and now I'm at my auntie's, living at
my auntie's. My Mum's on her own, and I never go round to

see her. She's getting married. My Dad's on his own and he's
getting married. And I hardly ever see them. I just fallen out
with them, because they only want me when it's convenient
for them, and show me off and all this. "Get off, I want to do
that, I've got my own life to lead." I want to make my own
decisions, not to do what they want to do, and be at their
beck and call. It was just brewed up—and it—my Mum and
Dad split up. It made me a bit upset and, well, they was
always trying to grab me and—they'd say "Well, I've give
him more than what you have. Now it's your turn to give
him more than what I can." And it was always like that. I
was always sort of in between. And they says "You've had
everything you've wanted" . . . . I didn't, though, did I? I
didn't have Mum and Dad live together. "You always
grabbing everything you wanted" and all this lot, "Oh, oh,
you don't know how lucky you are." I just couldn't stand it
any longer and just walked out on them.'

(Boy$_{22}$, Group C, 17)

'I don't want to get entangled in, you know, not having no
family or anything, you know, no one to help me, you know,
go off and leave them. I'd have no friends, no family, no
nothing.'

(Boy$_{24}$, Group C, 15)

Accounts such as these betray an expectation of an evaluative
kind which, it appears, is widely held by younger adolescents
throughout the social class system. It is that if a man and a woman
bring a child into the world they should attempt to live in
harmony, and provide the necessary security and care. The
supporting reasons are mainly egoistic in character; the evidence
of this research suggests that broader social considerations have
very little salience. Thus an 'old-fashioned' view of marriage
remains a major part of the taken-for-granted world of most
younger adolescents, despite an abundance of more 'objective'
evidence for the fallibility of the institution in modern industrial
society. It is against this background that the struggle for independence, and many accounts of conflict with parents, must be
judged.
    The presence of a step-parent highlights another issue, that of
the perceived legitimacy of parental authority. Expressed attitudes
towards a step-parent ranged from uneasy tolerance to outright
rejection. This predominantly negative view was based in part on a
denial of the validity of the role; in some cases also it appears that

adolescents received indications at the level of interpersonal perspectives that they themselves were not fully accepted.

'I don't get on with my step-dad at all. We, we just—we argue a lot and—he throws me out once a month, and then it's all better again and—he's pretty screwed up himself. I feel pretty sorry for him. I mean, like—um—he married my Mum partly for the money, I think, well I know, which I don't, I don't um—sort of resent. I'd do the same, but that was part of it and um, he had pictures of building up his business and doing all right and maybe having a kid. And all of a sudden he gets two children that aren't his own sort of turning up on his doorstep saying "We're coming to live with you, support us", which, which he has done, and he's done very generously. And he's very kind to us, in material terms he is anyway, you know, feeds and clothes us. But I think that was probably very difficult for him—and not, not what he had planned like, you know, all the responsibility. And then he had another kid, that's more responsibility. And although he's always bollocking me and all this, shouting me and saying I can't do this and can't do that he's, he's only doing it because he thinks that's what's best for me, and so I appreciate it in a way. He always means well, it just comes out wrong. He tells me how much he hates me, which, I don't think there's a lot, it don't really matter. But he doesn't mean to say it, it just comes out wrong, because he's not very good at delivering things.—He's got a very erratic temperament—we just don't meet eye to eye at all.'

(Boy$_{15}$, Group A, 17)

'Christmas Eve or Christmas Day it was. My mother was really ill. She couldn't get better and nothing, and she was always in a sweat . . . . She said "Help your Dad". And I answered "I'm not helping him. He's not my Dad" . . . . And my Mum said to me "Help him on, because he's"—and I said "No", and I said, I said, "I'd rather have the dog than help him." My Mum said "Please, Sarah," she said, "Help him." And I said "No," I said, "not for you," I said, "however sick you are. If you want to help him, you help him, but I'm not" . . . . I said to him "You want to get out of here," I said, "You're skippy." And, you know, and he said to me "Oh go away," he said, "you're not worth a balloon, you, the way you treat us." And I said "You're not worth a burst balloon,

you're not worth it." And my Mum saying to me "Go
upstairs, go to bed", you know, "If it takes all my energy to
get up, I'll hit you." She was laughing in a way, you know
. . . . and I saying "You mind your own business. It's got
nothing to do with you. I hate the way he treats you" . . . .
And then he just said to me "Oh go to bed, go to bed", he
was saying, "before I give you a belt." I said "That'll be the
day, love." He's only ever hit me once, and I hit him back.'

(Girl$_7$, Group C, 15)

Reactions to step-parents reveal certain background beliefs
about the place of real parents: they do have legitimate areas of
authority simply on the basis of their role, and (unless there is
decisive evidence to the contrary) they are to be given a degree of
respect. This is the generally unstated context of complaints about
parental restrictions, and descriptions of problems of communication. Here also is an explanation of why some parental actions that
an observer might judge arbitrary or vicious are accepted by
adolescents without demur.

The presence of a retarded child, or some other circumstance
that places a long-term strain on family life, appears from the small
but pungent evidence of this research generally to have a markedly
adverse effect on adolescents, who themselves still generally
expect a fair measure of care and attention, even while they are
psychologically moving away from their parents. On the other
hand there are certain kinds of family crisis, especially in working-
class homes (where, statistically, they are relatively more frequent), that enhance the salience of values associated with communication and co-operation. The death of one parent may draw
out even stronger loyalty to the one who remains, as witness these
two extracts from boys; in the first case it was the father who had
died, and in the second case the mother.

'Family, that's number one to my life. Mum and my family,
like, my Mum. And what she say goes, you know what I
mean? Because, er, you really realize it, your Mum must be
the be-better friend than any one else, you know. Like, erm,
if you're in trouble your family's there before your mates.
See, what I've realized a lot is people put their mates first,
and I would never do that. I mean, er, people think of their
mates more than their family and that. And you shouldn't do
that, because if you're in trouble with the police or anything
like that your mates wouldn't do nothing, but your mother
would, you know what I mean? Or your, or your brothers or
your sisters. And there's a lot of other differences, like, erm,

I don't know, with police, money differences, just general worries, like, you know. And your family go out, out the way to help you, which they should do, so, so I suppose you should think of, er, just try and think of your family more than, give you, more than yourself, you know what I mean?'

(Boy₃, Group C, 18)

'I guess I am the only thing that's left for him now. It sounds a bit corny, but it's really . . . . I like to help him out whenever I can, and I think by, or if I had got better exam results I, that'd been another way I could have pleased him, but only in that way really. But in doing my own—in doing what I'm doing now, and acting like I am, I suppose, I'm not so silly like other people, or other friends that he knows that were mine at the time and seen how they've ended up, not working. —I think he's glad that's the way it is. At home I help out, you know. We both put on the mother bit, you know. I do the beds and so on, you know—hoover and polishing and things like that because, because, if he comes home, because he does a twenty-four-hour shift which is nine o'clock to nine o'clock, and has twenty-four hours off and he's usually so tired he just goes to bed. And then he's at his point, really he would be a bit annoying, in a sense, he's moany and he's tired. So I just left him to go to bed, and when he wakes up and he sees that there's something done, it gives me a bit of pride. Says "Thanks", and then I get something back for it, see. I don't take that for granted, you know, that's again something we've got between us.'

(Boy₂₇, Group C, 17)

The existence of deep and widespread trauma in the family lives of adolescents, at a time when relatively traditional expectations about the character of a home and the duties of parents survive with remarkable strength, raises an important question, the inverse of what is conventionally asked. How is it that so many boys and girls, even from seriously disrupted families, emerge as adults without having become 'delinquent', or seriously depressed? Part of the answer lies, of course, in the wider human resources of the family. But there is another important aspect: the social environment provided by adolescents themselves, as the following chapter will show.

6
The Social Life-Worlds of Adolescence

There are two outstanding conditions that affect early adolescence, as a period of movement towards the fully independent status of adulthood. The first is puberty itself, and the awakening of sexual feelings of great intensity; for psychodynamic theorists this has tended to be the ultimate *explanans* for all other adolescent phenomena. The second is the amount of time that is available for boys and girls to spend as they choose, or in ways of their own making. The physical requirement for sleep becomes less, so that by the age of about fifteen many adolescents have seven or so hours available from the end of a school day until they go to bed. In addition there are many interstices in the official programme of school, and the holidays provide very long periods of unstructured time. It is in relation to these two features that some of the most characteristically 'adolescent' activities develop. Here special kinds of skill and awareness are required; the prizes for success are high, while failure may be disastrous. There are some refuges and escape-routes on the way, though these are far more available to those from affluent homes. Undoubtedly a 'moral education' of a kind is involved, and experiences may be of very high intensity. The expectation among many working-class adolescents is that an important stage will be complete when they are sixteen; there is, so to speak, a great deal to be done by the time that age arrives. Those who envisage staying on at school, however, perhaps intending to follow this by a period in further or higher education, have more time available; their characteristically adolescent phase need not be so concentrated.

The social life-worlds are, of course, already in existence before any boy or girl graduates into them from childhood. The rules, customs and prevailing ideas are handed on by those who are older, and are experienced subjectively as part of the 'natural' order of things. Some characteristics probably do not change greatly even over long periods, while others are only gradually modified as a result of external circumstances, such as decline in affluence, changes in the law or new provision for youth. The purpose of this chapter is to describe certain features of such social life-worlds, and to draw out from the interview data some of the values that relate to conduct within them. In keeping with the main tenor of the accounts, these values pertain more to inter-personal relationships than to the activities themselves.

Some General Features

Adolescence, then, generally means 'moving out' into a social environment that is neither childish nor adult. The requirements made by the outside world are full of internal contradictions; at one moment an excess of regulations seems to suggest that the adolescent is no more capable than a child, whereas at another the provisions and opportunities imply the full responsibility of an adult. Boys and girls in their early teens often have stores of physical vitality far in excess of what is commonly required of them, but relatively few channels into which to direct their energies. It is in response to this highly ambiguous situation that they develop patterns of social existence that are characteristically their own.

There is a marked difference between the sexes in the first experience of the social life-worlds of adolscence. For boys the transition may not be particularly clearly defined. The first activities are a simple extension of those of childhood, and if there is no change of locality previous friends may well be taken on into the early teens. Many boys around this age have developed their social skills mainly among those of the same age and sex. Since the demands made by parents, in the form of practical help at home, are generally light, it is they in particular who have a great deal of time on their hands. Girls, however, face a rather different situation. From the onset of puberty they have the status of potential girlfriends. Since their age is notoriously difficult to tell, they are able to go drinking in pubs unchecked from about fourteen onwards. Although they may have had little previous social experience with boys of comparable age, since there tends to be a separation between the sexes in the later years of childhood, they generally have acquired a broader range of social skills than boys; possibly this arises from their more extensive interaction with adults, for example through child-minding and giving help at home. The demand for help of this kind tends to continue, and perhaps to intensify, during adolescence.

Social class also makes a large difference in the first experience of adolescent life, and the chance to develop autonomous social life-worlds. This research indicates that those from working-class homes tend to 'move out' earlier than their middle-class counterparts and, as was shown in the previous chapter, to be bound by less stringent restrictions. If they have been accustomed to periods of unsupervised activity lasting several hours at a time (for example, 'playing out' in a street or the area near a block of flats), they often have already developed considerable skill in interacting with those of their own age. Usually they are not under strong pressure to do homework; the demands from this quarter are not severe, since they are generally in 'lower' bands or streams at school. Boys and girls from settled middle-class homes are likely to have access to greater privacy. They may well be encouraged by parents to take part in certain 'respectable' pursuits such as organized sport, amateur social work, holiday parties and the activities of church-based youth clubs. They are frequently urged by their parents to do well at school, and to be thorough in their homework; even if such exhortations are unwelcome, they often accept that a prudential wisdom lies behind it. As a result of factors such as these they tend to 'move out' about two years later than working-class adolescents; and when they do, they may well be relatively vulnerable, and less competent in interaction with their peers. By the age of about eighteen, however, differences of this kind seem largely to have disappeared; middle-class boys and girls by then have generally been successful in obtaining such freedom as they want, and are able to lead a full social life outside their homes. On the other hand most working-class adolescents, having left school at sixteen, are either in jobs or looking for employment; and by the late teens some girls are already married.

It is, of course, highly misleading to talk about 'the peer group' in a simple way, because there are several different forms of association among adolescents, which serve different purposes and express different values. A rough classification that emerges from this research is as follows. There is, first, the group of about three to ten boys who go around together, finding such occupation for their leisure time as they can. It is here that many boys, especially those in the 'lower' half of the social system, have their first experience of adolescent life; some, indeed, go through the whole teenage period participating in only this kind of group. Second, there is the girl–girl dyad (or, more rarely, triad), where the level of intimacy is very high. To have a close girlfriend in this kind of way is strongly characteristic of those who are 'moving out' for the first time. In this research there were far more instances of this among working-class girls than among middle-class girls; this may simply be a reflection of the fact that such girls achieve a measure of independence from home far sooner, and in so doing are in urgent need of social support.

A third kind of group arises as a result of some deliberately pursued activity or experience, such as making music, acting, sport, cadets or taking drugs. Here it is the activity itself, rather than interpersonal liking, that is the primary bond. Another characteristic type of group is the loosely-knit association of adolescents of both sexes, typically containing boys of around seventeen to twenty years old and girls of any age above about fourteen. Here there is often a partial integration into the life of young adults, particularly through the pub and through siblings who are already married. Fifth, there is what might be termed the 'artefact', the group that has arisen not because of organic ties, but as a result of the planned intervention of adults into the adolescent world. Perhaps the clearest example is the lower-stream school class, where boys and girls from a wide area, many of whom would not otherwise know each other, are brought together. Such groups are the least 'natural' in their genesis; yet, paradoxically, it is from the characteristics of these that inferences are often drawn about the nature of 'the peer group', since their behaviour is the most accessible to the perception of adults.

These five are the most typical of the peer groups of 'normal' adolescence shown up by this research. The 'gang' (at least in its male version) may be regarded as being in many respects an extension of the first type of group, with a hardening of the interface with the outside world and a differentiation of structure and function within. The more permanent relationship between a boy and a girl, leading to engagement or marriage, in so far as it is a characteristic of adolescent life (i.e. generally among those who do not extend their education beyond sixteen), is often an outgrowth of the fourth type of association. However, this is nothing more than a rough typology, and it is recognized that there are many kinds of group with intermediate characteristics. It must be said also that from the point of view of any individual such groups are not mutually exclusive. A boy or girl may belong to several, and experience a division of loyalty between them; even being a hooligan of some kind is not a full-time occupation.

Relationships within such groups are often of high intensity. Not only do boys and girls spend a great deal of time in such company; their skills in resolving conflicts of interest, and their ability to see one another's point of view, at first are relatively undeveloped. Within the items dealing with interpersonal conflict (nos 1, 5, and

14) about half of the material was concerned with peers, and there were many accounts of conflict among peers associated with other items. The picture conveyed by some of the literature, particularly that from the 'youth culture' tradition, that adolescent groups exhibit some kind of organic unity, aligned against, or at least indifferent to, the adult world is not supported by this inquiry. This question was taken up in one of the 'validation sessions' with some boys and girls who had not themselves taken part in the research. They confirmed that high levels of conflict among peers was a common experience; they also pointed out that, since so much of the 'real' life of adolescents is spent among people of their own age, harmony and conflict here often has a greater personal significance than elsewhere.

Although allowing scope for individual 'character', peer groups often exert strong pressures towards conformity upon their members.

'I have always had this from my friends. If they get to hear about something they will pressurize me, consciously, not just saying "What about?" but, well, you know, they will keep on at it until I give in, and I always do because I'm pretty weak about these things and they, they just brought it to a head themselves. We were just walking along . . . . I was feeling pretty depressed—obviously ashamed of myself and—I needed a boost, sort of thing, pretty quickly. And, er, we were just walking along with a group, sort of thing, and she was there, you know, and they sort of pressed me, you know. I said I wouldn't go out with her, I had originally intended to leave it until the sixth form. They sort of pressed it and it was brought to a headlong issue, whether I did or didn't, right then and there, and so I had to ask her out then, and that was expected. I would not have if I had the choice, but I was sort of pressurized into it, just by saying, er, they were sort of saying in a way "Look, she wants to go out with you and you said you would go out with her. What are you going to do about it now, right now?", you know. So I had to do something then, otherwise I would look an idiot.'

(Boy$_6$, Group A, 16)

This is a relatively mild example, because it comes from a person who was by many standards talented and successful, as well as being from a relatively prosperous home; also his friends were acting in a largely supportive capacity. There are other examples where the pressure is felt more painfully, and the consequences of not conforming may be very serious.

'There used to be about five or six of us. We used to "Oh, if we're going to do it, do it, we'd better do it in style." And we was going round, we used to have a great time. Then we'd start to flog the stuff—you know, to get the extra money, and then we'd probably go to a drug-pusher . . . . There was a couple of drug-pushers down there. So we used to go down there and get our money and go down and get some drugs. But I think it all started—when I was about fourteen. I was doing shoplifting, little things, then, but then I got in with this crowd. Kevin had been in prison, been in prison for stabbing somebody. He's been out now, he's out now. He was in there for two years. I was, I went out with him. We went round in a big crowd. Maybe—if I hadn't gone about with him I'd never have got on drugs. I wasn't on drugs really hard, you know, I was just on it to be like the others, you know, "I'd better do what they do, otherwise they won't want me around." And it's the same with the shoplifting, because shoplifting before was just a bit of a game, you know. We'll go out, nick a hairbrush or something stupid, because we didn't have enough money to buy it. But here, you know, it was something you know, it was something you had to do to be up to other people's standards.'

(Girl$_2$, Group B(N), 17½)

This general picture is confirmed by the categorization of the topics chosen in connection with item 9, 'When you were right on your own, with hardly any one taking your side'. Out of a total of seventy-four categorized choices there were only eleven cases of a boy or girl 'standing alone' for a value at the level of action (category 3), nine of which came from those who were over seventeen years old. The paucity of accounts of actively maintaining a value among peers, in relation to this item and throughout the tape-recordings, is striking, since there is no reason to suppose that participants would wish to withhold descriptions of actions that would show themselves to an adult in a favourable light. The probable inference is that standing alone in this way is indeed rare, and almost unknown in the younger age-group. This question was taken up in the validation session to which reference was made in chapter 4. The opinion of the boy who took part was that it was inconceivable for a person below the age of about sixteen to hold values in an individual way. Boys and girls below that age did, of course, have values, but these arose from participation in group activity.

'We had our own values that you get in a group. It's the way you do things, and it's the way you react to people, and it's your relationships—that are the values you build up. And I think the people you're with, and the different relationships you build, give you different values. So—I mean, at the time I, I probably had quite a few changing values then, because I was changing groups, and sort of going from group to group. And so in one place I'd fit in with what one people thinks, thought, and not necessarily fit in right, because at the time I was changing so much myself I didn't know what I thought, so I wouldn't really bother about it. But, um, your values do change, I think, with, with the different people.

'I don't think you make maybe, maybe, at that age, concrete—decisions on values. Rather, you fit in, and where things don't work out maybe you change them. Er—see, I can't think of at that age actually sitting down and thinking out, working out, "This is right way to do that thing." I think there was nothing concrete, but just in the way you lived and the way you reacted to people you must have had a set of values, of morals even. And—I found maybe a lot of the time mine didn't fit in with the group's. And in that time there was conflict where you, you wouldn't think it was nice to do one thing and others, you know, they, they don't mind at all. And maybe a lot of dishonest things were done that, that even at the time I didn't like doing. But, you know, everybody else did, so rather than make too much of fuss you fit in with them, even though it's not right in your mind and that you don't necessarily agree with doing it.—You tend to get left out if you, you start stating your values outside the group's, and you don't want to do that. So, so you fit in.'

(Boy$_4$, Group B(N), 18)

Thus in relation to the social existence of adolescents, at least in the age range fourteen to seventeen, it can be said with some assurance that the values that are implemented are mainly those that are embedded in the social life-worlds themselves, or that are held in a transitory way at the perspective level. Indeed, it is possible for a boy or girl to have as many sets of values as the groups in which he or she participates, and without necessarily noticing that these are mutually inconsistent. In the light of this the idea of making simple measurements among those of this age, to determine the constituents of a 'personal value system', is virtually meaningless. Insight will be gained, rather, by looking at the values that are associated with particular kinds of group activity.

From Childhood to Adolescence

Although there are many middle-class boys and girls who continue a more or less 'privatized' existence in the early years of adolescence, their social life being centred on the home and a few carefully selected pursuits, the pattern for the majority of adolescents is that of being given a considerable and increasing degree of freedom. It is in the using of this that two of the most characteristic types of association of younger adolescents develop.

Boys

For many boys the first adolescent peer group is very much like that of childhood, a loosely knit affiliation of several boys of about the same age. Objectively the new factors in the situation are the increase in physical size and vitality, and in many cases a small increase in spending power as a result of receiving more pocket-money or having a part-time job. There is a greater freedom of movement, and although the immediate locality is still highly important life is not bounded by it as it was before. Subjectively there are several developments, such as a growing ability to imagine the feelings and perceptions of others, and the awakening of sexual desire. For younger boys the activities mentioned in this context included sport, supporting a football team, 'hanging around', exploring, fishing, vandalism, experimenting with gunpowder, using air-rifles, playing cards, and 'having a laugh'. The two main later additions are the motorcycle and the pub.

'When I first come round here—I kept on having fights and that. But then after a while made mates, like. "Mate and me", and that. And he, we go to football and things like that, and have a laugh and that. But if I'd been having no mates I'd be lonely and that. So I just pick them up wherever I go, —and, and they, they do real good to me and that.

'See, lately they help me out and things like that. But if I'd had no mates. I don't know what to do without mates, you know.

'I wanted to go Swindon. Millwall was playing at Swindon, and that. And—I didn't have the money. So I went over the park and I was thinking about it all the time, what I could do down there, have a laugh and that. Then my mate come up to me. He goes "You can't go, because you haven't got the money", and that. So he walked off. And I was playing football and he come back. He goes "You can go", so I was

really happy, because I could go footballing. Just got in the
van and went there. It was really good. Now I'm glad I went
there, because it was one of the best matches I've been. So
that's one way he's helped me out, things like that.'

(Boy$_2$, Group B(M), 15)

'There's three of us in the fourth year. We're always around
with each other at night. And, I mean . . . . but we seem to
know everything, I mean, we always seem to do the same
things together. I mean, we always go the same places . . . .
we all know everything about each other. I mean, we always
go the same places, you know . . . . the docks, you know
. . . . we don't go "I'm going down the docks today. See you
tomorrow", something like that . . . . all ready to go, and one
says "Well, I can't go, I can't get the money", or something,
we, well we don't say "The rest of us'll go, see you tomorrow." We'll wait until he can go. That's what we do. We
won't wait, you know, we won't just leave him on his own.
We'll wait until he can go.'

(Boy$_{12}$, Group C, 14½)

'Having races with my mates . . . . on dual carriageway . . . .
Well, we just stand there and somebody'll say, er, "Go", or
something like that, and we just clear off . . . . sometimes we
go down back roads where there's loads of bends, see if we
can take the bend a bit . . . . I don't do too badly sometimes.
All depends, because if you haven't got much petrol left all
the oil comes through in the bottom, so that take longer to
get through. Not much petrol gets through, so you don't get
such a good performance. I've done, suppose I've won about
six out of ten.'

(Boy$_{17}$, Group C, 16)

'At home he's always bloody, you know, trying to come hard,
like. Gets on my wick. Well, once, when we first come down
here, because we were used to fighting in the streets, right?
And, er, there was all these kids and they all started, er,
pissing about with my brother. And me and John, we chased
them off, like. And he started acting it hard. "I chased them
off, didn't I?" he goes . . . . I started having a fight with him in
the middle of the road . . . . and we started fighting in the
middle of the road, and a bloody car pulled up and nearly
knocked us down. And he get, he gets on your wick, you
know, he's always, he's always trying to be hard.'

(Boy$_{19}$, Group C, 16)

These extracts show something of the characteristic spirit of the group of younger boys, whose typical implicit values are loyalty, tolerance and mutual help, together with a general consensus that it is better to do things together than to do them alone. There often appears to be a delicate balance of power and status; it is important not to lose face, and to be severely discredited may entail leaving a group altogether.

'He said, "Well, mice've got no bones, it's a well known fact." I said, er, "I think you're wrong there." He said "What do you mean?" I said "Well, a mouse is a mammal," I said, "If you look in your classification list in biology you'll find all mammals are vertebrates, so they've got to at least have a spine." And he said—"No they haven't". I said "They, they've got to have bones in their legs. How would they walk?" I said. "If they had no bones they'd just be like a lump of jelly on the floor." "Oh no," he said "you've just got to have a very tough skin." I said "Oh, you've got to have bones." He said "Oh no, they haven't got bones, it's a—well-known fact." I said "Well, they've got to have bones." He said "Oh no they haven't." And then, you know, the two of them saying "Oh, mice have got no bones." But I knew I was right, that they have bones, you know, but I just couldn't argue any further with the two saying, you know, they haven't. And, and all the others, just, just not worth it. So I said "Oh, leave it at that." But, you know, I knew. And I said to Mr Evans the next day, "I know it sounds a soft question. Mice have bones, don't they?" He said "quite right", he said.'

[Later a group of them, including the boy who claimed mice had no bones, were with the biology teacher.]

'I said "Do you still say mice have got no bones?" And, er, I deliberately said this . . . . in front of all my mates. You see we were all standing at the end . . . . we all sat there having a long talk, things like that. And I stood there and I deliberately said it when everyone was around. And he said "No they haven't" and everyone laughed. And he just sort of went a bright shade of red and he, er, said, "They haven't". And everyone was laughing at him and saying "Who told you that?"

'So we asked Mr Evans, and he said "Was you the one er —who said that mice have no bones?" He said "Yeah, but my sister told me." "Don't try to get out of it." He said "It was my sister that told me." So I said "Go away, you're lying, it was you. You was the first one to say it." So he said, er, "Oh well". And he's never bothered with us no more.'

(Boy$_{12}$, Group C, 14½)

The importance of the all-male peer group generally recedes as new interests develop, such as having a girlfriend, and perhaps having a job, though there are some whose social orientation continues to be mainly towards their own sex, because of their lack of social skill.

'It's, like, when we went, when we went to this place—just before Christmas, like, you know what I mean? And um er—when I heard there was niggers going, right? You know what I mean? I went "Fucking black bastards", like, you know what I mean? But ended up, like, had a right good time, and they really—good people, right, you know what I mean? . . . . They, they're really genuine geezers, like, you know what I mean? They may have been a bit flash, like, but they was really good geezers.

'You could talk to them, and, you know, you have a laugh with them. You say, you say to them "You black bastards", and they won't say nothing. They just "Yeah, yeah", you know, have a laugh with them, right, you know what I mean? Like, you—I went up to one of them, I went "You black cunt", and he said, he said, "Shut up, Yorky", you know. They, just had a laugh with them, you know what I mean? Really decent geezers, like, you know what I mean?

'I don't really talk to girls, do I?—Only, only girls I know, like, you know what I mean? Girls I like, I like, just ain't got the bottle to talk to them, like, you know what I mean?'

(Boy$_1$, Group C, 17)

Boys from affluent middle-class homes seem to be less likely to form peer groups such as those described here as typical of early adolescence, though as they obtain greater independence a wide range of typically 'adolescent' activities becomes available to them, some of which are mainly in male company.

'I like lads of my own age, really, you know, and older. I don't like young kids. Um, I get on pretty well with girls. And —I think I get on a lot, I meet more people, as I, I meet more people, because they know different people, you know. And, erm, and I don't have many arguments. And they, they come up our farm, and I go down their house.

'Like me they've most of them got bikes, the lads. We go to the same places at night. They're all my age. Most of them used to go to my school, or are Stoke supporters.

'In this area the, the police are having a big clamp-down on drinking. We go to a private club, cricket club. Um, there's about ten—lads that go down there, um, each night, and, um, seven will come down one or two nights. Er, there's quite a lot of—people in late twenties, and they all get together, play darts, cards—you know, drink.

'I don't like to get too involved with my girlfriend, because I like to keep my mates as well. I've found out in the past, you spend too much time with her you tend to lose contact with your mates and you don't know what's going on when you go back. So, um, I don't spend too much—time with her. But she's, she's, erm—she's got a nice personality, she talks a lot, and, you know, she listens to you.'

(Boy$_8$, Group A, 16½)

These comments on the all-male peer groups of 'normal' adolescence must be qualified by one further observation. Throughout the whole range of social class there appear to be some boys who are relatively solitary, and if they make friends they tend to do so with individuals, rather than participating in a group. To be solitary in an affluent environment, though a social handicap, is no great hardship, and may even present an opportunity to develop particular talents. But for a working-class boy to be without a group of friends, especially if he is physically small or weak, is a very serious plight.

Girls

The situation for girls at the start of adolescence is very different from that of boys. As soon as they have ceased, physically, to be children, they are viewed as potential girlfriends; ideally (from their point of view) for older boys. Many middle-class parents, eager for their daughters to do well at school and have further success in the future, and aware of potential dangers, are reluctant to give them a large degree of freedom, especially at first; girls from 'lower' in the social class hierarchy have a more easy access to social life. Here, however, their predicament is by no means an easy one. The number of boys who are sufficiently competent to make enduring relationships is far smaller than the total of girls available; and since having a boyfriend is one of the few major sources of status and self-esteem to which they have access, the situation is often one of intense competition and jealousy. Moreover, the prevailing etiquette does not generally allow a girl to take direct initiative in approaching a boy whom she 'fancies'. One of the most common solutions to this problem is for a girl to have one or more close girlfriends, with whom there is an intimacy much deeper than that that obtains between boys of comparable age. This person has several important functions. In public, she is someone to go around with, a source of confidence and a safeguard against the stigma of being solitary. In private, she is someone with whom to talk over problems and plans, and with whom to have lengthy discussions about other people. But perhaps her most important service is that of promoting interests and monitoring progress in the field of boy–girl relationships. It is quite legitimate for her to tell a boy that her friend likes him, and thus help to get a relationship started. Later, from what she has heard, she can relay back information about how the boy thinks the liaison is progressing; she can also warn her friend of any signs of treachery or deterioration.

'I, I couldn't mix with anybody and, erm—Karen was, was much different from me. She's, she's, everything's different from her than it is to me. Like, way, what, what, what job she wanted to do and everything. And, erm—I've been friends with her for about three years now. Before, I couldn't mix with anybody. I used to be all by myself. But since I've met her I'm, I'm getting, I'm getting more involved with people than I do nowadays, you know, than I did when I was twelve. I'm all right now.

'I can understand their problems. If they say they've got problems, things like that, I try to sort them out and everything. But—but she has changed my life completely, like, you know what I mean?

'She's got loads and loads of friends, you see. And I went up to her house one day. She, she said, I said "I don't want to meet any of them. I'm shy", you know, and she said "If you don't, if you don't come with me I'm not going to speak to you again", and I didn't want that to happen. So erm, I went round there and I met John, and—erm, that was it, I think. You know she's, erm, she's my best mate now because she, she helps me, you know, with my problems as well as her problems, like everybody else's.'

(Girl$_{11}$, Group C, 15)

'When I go out it's with my friend Bernadette. And she's a really nice girl, you know, but she's—how can I put, she takes things serious, she's a right laugh . . . . and I'm always mucking about and she's like that, you know, if ever I ask her. But she'll take things serious especially about boys, you know, and I won't do that, because I don't think it's worth it, you know. If ever she gets upset over a boy she likes I'll talk to her or something like that, whereas I don't, I think, well, you know, ... and, er, most of the time I get on right well with her. But we're both Leos and clash a bit, you know, we both want to be sort of, rule one another, and in fact sometimes we have little rows.

'She, she, she's deeper in Leo than me. I'm, I'm only in on July 24th which is the day after, so I've got a bit of Cancer and all. I suppose that evens it out, but she's right in August and so she's got, you know, definitely a Leo. But I like to rule people—and so does she, but we've, you know, it doesn't seem to matter that much really, because we're just—one another. We're just all right together, you know.'

(Girl$_6$, Group C, 14½)

The most valued characteristics in a younger girl's close girl-friend seem to be trustworthiness, social skill, the ability to listen and the capacity to raise morale in times of difficulty. But with the security come certain dangers. A girl who has taken the time to cultivate such a friendship has a great deal to lose if for some reason it disintegrates; having shared some of her most intimate secrets she is also very vulnerable, and can be highly sensitive that her confidences might be betrayed. There are endless possibilities for misunderstanding and misrepresentation.

'I said something to a girl I was on duty with about my best friend. But it wasn't meant to be offensive really, and I, it was just that I said it. Well, she started saying that, erm, I'd said something else and took it the wrong way. But it started going round the school and my best friend came up to me and said, you know, she found out that, you know, what was it, what was it all about, you know. She got a bit angry, like, you know, and I said, "Well, what, what have you been told?" Well, but the version what she got and the version I said were totally different. So when I explained to her what I had said . . . . she said "Tell it to my face next time and don't say it behind my back." But, I didn't mean to be offensive, but, you know, it was just that I said it. And she says "OK," she says, "Well, forget it".

'We've really come very best mates . . . . "Wherever Lynn goes, Tracey's there", sort of thing. And, erm, when, when we have a problem or something like that, go, really go to each other for help, you know . . . . and if she has a problem

she comes to me and tells me about it and I try to help her
and the same with me with her, you see. So we have that
good understanding and . . . . couldn't do without her.'

(Girl₆, Group B(N), 15)

In this instance the rift was easily healed. With more serious
cases the misunderstanding may go on for a long time, or even
result in violence. Perhaps the worst offence that a girl can commit
against one of her intimate friends is to try to take her boyfriend.

'My mates were in, we went along to this, ballroom classes,
and I'd just introduced them. And there is one lad, Brian,
who I think, you know, is really nice, and we usually get on
very well together. And this, certainly, well, one of my
friends who I have, you know, I've been doing my best to get
off with, you know, trying to—pair off with the lad she likes,
well she went all out to get him, you know, sort of thing. She
was—always talking with him. And when I came he really,
you know, they was really, you know, they was really, sort of,
pushing me out. And she started dancing with him. And at
the end, you know, she came in and she says "You know, I'm
awful sorry", you know. And I just turned round and I went
"Get lost, I don't want to know you any more. You take
him," I said. I said, "You can have him for all I care." She
said . . . . and she said "And you're not going to do nothing
about it." That made me lose my temper more, and I was
saying, I said, I said "Well, you can have him, and I don't
mind", you know, I said, "To think I", you know, "trying to
get you off with the lad you like a lot," I said, "and all you
can do is go and play a dirty trick like that on me." I was
really very disgusted with him, you know. And I said "Don't
talk to me no more," I said, "Don't want nothing to do with
you", you know. And—she was, you know, they were sort of
all standing there watching me. And, but—the people who
were watching were . . . . I was doing something that I should
have done a long time ago, you know, telling her, straight.'

(Girl₃, Group B(M), 16)

As girls gain in confidence and social experience their sense of
need for a close associate of the same sex becomes less urgent.
After they have been successful in securing a steady boyfriend,
with whom perhaps even greater intimacies are shared, they gain
in self-esteem, and the girl upon whom there was formerly such
reliance may even become redundant.
Although this research indicates that some upper-middle-class

girls do have close girlfriends of a similar kind, their function is not so vital. For such girls are often able to derive a sense of personal worth from other sources; and generally they 'move out' into an adolescent social milieu at an older age, when they may well be able to manage the details of their social life singlehanded. It must also be said that, just as some boys go through the whole of the teenage period without making a close relationship with a girl, there are some girls who throughout this period have no success in male company, and make such social life as they can either with girls or with those of a different age. As with boys, failure in the sphere of peer relationships brings far more serious consequences for those from working-class backgrounds.

Violence among Adolescents

Those who 'move out' into the society of their peers may well find that this new world can be daunting and violent, as well as offering many new social opportunities. Conflict is given a new dimension compared with childhood by the fact that adolescence involves huge discrepancies in physical size and strength, for both sexes; among older working-class boys who were interviewed the largest was about six feet tall and looked at least fourteen stone in weight, whereas the smallest was not much over five feet, and in many ways appeared to be about fifteen years old. In keeping with the comments made in chapter 4, it is likely that successful aggressors may have highlighted the extent of their victories, and the down-trodden underplayed the extent of their defeats. The accounts, which were particularly associated with items 1, 5, 9 and 14, gave evidence of several types of violent conflict, of which three seem to be especially significant. First, there were quarrels arising between people who already knew each other fairly well, and shared to some extent in the same activities; second, there were violent or quasi-violent episodes between strangers from similar kinds of background, either on an individual or group basis; third, there were acts of aggression between members of different social classes (even though the participants themselves may not have seen the matter in social class terms). The values in relation to which action is guided in the three types of case are rather different.

Violent interpersonal conflict among boys

Almost all the accounts in this category come from members of the working class. It appears that the underlying ground for a fight is generally a boy's status or dignity within a broad group whose members are known to one another. The immediate 'occasion' is a physical or verbal insult, mockery, making a person look foolish, or an attempt to exclude him from a group. A fight may occur spontaneously when the affronts have exceeded a certain threshold, or at a deliberately chosen opportunity.

'One night when I was up here . . . . he turns around and he called me . . . . a wanker, and I turns around and calls him a wanker back. And he says "What?" and I says "Wanker". So he just stood there and looked me up and down, and I thought to myself "Aye Aye", and I was just ready for a fight. And he just turned his back on me. And that really annoyed me, that did, a person doing that, and I thought "I'll get you one day for that" . . . . He thinks his self so hard, and yet he thought he could have me, and he turned his back on me and walked away. He wouldn't kind of face me like a bloke. I, I, when you fight, I don't think you're a man because you fight, but in that sense, you know—he thought his self a man, man enough to have me . . . . he's a coward. He didn't want to be shown up by this lot, because once he know, once they saw a fight they'd take the piss out of him something chronic up here. Anyway, I walked home that night, and that cunt's down at the end, the top of my road with my other mate. And I . . . . all the way across the road say "Come on then". I got half way down the road and he come up behind me, and I turned around . . . . he said "I don't want you running off, I ain't having you running off, Mick, when I get started in to you. I'm going to do you in." I said "Good, come on then" . . . . He held my coat and then he said "Come on then". And he come up and stood, and didn't move for a couple of seconds, and he started to laugh, and I had him then. He wished he's never started on me. And after that he stood up and he, every time he sees me he said "Hello, Mick, how are you getting on?" Creep. Creep. And my other mate, he say to me, my other mate telling before we had that fight, he says "If I gets too, if I starts to smash his head against the ground, gets too nasty with him, pull me back", and yet he didn't do nothing. And instead of saying "Mick, yeah", instead of saying "Right, Mick you are . . . . You can have me", he said "Oh well, I wasn't fighting my hardest, I weren't on form that night", you know. And it gets right up my nose people doing that.'

(Boy$_{23}$, Group C, 17)

'I know it's, er, wrong, but I like seeing a good, watching a good fight. Er, well, most boys do, er, erm. If there's something really going I like to stop it most of the time, you know. A lot of the time I just don't like getting involved. But if it's any of my friends and there's more than one on to him I'll go in and help.

'Just before Christmas there was a boy who was going on, going on at me for over two years . . . At school, erm, started pushing me about. I said "No, don't be so stupid. Go away", you know, and, er, he kept on pushing me about. And I came away, I walked away. And he punched me in the back which I, I can't stand being punched in the back. And I just turned around and had a good old go at him. And, er, well he had to have, er, had to go to hospital . . . . He wasn't really bad, just, er, sort of, er, er, you know. He said "I'll get you for this", but he didn't, you know.'

(Boy$_{16}$, Group C, 16½)

'Yeah, I doing a lot of fights. I like fighting. People who aggravate me, I get satisfaction out of hitting them. People who don't, I don't hit anyway. I don't think I'm particularly good at fighting. I only pick on people I think I can beat. People I don't beat I just lump it, because, er, people who can beat me I just lump, I just respect them anyway.'

(Boy$_4$, Group C, 17)

These three extracts were from boys who were physically well equipped to handle the situation they were describing. The situation looks rather different from the standpoint of a boy who is small or weak.

'When I went into work I had to hunt, like, you know. Didn't feel too good and, er, you know, all my friends came round scrounging my fags. And there's one particular kid who come up to me and, er, just punched me like, and . . . . my fags. And when I went and got them back he threw something at me like, you know. I really got uptight about that and I threw something back at him and just stormed out. And that was about it, really.

'Didn't talk to him after that. And I went home. Course, I lost a day's pay, half, half a day's pay for it, like.

'Well the only reason they, why they gang up on me, like, because as I told you I don't like violence unless I'm really pushed into it, like. So they know every time they pick on me, they know they're not going to get hit back. So that's when, that's when I really feel annoyed, like, you know, because that's when everybody really picks on me. It's the only reason why.

'Well, they just take the mick out of me, that's all, like . . . . just take the mick. Keep pushing me about. Meanwhile I take no notice, like. It's the only way.'

(Boy$_2$, Group C, 19)

There appear to be certain rules whose function is to ensure that fights among those who know one another, and will have to live with one another afterwards, are tolerably fair, and that injury is not excessive.

'That's the way I am, not a trouble-maker really, but [Laughter] I'd always help somebody out. I suppose it's because I'll always help somebody out, if it's not fair. — I'll, I'll never go and fight in a fight with bottles and things. That is really disgusting. If you can't fight using yourself, it's not worth fighting using bottles. — People say it's . . . . you've got to be mad in the head to use bottles. Look at the consequences that come out. You get a bottle in your face, you know it — you get a punch in the nose, you know it. But — you don't get injured for life, same as if you go with a chain or something. — Get that wrapped around your hand it'd break your arm in half, easy. And pick-axe handles and things like that . . . . People say that people are hard, but they ain't only because they pick up bits of wood and they threaten people with them. — And half the time people have been beat up anyway, and they're just lying on the ground, and they go and pick up a bit of wood and hit them over — "Cor, he's hard, he just hit that mush over the head with a bit of wood." Oh, I could never do that. It's not hard, it's just having no brain.'

(Boy$_{31}$, Group C, 17)

'I went to a discotheque . . . . and, er, my friend said he was going to have a go at this bloke. So after the discotheque was finished he went outside and started having a go. And this other fellow was getting the better of him. So I joined in, and, er, er, this other fellow got pretty hurt . . . . and so we ran off. We never thought no more about it until we went back to school on the Monday, and the police was waiting for us.

'We went to court. Really scared, you know. And I only

got fined five pounds, and that. I felt I'd been disgraced.
'It was a sort of one-to-one fight. After all, my mate did
start it. So I thought it was a bit, not very friendly of me to
join in . . . . he was a bit smaller than what I was.'

$$(Boy_{15}, Group C, 16\frac{1}{2})$$

It is possible to abstract from the material dealing with conflict
of this kind a set of guidelines concerned with the initiation and
conduct of fights, which may be summarized in the following
points.

1 If one's dignity, status or rights are seriously violated, one
   ought to fight.
2 If one is attacked physically, one ought to fight back.
3 There are some circumstances where a largely ritual conflict
   will suffice instead of a genuine fight.
4 If the odds against one are very strong, it is wiser to avoid a
   fight.
5 If a fight is becoming more serious than its 'occasion' merits,
   it is right to intervene to try to stop it.
6 Some people are so despicable that they 'deserve' to be
   beaten up.
7 It is wise to adopt a general manner of a kind that will enable
   one to avoid being a case under rule 6.

Although there are some mutual contradictions between these
rules, they appear to have certain general functions, of which the
most important is the establishment of status. A boy may sometimes be faced with a difficult decision here, because of the
uncertainty of the outcome from a fight, though to have fought
well and lost may be better than not to have fought at all. But
there are also prudential considerations. With a near equal, and
when the 'occasion' is not serious, a display of aggression may be
all that is necessary; and when the physical discrepancy is very
great the weaker may 'back down', judging it wiser to accept the
loss of status that this entails. The sixth and seventh rules are put
forward here rather tentatively. It seems that some boys are
perceived virtually as a 'disgrace to the tribe', not because of
anything they have done, but simply because of the kind of people
they appear to be. It is a plausible hypothesis that under the
conditions that many working-class adolescents now face, where it
may be difficult to establish a sense of personal worth elsewhere
than among themselves, anyone who is evidently despicable is a
kind of threat to the rest, a reminder of what they themselves
might easily be.

Aggression between strangers of similar background

In comparison with the first category of conflict much less was said on this topic; there is some ground for thinking that this may in part be an artefact of the research instrument, which tended to highlight episodes of a highly personal character. This general category includes clashes between gangs, aggression at football matches (cf. Marsh, Rosser, and Harré, 1978) and casual encounters between strangers. From the little evidence available from this research, it would appear that, since those involved recognize each other as coming from the same kind of background, some of the signs and rules that guide interpersonal conflict are still operative to some extent.

> 'I was fishing in the breeding place, I was catching some fish and then we heard this gate, just close together. So we run along and a kid, some kid, about, he reckons he was about twenty-two but he only looked about eighteen, something like that. So we run down . . . . and he started pushing us about. So I swore at him and things like that, and said "Don't push me about" and other things. And he kept pushing me about and he reckons that he used to . . . . and I don't care.
> 'And he kept pushing me about and my other mate was there and he was blinding, going "Come on right out", and I just felt a bit scared because I was thinking that he was twenty-two and, and he done a lot of fighting and that. And I thought I might get beaten up, so I left him alone . . . . the next day and I wanted to fight him because I felt bad after it. I couldn't hit him or touch him or nothing. So I went out the next day and I didn't see him. So next time I go up there, if I see him I'm going to just hit him.
> 'He was pushing me around and I had my bomber jacket on, and I only bought it a couple of weeks earlier. And he, he kept pushing it and pulling it and that . . . . and he kept kicking me and things like that and he just got me angry. And I just don't know, don't know, don't know why I just didn't hit him. Just left it. And when I got out the park he just went off and I felt really bad.'
>
> (Boy$_2$, Group B(M), 15)

There is, however, one major difference in conflict of this kind. A general principle of loyalty to the group to which a boy belongs may be judged to outweigh other kinds of consideration such as fairness.

'If I don't get on with somebody and, er, they keep making an issue of the fact I don't get on with them, and coming up to me and trying to start trouble, then I'll steer clear of them. And if they follow me, you know, and really try it then I'll have a fight, I expect. I don't know why, I just will . . . . I mean, all the time there was trouble up here about, when was it, a couple of months ago, we expecting youth clubs from all around to come up and beat up the nippers from up here. That was causing me unrest. I thought "I've got to go up there tonight, and we've got to fight, because I'm not going to stand there and let my friends get beat up. I don't want to fight, but I'm not going to stand and let them get beat up. So I've got to jump in and have a fight, you know."'

(Boy$_{15}$, Group B(M), 17)

'A lot of people say, like, "He's from Manchester. Let's go and batter him up", like, you know.'

(Boy$_{12}$, Group C, 14½)

Conflict between those of different social class

This category is typified by the assaulting of boys who are 'higher' by those who are 'lower' in social background, for whom the perception of class is often transmuted into a matter of personality; middle-class boys are 'soft' or unmanly in some way. There appears to be no clear etiquette governing this kind of violence. The main controlling factor is probably the simple prudential consideration of possible repercussions from the police. Whereas there was only one clear account from an aggressor in this kind of conflict (perhaps because the interviewers themselves were evidently middle-class), several boys in group A described how they had been attacked.

'One of us had a long coat. We went up behind this bloke . . . . sort of university student, you know, looked really drugged up and that. Our bloke had a long coat, put it over his head, pulled him on to the floor, and we started booting him and that, and searched his pockets, and just run off and left him there.
'Felt sorry for the poor bloke . . . . but he didn't know much about it . . . . makes me feel sick to see blokes like that.'

(Boy$_{15}$, Group C, 16½)

'Because I am different to everyone else I get picked out
quite a lot by the general mob, me and my friends. I mean,
when we were in the third year we all had long hair and holey
jeans, well when we were in the third and fourth year, we all
had long hair and holey jeans. So we were all hippies, which,
well everyone else thought we were hippies and junkies,
which we weren't particularly. Well some were, some weren't,
so we all get persecuted for that. Then er, then we were all
punks—or all are punks—and they seem to have laid off a
bit. I mean, I still get kids calling me "junky", because they
remember I had long hair I suppose.

'I get beaten up quite a lot—which is just because of my
appearance and nothing else, or occasionally I have a big
argument or disagreement with somebody. And they, I might
have a fight with some kid, and he brings his brother and his
mates . . . . I can run fast! I've only been beaten up three
times—since I've been here . . . . I've got my nose broken a
couple of times, things like that, black eyes, couple of toes
broken . . . . bruises, ribs and that, enough to crawl home!
[Laughter] I haven't been put in hospital yet. I've got a bit
paranoid about it. I'm becoming more paranoid about it now,
because there are people who are after me. I mean, I'm not
friends with the hippies or friends with the punks. I just do
what I want.'

(Boy$_{15}$, Group A, 17)

'About two years ago, used to go to a youth group at my
local church, and on the way to the youth group we were
being followed by a load of lads from one of the local estates.
They were sort of jeering at us and saying "You good-for-
nothing Christians", etcetera. We sort of walked on, ignoring
them. Then after the youth group was over we were walking
along a little passageway which leads to a middle-class area
and, er, we found out that we were being followed by five
blokes and six or seven girls. That's a lot. So we sort of put
the girls to the front, and five blokes walked behind them.
And, all of a sudden the lads started chasing us, jumped on
us, and of course a little scramble . . . . and they ran away.
We went into a girl's house and 'phoned up the police . . . .
About an hour and a half later a couple of bricks were
thrown in through the window—and, um, it was presumably
some of the lads, so we 'phoned up the police again, and
they came around.'

He goes on to describe how, shortly afterwards, he was 'collected' by two of the boys concerned, and taken out for a fight.

'And then, at the end of January, er, I was supposed to go to court to be a witness and, um, it was decided to drop the charges. But the police decided to continue them, and fortunately I didn't have to be a witness or anything . . . . That was it for a couple of months, and then I heard that this lad was looking for me again, and so we sort of met and we had a fight. [Laughter] Both come off as badly as each other, really . . . . I'd read about things like this, but before I'd never imagine that it'd happen to me. I, I just thought it was a really exciting thing really. [Laughter] It hasn't really, I suppose it's made me angry with him about, er, hurting other people.

'About a year and a half ago I was walking home from a disco by myself. Just outside the main gate there was another fifteen of them. "Ah, here comes a middle-class person", or words to that effect. They sort of chased me around a bit, and they caught up with me, and one of them said "Hang on just a minute. Just want to make sure I don't know him", and they sort of turned my face around, "Nah, that's all right", and started laying in to me.

'Things like this happen all over this district—especially Friday nights going down the Hill, which is a local place for punks and teds, meeting place round here. About once a month there's rather a big fight there . . . . I suppose it does affect me a bit more when it does, actually does happen to me. It just sort of makes the realization come true.

'I think it's all very isolated cases apart from this ted and punk business—just I've met up with it a couple of more times than other people. Don't know why. Why me? [Laughter] . . . . The first incident, er, I got taken home by a policeman and I broke down then because I couldn't understand it. But, er, the time I got beaten up at the disco, walked home making up my excuses, got in and went to bed.'

(Boy$_{14}$, Group A, 18)

Violence among girls

While the interviews produced an abundance of evidence relating to milder forms of conflict among girls, the number of reported incidents relating to actual violence was relatively small. Even so, this was sufficient to indicate that it is markedly different in character from that among boys. All the accounts were of conflict in the interpersonal category; some of it was between sisters. There appear to be three main types of cause for an outbreak of physical violence: taking, or attempting to take, another's boy-friend, defamation of character, and jealousy of various kinds.

'We were in the house and my older sister, you know. I'd just come in from school, and it was her day off work, and she hadn't done any, you know, any housework at all, and she'd just left it all for me. So when I came in I was sort of very annoyed and . . . . and I was really annoyed because, you know, I mean, if it was my day off I think I'd have done it. And then—she told me to, er, go to the shop for her, and I said "No", and I said "All this," I said, "and to think you couldn't do it right," I said, "seeing it's your day off, I mean." We were arguing, and she hit me across the face. And I said "Get out", you know, I said, "and take, take your stupid child with you," I said, "Don't come back to this house because I, we didn't want you there. You just a lumber. You been living off my mother for two years."'

(Girl$_3$, Group B(M), 16)

'On Saturday night we'd been invited to an eighteenth party, Jill and I. We went, and we'd arranged that we were getting a lift home by Susan's sister. Anyway, the party finished about a quarter of an hour early, so we went for some chips, you see, and we were walking through the centre of town when we were stopped by these two boys. And we knew the girls from school—sort of go round with them at school.—So we went on—got talking, then got our lift and thought nothing more about it. This was on Saturday night. Then on Sunday night when we came in . . . we stood behind the records, Jill and I, and, um—getting dirty looks from everyone. And we thought—"What have we done wrong?" Someone must have told these two lasses that we were sort of messing around with their boyfriends.

'This girl came up and started, you know, started shouting and making accusations at Jill and then she started.—She hit her across the face, and Jill didn't do anything, she carried on. Anyway, then this other girl come and she started, she hit me—so then there were Jill and the other girl, and me and this other girl, and we were all fighting behind records. And I remember looking up and seeing everybody stood round.

'There were everybody there. All I can remember is looking up—everybody were watching, and even somebody else, this girl, one of the girls—said "I'm going to get a, get on to you personally." She's one who comes and says we don't like her, so "Bash her up", and they all follow. And there were a few more as well who were sort of shouting, and they were involved as well. Anyway, they got banned from the youth club.'

(Girl$_{14}$, Group C, 16)

'There is one girl in particular, you know, she was "Oh, I'm Miss fantastic. Look at me, I can do everything." And then I came along, more or less on to the scene, and I could outdo her. So it was her, more or less the ringleader, and her friends, you see.

'One night after the match, you know, we played the match, and these girls came down saying they . . . . and they beat me up afterwards the match, you see, because the girl wanted to play the same position as I did. So, er, they got away with that and then carried on for a certain length of time. And, and, my Mum come down and got it stopped.

'I got them back in my own way, you know. If they wanted to start a fight, you know, I normally used to back down and go in a corner and shut up, you know, and leave them to it. And after a while, you know, I thought "They're not getting away with it no more, so I'll get them by myself", you know, "while they're by themselves." So I did that and they just didn't want to bother me any more.

'I got them back, what they did to me.'

(Girl$_2$, Group B(M), 18)

'He asked me if I'd go out with him and I said "Yeah", but then I found he was two-timing me and going out with somebody else. I couldn't stand that. I said "I'll smack her head in" if, if he didn't tell me, he wouldn't tell me. He hadn't told her, but if he'd packed me up and then gone out with her or whatever . . . . "I'll smack her head in".

'I would hit her, but I wouldn't really, because she had him first. But if I had him first I'd fight for him. But she had him first.'

(Girl$_{12}$, Group C, 15½)

The aggression of working-class girls can be related to their social position as it was characterized earlier in this chapter. Whereas interpersonal conflict among boys often appears to be that of the relatively powerful, and to be backed by certain considerations of honour, that among girls looks much more like that of an underclass, struggling for limited resources. Whereas boys may find it necessary to fight in order to increase or maintain their status, girls are more likely to fight when almost all status is at risk, when pyschological survival itself is threatened. Some girls, however, gave evidence of remorse at having been involved in fighting, as if this was not compatible with their view of right behaviour for their sex. Fighting among boys is well established, and a series of safeguards, particularly through ritualization of conflict, have evolved; among adolescent girls, however, fighting is a more recent phenomenon, and appears to be less structured. Only one participant in this research reported a permanent physical injury resulting from adolescent violence. As it happened, this was a girl; another girl had literally (not metaphorically, as is often the case with boys) kicked her in the head, and damaged her inner ear.

Relationships between the Sexes

The tape-recordings contained an abundance of material concerned with friendships of various kinds between boys and girls, scattered throughout the items of the interview schedule. As was pointed out in chapter 4, directly sexual aspects were generally indicated by oblique rather than direct reference; the most detailed descriptions were concerned with the circumstances under which relationships were made and broken. Even here some social class differences were apparent. In keeping with the observations made earlier in this chapter, those from working-class backgrounds tend to form such friendships at an earlier age and under stronger social pressure, even if initially their liaisons are of short duration. There was also some indication that middle-class adolescents, perhaps unwittingly following their parents' mode of life, are more 'privatized' and less based on a single locality in the way they form their attachments.

A girl in the 'lower' part of the social class system, even if she does not go to a youth club, is likely to be visible in her own neighbourhood and at school, 'available' for a friendship with the opposite sex. The first relationships she makes with boys may well be brief and superficial, though after a year or two she will perhaps go on to make a more serious attachment, probably to a boy who is somewhat older. To have a boyfriend is an important source of status, for which it is worth making certain sacrifices. If she is not successful in forming a suitable relationship she may, as a temporary expedient, take on a boy of her own age or even younger. Under the circumstances it is better to have some kind of boyfriend than none at all; and even if his company provides little intrinsic satisfaction he is at least a stop-gap; in his absence his virtues can be magnified a little, and he is a topic for discussion with female friends. The first genuine boyfriend is an important milestone, a token of success.

'My friend fixed me up with this boy named Frank . . . . who was, I didn't want, I didn't know I'd ever go out with a boy. I thought "Oh no, I'd never go out with a boy, nobody'd fancy me." But this boy named Frank, he told my friend Ann that he fancied me, but he didn't know whether to ask me out or not. So Ann thought "Oh, I'm going to do a bit of stirring." So she went and told her brother Peter, who's—Frank's mate, and, erm, he, he told Ann to come over and tell me that he fancied me and wanted to go out with me. So, I said "I'll, I don't know, I don't know really whether I want to." So she said "Oh, go on", so I said "Oh, all right, then". So she said he's coming down the next day, so I thought "Well, I'm going to wash my hair, so when she comes round I won't see him." So I washed my hair and she came over and called for me, but I was washing my hair so I couldn't come down and see him. So he went, because he didn't really want to see me, I don't think. And then about a week later, he, erm, he come down and I was, I didn't realize he was going to come down, so I had to go over. So Ann and her brother said "Oh, this is Frank", and "Frank, this is Elaine". So I just said "Hello". And, erm, Ann said to her brother "Oh, let's, erm, let's go in and have our tea now, Peter." So, so Peter goes "Yeah, all right then". So they both left me and Frank outside then, you see. It was all fixed, all arranged, I was so annoyed. [Laughter] And he asked me out and he took me out, and it lasted for a whole month, well, longer than a month, actually, and it was about one month and two weeks. And, erm, when my friend saw him, he'd left school, in the fifth year, and my friend saw him with another girl. And, erm, it got me because I thought "Oh, he liked me a lot and I'll go out with him for ages". And he said "Oh, we'll probably last for three months". Well, three months is, well, "I doubt whether that would last", I said. Obviously it didn't because he was with this other girl, and I'd love to have found out who she was, really wanted to tell her what he's like. And then the next day she saw him with another—girl, and it just carried on like that. Day after day he was with somebody else. Now, he used to see me on Tuesdays, Wednesdays, Sun- Saturdays, just three days. And I wondered what he was doing on the days in between, but he said he was studying for his—O levels. And, erm, well, he said he'd come down one day and he didn't. So I thought, "Well, I'll go and ring him up." And I rang him up and his Mum said "No, I'm sorry, he's gone out." So I thought "Ah, he's meant to be studying for his exams." So, erm, I rung him up the next day, and he still wasn't, he wasn't in again. So I thought "Well, that's funny, what's he been up to?" And after my friend telling me he was going out with this other girl—I got a bit upset. I, I was going to chuck him, but I didn't know whether to or not, and I was really upset. And I was crying and everything, and I didn't know what to do. And then one day he come down and, erm, he didn't come over to see me. And I saw him and I thought, "Oh, this is annoying." So I walked over from there, and I said just "Hello, Ann", and "Hello, Peter", and I didn't say hello to him. So he drove round my friend's house because he'd found out where my friend, and he asked her out, while he was still going out with me. And I was so upset I walked round Jackie's, but I didn't know he was round there. And I saw his bike, because he rides his bike, you see. I saw his bike and I said "Hello, his bike's outside my friend Jackie's house." And I went up there and he was standing there speaking to Jackie. Oh, I was so annoyed, and I, so Jackie, Jackie, I was crying, I was really crying, and he saw me and he thought it was funny. He was standing there laughing his head off, and I really were annoyed. And Jackie goes to me, she said, "He's just come round to ask what was the matter with you, and why you didn't say hello." And I felt, "Oh", so I believed that, but it obviously wasn't true, and she didn't want to tell me that he'd asked her out. But she had told one of her other friends, and this girl thought it would be wise to tell me, because if I wasn't told I'd be really upset, and I'd be going out with him still. And she told me, and I was upset and that. So she said "Well, why don't you chuck him?" And I said "I can't". So she goes "Why not?" So I said "Well, I like him too much." So she goes "You've got to chuck him sometime, because you can't carry on if he, especially if he's going out with all those other girls." So I thought "Well, yeah, is Jackie going out with him?" So she goes "No, Jackie won't go, go out with him because she's a good friend of yours, and she wouldn't go out with one of your boyfriends." So I thought "Oh". So the next day he come down and I said to him "Look, I've found out that you've been two-timing me." And he denied every word of it. And he, we had a big argument, and it was all over this and that, and he said "And I wasn't two-timing you", and he, I said "Well, you was also with these other girls." So he goes "I wasn't with all these other girls", and, sort of, looking down at the floor. And I said "Oh, do you like the pavement, or something?" because he kept on looking at the pavement. So he goes "Yeah", he said, "it's quite interesting". So I said, said, "Oh", so I said, "Anyway, I don't want to go out with you no more." So he goes, "Oh, that's good", and rode off. And I was really upset. I, I, I think I was really broken-hearted, but it took, mended up in a week when, when I was asked out by somebody else. [Laughter] And that was it, you know. But it was really, it hurt me because I didn't really want to chuck, chuck him, because I liked him a lot, and I think I still like him.

'He wasn't really good looking. He had a bit of a nice personality until I found out what he was like. Erm, he was shy, but he started to speak more and that. And he took me loads of places and everything, like the pictures, parks, and everything. And he come round my house to see me, you know, most days. He was nice, he was nice towards my parents and everything. My Mum, my Mum thought he was nice. But—when I found out what he was like, I don't hate him, I don't dislike him, I like him still, but, I see him now because he still comes round to see Peter. Well, I was round his house once, round Ann's house once, and he turned up. But he just said "Hello", and that. And Ann said, "Well, why don't you just start speaking to him, and just, just be friends?" So I don't mind that as long as he's nice towards me, so—I think that's it.'

(Girl$_7$, Group B(N), 14½)

A girl who 'moves out' into adolescent social life at a later age, perhaps coming from a more protective home, or having given a lot of her time to schoolwork, is likely to experience greater depth in the relationship with her first real boyfriend; and even though she may be lacking in certain kinds of social skill, she is less likely to need another girl as a close ally in her cause.

'Well I, sort of, I'd never really been out seriously with a boy, not, you know, going with him for several months. I'd only just, sort of one-night stands and that sort of thing. [Laughter] And, and then, um, this boy who had actually been working at Tesco's, and it, and, um, started sort of going out seriously. And, sort of, my whole life had been, sort of, wrapped round the family until then, sort of, sort of changed towards going out, meeting him sort of more or less—every night, and sort of getting really involved with him instead of, you know, just sitting at home, watching telly with the family, sort of involved with all the family, you know, routine. Sort of got out of the routine and started going—out more and meeting more people, sort of a whole range. Sort of changed quite drastically. And, you know, my whole life sort of changed from family, sort of, towards the boy, you know.'

(Girl$_5$, Group B(N), 17)

The position of boys is very different from that of girls. The prevailing etiquette allows them to take virtually all the initiative, and for practical purposes they are in a minority. Thus almost any boy who wishes to have a girlfriend, and who is prepared to take the necessary steps, is likely to succeed.

'I went out, and I said "I'm going up that youth club on my own, and I'm going to pick up a bird", because there's hundreds of them up there, just waiting to be picked up.

'So I went up, and, er, just sat around. I got myself all dolled up, went and sat up there. Three birds came talking to me. And, er, I knew two of them, I didn't know one. The two I knew were right scrubbers, to put it—crudely, they really were. In fact one of them is now married—and pregnant. Look where I got myself . . . . And, er, they were both sort of saying, you know, "How about going with her, how about going with her?" But I never thought about this, and the one that wasn't doing all the talking "Um", you know, "I like that, she's quiet. She doesn't look quite as tartish as the other two." And I knew the other two really well. So, well, I'd seen her around but I'd never even spoken to her. Thought—"I fancy that". And I was just out to pick a bird. I wasn't interested in, as long as she was good looking, you know, that was it. I wasn't bothered what she was like. It was a one-night stand or anything. "What, whatever comes, comes, but I'm determined to pick a bird up." And I looked at her, and sort of asked her her name, or something "Give us a kiss", and she did. We never looked back. Just spent the rest of the night with her. The other two, we got rid of them. They were both, ah, you know, and, er, I says, you know, "What you doing tomorrow, what you doing the night after, what you doing the night after?" And it's just progressed. And I gradually, it took a long time. She were just a bird to take out—and then I realized, "Well, I like this lass", you know. I'd been going out with her about two months till, before I realized I liked her. It, it, it's really weird, is that. I usually like them and then decide I want to go out with them. And

with her it's the other way round . . . . She were just a status
symbol, a woman to take out, "Oh, this is my bird, you
know, call her Sharon".

'I decided I liked her. Then I got talking to her friend. She
says "Oh, she's really cracked up on you. You, you're on to a
good thing." Well I am, and I realized I liked Sharon.

'We just tolerate each other. We like completely different
kind of music—erm, she's always wanting to have her hair
cut, and I say she isn't going to have her hair cut. She likes to
wear long skirts . . . . fantastic hair, she's gorgeous looking,
which she won't have it. Um, and I keep talking about
shaving my 'tache off and she won't have that. I keep talking
about having my hair cut, she won't have that. She wears long
skirts, and I tell her "Get . . . . get shorter skirts on", you
know. We just, we don't, we don't even compromise. We just
get downright—er, disagree with each other but we don't
argue about it. We just tolerate it. And we go out places,
and we just, we talk together well, and we talk to each other.
She says "If I was clever I wouldn't get on with you", and
she says, "That's why we get on, because you're brainy and
I'm not" . . . . She puts on a pretence of being incredibly
thick sometimes, which is annoying. But—I just tolerate her
and she tolerates me. We just, I think I've got a, a quite a, a
funny sense of humour which has taken a long time, but she
now understands me, to a fashion, and she understands my
sense of humour and what makes me tick, and that. We just
get on.

'She's been out while I've been away. She's picked other
fellows up. I've picked other women up but we always come
back, end up back together. We've never actually split up,
but, er—when I've been out with other women I've, I've
thought more of Sharon. I've thought, "Well, she's not a
patch on Sharon", you know, gone back.

'She's seen the characters that she picked up in town since.
If she thought that much of them she'd have gone back to
them. She had all the chance she wanted, but she wouldn't.
So that was fair enough. It was an ego-trip for me too.—We
just, I don't know, it's just accepted that we get on. We just
accept it. She says "Oh, I want you to have a row with me."
So I start shouting abuse at her and calling her all the names I
could think of. "No, don't bother", you know . . . . We never
had a proper, serious row, no, never. We've sort of fallen
out, but it's been "I hate you", kiss, "I hate you", kiss. And
also, we—two of the lads in the group have girlfriends. Now,
she hates the music we do. All three of them really do, but

they don't, they don't, they don't, say owt about it, but they
do. When we go up to rehearse, the three of them hang
around, talking girl-talk in the corner, which is convenient.
And, er, that, that keeps us together in that respect. You
know, she'll come up to see the other girls when I have to be
there. And then we'll go to the pub afterwards, Sharon and I.
They all come up, you know, but I'm with Sharon afterwards.
Er, we hardly speak when we're rehearsing, simply because
we're there to rehearse, and we have an understanding on
this. But we're quite, we see each other every day of the
week. Er, when we started it was three days a week, now it's
seven.'

(Boy$_3$, Group B(N), 18)

Although the position is immensely favourable to boys who
have developed a degree of confidence and social skill, this fact
brings its responsibilities. A certain shyness is judged to be acceptable (and perhaps even commendable) in a girl, since her part is
mainly to respond. Boys however, are often anxious about the part
that they have to play. Anyone who is not sure of his ability or
attractiveness puts his self-esteem at considerable risk in approaching a girl. If his initiative is rejected it would be better never to
have made the attempt.

'I'm tongue-tied to a terrible extent. Especially in the
presence of girls, I don't know why. I don't mind when
there's a gathering of them there, and I'm feeling, um—I'm
feeling quite reasonably happy, you know. I, I, I occasionally
go into sort of states of depression. I think it's, this goes back
to when I was just left my first secondary school, I'm nervous
wreck. And, er, and I've more or less psychoanalysed myself
to get rid of that, as far as that goes, and can draw my own
conclusions.
 'On subjects which are of mutual interest to her and me
I've, it's difficult to find subjects, and when I do find a
subject, it, it's usually very sparse chatter, and it lasts for
about forty seconds if I'm lucky, and then we both dry up. I
don't know—if it's a failing on her part or not, as well. But,
you know, I'm, I'm quite keen on going out with this one,
because she's rather nice. And yet, I don't want it to fall
apart just because I, we can't communicate with each other.
 'Until recently I've not needed the, to be able to talk to
girls. Because I mean with Angela she's very intelligent
indeed and she can, if she sees that I'm tongue-tied at all she
can talk, and she can talk in such a way that it will get me

talking as well, which is one way we, that, that we used to get on so well, and we still do. You know, she's, we can still hold a reasonable conversation without me getting tongue-tied so. But when you're two of a kind meet, and you're not particularly good at talking to each other—I don't know what she thinks of me yet in fact, I don't know whether to ask her or not, you know—I don't know whether it would be fatal or not. As you can tell I'm, my experience with fe- girls is non-existent at all.'

(Boy$_2$, Group B(N), 18)

Sexuality is by no means the only important component in friendships between boys and girls. Indeed, a few relationships were explicitly characterized as being more like that of a brother and sister. To have a friend of the opposite sex is often a source of status among peers in general; and if the relationship develops favourably, it can serve as a very important means of social support. This is especially the case for those whose lives in other respects are in disarray.

'I took her for granted at first. The main reason being that I went out with her for so long—up to that time was because I made up my mind to have a permanent girlfriend. Probably because of, er—it was some, two girls were taking the mickey out of me when I was working at Woolies', and told me that I ought to get a permanent girlfriend and get myself sorted out. It didn't, it didn't actually influence me about that. That's just a reason I just sort of thought I'd bring up, but I thought I might try and have a permanent girlfriend, see how I'd get along . . . . I don't know whether—I'm so fond of her because I've been going out with her for so long and she's the first girl I've ever bothered going out with for so long. I don't think so, because I wouldn't bother going out with her so long —if I didn't like her, because things I don't like I get rid of. Um, now of course, I wouldn't want to be away from her for more than a day.

'Erm—when I first went out with her she was sweet and innocent. And that, that just goes. I mean, if she hadn't have been I don't think it'd have made much difference, but that makes it better now, looking back on it. Er, she's certainly not sweet and innocent any more. Erm—she's, er, just a very nice sort of girl. Didn't used to argue with me. She only argues with me now because she knows me well enough, and know how far she can go, and the rest of it.'

(Boy$_4$, Group C, 17)

'I used to hang about where I lived. My friends used to come round for me and we used to go out causing trouble and that, knocking on people's doors, and we always used to have the police round our houses. But since I've been going out with her I've, I've only had the police round my house once.

'I used to always be nervous, you know, because people used to come after us a lot. Not that I much bothered about it —except that I'd get a bad name, which I did have. But since I been going out with her, there, there's, you know, feel that there's nobody after me and I got a clear conscience.'

(Boy₁₇, Group C, 15)

'I think he gives a, me a help because as well as a few of the group he knows my past, most of my past. He doesn't know all of it because . . . . but he didn't know I was on drugs. He knows most of my past, he, you know, the things I get up to [Laughter], shoplifting, he knows most of it. But I've, it's just that—I've got, if he tells me I shouldn't be doing something I will listen more to him than any of the others. It's mainly because I've known him for so long—you know, and he is more like a brother. We treat each other like brother and sister—you know. We borrow each other's fags, we lick them for each other, you know. Say "Oh, I'll give you one back another day", you know, "Oh, come on", you know. It's, maybe it's because we've known each other so long we've managed—to be able to turn to it. Say if any problem happens in my life, I'm used to being, be able to talk to him because he's been through the same thing.'

(Girl₂, Group B(N), 17)

A number of boys and girls enlarged on the characteristics which they particularly valued in a friend of the opposite sex. There is a wide consensus among boys that a girl worth having should possess, besides a pleasing appearance, certain qualities of character and personality: notably loyalty, tolerance, docility and good humour. It appears that to respect a girl as a person with her own interests and opinions is relatively rare.

'This girl called Loraine, like. Only young, but she's nice, like, and I like her a lot. And June, like, she knows. And she, kind of, like, I go up to her all friendly, like, put my arm round her, kind for a laugh, and June gets all narked, right? And she goes "I suppose you'll be going, wanting to ask her out next." I goes "If you don't watch it I might, I might do that." Been going on like that.

'I see, I see Loraine nearly every day. It's like, she lives up near me. I see her going to school, dinner times, coming back. See her in the park, see her taking the dog for a walk, like. And go with her sometimes. Sometimes she comes up for me, sometimes I go up for her.
'She's nice looking, got a nice personality, like. Well some girls, like, they talk all hard, like, all the, like, all the coloureds. I can't, I don't like that. I like girls, like, to be nice and have a nice personality. Because I like, you're not walking down the road, like, and you're walking with her and she sees some of her mates and she says "Ooey" and that, something like that . . . . I like nice and calm, like. Some, well, um, well I wouldn't say I'm quiet. I'm, well, I'm about half in half, say, I am. And Loraine really got a nice personality. I haven't heard her shout at no one except her sister, but that's what you get with being, being the youngest.

(Boy₃, Group B(M), 15)

Girls, on the other hand, are often less exacting in what they require from a boy, and more willing to forgive or ignore certain deficiencies and infidelities. At the same time, the most coveted personal quality is probably that of loyalty.

'I was told I couldn't see him any more. That was by my Dad, that was for coming in late one night and drinking. So he said, like, I had to finish with him. Well, it was either doing what he said, or seeing him without my Dad knowing. I'm seeing him without my Dad knowing. I'm defying what my Dad said.
'He wanted to get engaged to me. Well, I said "No". He said "Why?" I just said "Well, I've had that, I've been engaged once and realized what a mistake I made and I wouldn't want to do it again." I was fourteen at the time. So it was a mistake. I realized that, and the lad I did get engaged to, he was, how old would he be? seventeen, so he was too old. If I got engaged now I would sort of think back, because I still think he's too old for me.
'Well, he's so jealous! He'll stick up for me. Say, like, one of his mates says something and, like, his mates was joking, he takes it seriously and sticks up for me. That's what I like about him. He can be well-mannered at times, all depends on what cases. He's not got anything really to say about other people.
'He never comes into the house with my Dad. And my Mum, she's a bit nervous now, in case he catches us, you

know, together. She knows I'm meeting him all the time. And
if I say "going with friends" she knows where I'm going
because she watches. She sees me knocking at the door and
walking in.'

(Girl₇, Group C, 15)

'He's much young- , well he's not, he's not very much
younger, he's two years younger than me.
'He won't go behind your back, like, I thought he would,
but he didn't. And he will try to get up and see me when he
could, but um—he never had no money, so he hasn't been up
to my place yet, but I been up to him. And um—he's, he's
not like other boys, you know. They all want, all want one
thing [Laughter], but he doesn't.'

(Girl₁₁, Group C, 15)

There is a great variation in the seriousness with which relationships between the sexes are treated. Middle-class boys and girls
generally appear to expect more permanence and depth, and to
have a sharper sense of hurt when a promising attachment is
severed; perhaps it is not a coincidence that they are generally
both older and less experienced when faced with such situations. If
a consensus exists among those of working-class backgrounds, it is
that it is unwise to invest too much of oneself, or to expect too
much of any one relationship.

'I was, I finished with a boy who, with whom I'd been going
out with a year, and felt very lonely. And—another male
friend phoned up to talk to me and he asked me out. And I
went out, even though I knew at the time he was going out
with a close friend of mine. And I discovered that I was a lot
more selfish than I had ever thought. It was my one scruple,
that I would not go out with a boyfriend of a friend of mine
. . . . And he finished with the girl to go out with me even
though I, I wasn't that keen on him.
'It was, there was no real necessity. I needed somebody to
talk to, but it needn't have been him. And, well, I was using
him really to restore my confidence I think, and taking no
notice of the fact that this girl I was very fond of was in love
with him. She'd been going out with him for more than a year
—and at the time I thought "Oh, well, all's fair", but looking
back on it it seems—very much nastier, I think.
'I, we, got very tired of each other, and he went back to
the girl. But she started to enjoy herself so much without
him, she left him after a week.—It was a total mess by the
end.

'What it really was, I ruined a perfectly good relationship.—
I hope I'll know better next time. But I can't guarantee
anything now.'

(Girl$_8$, Group A, 16½)

'My friends like to joke about it, actually. Call me, you know,
"under the thumb" and all this. It's like, it's practically like
being, being like a married man. But it's nice to relate to
somebody, you know, always have somebody there any time
anything goes wrong. And, um, you know, it's, I never used,
I don't, I don't now, you know, go boozing every, every such
and such a night, you know. We go where we want to, you
know, pictures or whatever.'

(Boy$_2$, Group A, 17)

'We'd had erm—we'd been going out together for ten
months. And, you know, I thought "Oh, great, ten months",
you know, "must really be",—you know, "everlasting", you
know, because, you know, ten months is quite a long time. I
though "Oh, it must really last now", you know, and I was all
prepared, you know. And, um, one night we were sitting in
our house and he all of a sudden just said "Not going out
with you any more." "Oh", I thought, "Well", you know.
And he was going "Oh, I've met someone who I like better",
you know. "Really," you know, "who is she?", you know,
"Who can you like better than me?", sort of thing, you know.
And he went "Oh," he said, "some other girl", you know.
And—I was going, I was really worried because I thought
"What's she like?", you know, "What have I done?", you
know.

'And I found that all my schoolwork had really gone right
down, you know. I was prepared to do this, like, because I
thought that, you know, without him it wasn't really worth
living, so why do anything anyway? And I just, you know,
while I was in school I used to just sit there and not take a
blind bit of notice of what they were saying to me. And I just
sit there, and I wouldn't do nothing.

'And my Mum said "Well, you've gone down quite a lot",
she said. And she said "If it's because of the lad," she said,
"You're not going to see any more of him anyway," she said,
"because they're not worth it," she said, "You might think
they are now", you know, she said, "but they're not." And
we sat down and we talked. And I realized . . . . that it

wasn't worth it, to let my life go away because of a stupid little incident, you know, that wasn't my fault, which wasn't anyone's fault, really.'

(Girl$_3$, Group B(M), 16)

From the many accounts of relationships between the sexes, a sample of which has been reproduced in this chapter, it is possible to abstract a kind of moral code, relevant to the younger part of adolescence. It appears to apply widely across social class groups B and C, and also, to some extent, to group A. Reference to it often seems to be implicit rather than explicit, and like many codes it is honoured as much in the breach as in the keeping. Among its main precepts are the following.

1 It is good to try to help another person form a friendship with someone of the opposite sex.
2 It is good to help a boy and girl who have quarrelled to be reconciled with one another.
3 It is wrong for a boy to take someone else's girlfriend (and vice versa).
4 It is wrong to two-time a friend of the opposite sex (i.e. to be taking out someone else as well, without letting it be known).
5 It is wrong to spread rumours, or to gossip about others, in such a way as would damage their prospects in forming relationships.
6 When one wishes to end a relationship with a person of the opposite sex, one should declare it openly.
7 It is wise to keep a sense of proportion about a relationship with someone of the opposite sex.

A function for this code may be hypothesized, especially in relation to the conditions in which adolescents from the 'lower' part of the social class system are now placed. The rules appear to be part of an evolved set of tactics for survival in a social environment that is often harsh, vindictive and capricious, and where support from other sources may be limited; not necessarily because of lack of good will or desire, but because of the objective circumstances of existence. Many boys and girls know well, because of events they have witnessed, the precarious nature of the relationships from which they derive much of their sense of worth and wellbeing. If these rules were broken too often their social life among themselves might well disintegrate. For some, after that, there would be almost nothing left.

7
Formal and Informal Work

One of the most significant, though not necessarily the most wide-spread, of the personal changes occurring during adolescence is the development of a powerful sense of capability and creativity. While childhood provides some opportunities of this kind the span of attention is shorter, the capacity to conceptualize is more limited, and physical skills are relatively undeveloped. From the early teens onwards, however, boys and girls quickly become able to equal adults in many areas of productive activity, and experience their own powers to an extent that may, in some cases, never be surpassed in later life. This has many implications for the development of values, especially in relation to the personal project.

Besides being productive in ways that are largely of their own making, adolescents have the opportunity to find paid employment. At first, of course, this is only in a part-time job, though after the age of sixteen a considerable proportion hope to enter the world of 'work' full-time. Employment brings its own satisfactions and disillusionments. It becomes necessary to make decisions about how to handle various contingencies, and under what circumstances to leave an unsatisfactory position in order to look elsewhere. There is also the possibility, especially for working-class adolescents in relatively depressed areas, that work will not be available. There are thus some who, having come to recognize something of themselves as productive beings, find that their abilities are neither acknowledged nor wanted by society.

These are the main themes of this chapter. Although social class differences are apparent in virtually every aspect of adolescent values, it is here that they are most immediately obvious. At the time of being interviewed the participants in this research were already set on paths that would, in a few years, lead to great discrepancies in income and wellbeing, though few showed a strong awareness of the extent to which this was the case. Sociological studies in this general area have tended to focus particularly on the processes by which people are drawn into different occupational categories. This chapter, though having common ground with such work, has a different emphasis: it is on the productive capabilities of the individual, the way in which they are drawn out or inhibited during adolescence, and the values in relation to which they are directed and given significance.

Experiences of 'Informal Work'

In a fundamental (but by the standards of the present day possibly romantic) sense, work may be regarded as the exercise of a person's powers in the constructive transformation of the world: an expression of individuality, an enhancement of the sense of being alive, and one of the most powerful of social bonds beyond the family. It would appear from the accounts that the main source of such experience for adolescents is personally initiated activity, outside the academic curriculum of school and often unconnected with paid employment. References to what may thus be termed 'informal work' were scattered through the interview material. There are, however, five categories that gather together data specifically on this topic:

1 item 4, category 3: discovery of skills and competence of 'other' (i.e. not mainly interpersonal) kinds;
2 item 7, category 5: taking up or abandoning some interest or leisure-time activity;
3 item 8, category 5: some form of achievement in leisure-time pursuits;
4 item 13, category 2: poor performance in leisure-time activities, including sport;
5 item 15, category 3: beginning to take a leisure-time activity seriously.

Although these clearly deal with different aspects of 'informal work', they all can be taken to indicate whether or not this topic had salience for the participants. Since there is no obvious reason for thinking that material on subject matter of this kind would be judged unsuitable for discussion in the interview, according to criteria such as those discussed in chapter 4, the frequencies in the six main cells of the 'sample' may be treated cumulatively, as shown in table 7.1.

Table 7.1 Frequencies in categories dealing with 'informal work'

		1	2	3	4	5	Uncorrected total	Total per 20 participants in each cell
Boys	A	3	3	5	5	1	17	20
	B	4	6	11	4	4	29	20
	C	8	2	4	7	3	24	15
Girls	A	5	2	1	2	1	11	12
	B	3	1	8	0	1	13	9
	C	0	1	3	0	1	5	4

The evidence of this quantified data is very much in keeping with the tenor of the accounts. It suggests that girls generally do not tend to characterize themselves as productive beings to the same extent as boys; moreover, the discrepancy between the sexes increases towards the 'lower' end of the social class system. Possibly the main general explanation is that the expectations placed upon the two sexes are different. Among peers girls are often given a relatively passive role, as was indicated in chapter 6; their position is one that demands considerable interpersonal skill, but not much creativity in a directly material sense. At home they are expected to give help in many ways; this, however, has largely lost its charm and become a matter of routine by the time that they are in their teens. Boys, on the other hand, are seen to be those who take initiative, in social life-worlds that strangely mirror the traditional demarcation of sex roles in adult life. It is not necessary for them to study hard how to make themselves acceptable to the opposite sex; and if for some reason they do not try to find a girlfriend other kinds of powerful commitment are legitimate.

As a consequence of both material and cultural aspects of life-style the range of possibilities for 'informal work' is greatest for the offspring of relatively affluent parents. The demands of social life are often experienced at a slightly later age, and with less intensity; there is usually a greater degree of privacy available at home; the immediate locality does not have a strong confining influence. Especially in the case of girls, leisure-time pursuits perceived by parents as worthwhile are likely to receive marked encouragement, since these may perhaps deflect their children's interest from 'typically' adolescent pursuits and possibly be useful in the future.

'For a while I've been sitting about and not doing much, just
coming to this youth club twice a week when we're allowed
out, because my parents say "Oh, that's plenty of social life.
You're not doing anything, you're just sitting about", and
"Why can't you do something interesting and constructive?"
And, um—I've always thought "Well what a load of rot.
What can I do?" And they suggested things like embroidery,
and awful things like that, you know, "Why don't you read
interesting books instead of all those novels you read?" and—
all this. And, um—the suggestions that they've made completely turned me off, so I've just been sitting about . . . .
But um—just recently I've started doing quite a lot of things.
I've started doing ballet, which I like because it gives
precision and it can, you can control your body, and you
know exactly where you are and . . . . but I don't know
whether to pack it up now. But I enjoy doing that. I've also,
just recently I've, I've just, you know, started doing things,
and I've joined youth theatre to make an outlet for my
character and you know . . . . And I've started, I thought I'd
try an evening course at the tech. So I'm doing print-making,
and I'm putting everything on and I really love this because
I've got something on most evenings. You know, most of the
day I've always got something to think about—and before I
didn't used to like this, because it used to worry me. "Oh,
now what have I got to remember now?", "Oh, I know, I've
got something on my mind. What is it?" But now I've got so
. . . . of my mind that I like the power of being able to cope
with it. And thinking that I'm doing something, whereas
before I was being lazy sitting about and watching television.'

                                                      (Girl$_{16}$, Group A, 16)

'When I went on holiday I did some sculpture, like, and, er,
I discovered I had something in me to do some. Well, um—
did sort of painting and er . . . . At first I thought "Oh, I'll
go along". I hadn't really met anybody to talk to at all,
though there was a lot of people there. Nothing happened
until I got to know some people there, and they also decided
to do a face . . . . I found once I got into it, it was OK in the
end. And skating, I'd never done skating before, and I used
to watch the television, all these, er, skaters did it very well,
and I used to think "Oh, if only I could do it". So, at school
they organized skating classes . . . . At first I was holding on
to the side, but now I can go around . . . . I thought I'd never
learn to skate, as the first few times I just fell off, you know,

on to the floor all the time . . . . so that surprised me,
because I had it in me.'

(Girl₉, Group A, 16)

The impression conveyed by parallel accounts from middle-class
boys is that there is a wider range of possibilities that they
themselves see as attractive, and often a greater degree of personal
involvement and satisfaction in what they undertake.

'It was mainly a protest song, though. It perhaps didn't really
have a hopeful note. It suggested that, er, money spent on
space travel was a waste of money really.

'My family's heard it, and they think, think that it's really
good. And I think their first reaction was "Well how—do you
get a song published?" I don't know that it is that good
really, but I don't know—I, I think it might be something
that's worth looking into.—Even if it did get published it
might not sell much. I also sang it to one or two people at the
youth club, that's the church youth club. They are—well
they're quite keen on Bob Dylan and they felt it was—well,
quite good, I think.

'I'm tempted to say that it's a sort of creative urge inside
me, but . . . . I think that's a bit trite really, and it might not
even be true. I think that certainly with the last song it has
been something like that. It was, um, the result of hearing
something on the radio and that was just it, and I went up
and wrote the first draft.

'As for performing, er—well I don't do a great deal of
public performing, but just sit in my room and play on my
own. It's, I think it sorts of helps me to unwind, really.'

(Boy₁, Group A, 17½)

'Apart from Susan, you see, Susan was a lot of my life, but
er, apart er—er, a lot of it I didn't have something to do, you
see, or quite a bit of it. So—I took up bass guitar at first,
which erm, I got fairly good at, but we were playing folk
music and things like that, a "dear little folk group", which
didn't really do anything. And then we um, sort of graduated
to—a smaller version of a rock group. And er, that fell
through a bit. And er, I decided that I'd like to take up
drumming after what I'd learned from Chris, and er, he told
me that I'd make quite a good drummer. So I thought "Well,
why not give it a try?"

'I like nearly every sort of music. As far as drumming goes,
I think I just like the type of music that we play at the

moment, which is heavy rock, just rock, and er, sort of
blues-ey rock. That's what I like to play, but I like any sort of
music.

'I, I won't ever be satisfied with anything. If I play something I could do better, you know. Nothing is too good. You
know, I like to improve on it . . . . I wouldn't stop at anything till it's perfect; or I, I just won't stop at anything until
I'm stopped and told it's perfect, you know.'

(Boy$_9$, Group B(N), 16)

'I was the only one who became interested in Esperanto.
There was—about sixty who learned it, and we were taught by
a club instructor who was, well, I'm quite friendly with him
now, but he was not, not a very good teacher.

'Because of the congress for Esperantists, I was teaching
before that, but bec-because of the congress, coming to know
these people, I've been asked to edit a magazine, and I do
quite a bit of other things. Like this summer for instance, I
was away for a fortnight teaching at this international camp,
children's camp, you know, and these sort of things, you
know. They keep roping me in because they know I'll do it,
really. That's always happening to me.

'I really do enjoy preparing lessons, although I don't always
do it. You know, I, I can, I can do it off-the-cuff often,
because I know what I'm doing, but I really do enjoy preparing these things. And it's, um—I don't know, it's hard, I
don't think you can put things like that into words.

'Really, you see, it encompasses everything I'm interested
in, because it's not, it's er . . . . I'm, I won't use the word
intellectual, but it is that side of the things I'm interested in,
and it's also, it's social life as well, albeit not very often, but
it is that as well, you see. It's—holidays, and, you know, it's,
it, sort of brings everything into it really.'

(Boy$_5$, Group B(N), 17)

The accounts of 'informal work' given by working-class adolescents often convey more vitality and intensity than those of their
middle-class contemporaries. In some cases it is as if the discovery
of personal powers were almost a surprise, which may well reflect
the way the process of schooling often impinges upon them.
Where there is no credible social life-world within which achieve-
ments can be assessed objectively, the standards for judging work
must be found within the individual person.

'I went out and spent about fifty quid and bought a guitar
. . . . I just went out and bought it, because I fancied playing
it, that sort of thing. Everybody said I was mad, sort of thing
. . . . electric, I went out and bought one.
'It makes people happy . . . . I just thought I'd—do it, sort
of thing. We used to—my Dad and Mum used to say "Go up
and do some revision", sort of thing, so I'd go up and—play
my guitar. He'd think I was doing revision. But I enjoy
playing my guitar, you see . . . . And er, you know, if I can
make people laugh or something, you know, quite, quite a
good feeling.
'Today, probably practise from, well, practise all dinner
time . . . . four o'clock till six o'clock, then half past six to
half nine . . . . I just like to—like to play it . . . . taught
myself everything I know.'

(Boy$_4$, Group B(M), 16½)

'A few years ago I'd got this garden going. Put all these seeds
on it. I spent about two quid on putting all these seeds and
potatoes in it . . . . Nothing come up . . . . I put lettuce,
cabbage, er, cucumbers, er, all that, potatoes, marrows, all
that, and they still didn't come up. And, er, probably because
I watered them too much, because I watered them too much.
And they didn't come up . . . . And then I tried, I tried again
this year and they're coming up, they're coming up better
than my Mum's and Dad's are.
'My Dad was doing it, and I was doing his work, and I
thought "I could do this myself". So I asked him for a patch
and I did it.
'I did nearly all his gardening and digging, and then I
thought "Well, I'd like to do it myself". So I did it. It turned
out all right now.
'I've got, er, I've just put some lettuce in, potatoes that
come up from last year, and, er, spring onions, beans. I put
some flowers round the outside. I put all that in, and they're
coming up well now.
'I like to see, when I've put them in and you wait a few
weeks. I like to see them coming up, you know. I keep having
. . . . my Dad's coming up . . . . and, er, great satisfaction
when they come up in the end, though, when you can say
"Oh, I did that and it's all come up well this time". Yeah,
and I can say to my Mum "Beaten yours now".'

(Boy$_6$, Group B(M), 16)

'I do a lot of art work. And, ever since the age of five I been scribbling little matchsticks, making things like that. But gradually I been going on with, you know, and, you know, I've just taken each practice as—a good idea to, er, as a leisure, like. And, you know, I like to draw things of beauty, mainly . . . . something like a horse, or a scenery, anything in that sort of region, an animal or, you know, a lake, er, trees, anything.

'When I feel disappointed with myself is when I take a lot of time over a drawing or a model, and it doesn't look as good as what I could have expected it as. So—you know, I'm, I feel disappointed, you know, after spending so much time, but it's not good enough. Because I, because I've, I know, I can know, I know when it's good and I know when it's not good.'

(Boy$_{18}$, Group C, 15)

An appreciation of the social nature of work is present in many of the accounts, but is most strikingly present in some of those given by working-class adolescents.

'I like pigeons, see. When I get older I'm going to keep pigeons . . . . And, er, my Dad asked me, would I like to build an extension . . . . the main shed which we built about —twelve years ago . . . . When they built the, what the house stands on, the concrete pillars, we had to scrape the concrete off the edges, just to make it nice.

'Then I got a bit older. I was—twelve or thirteen. We built another end on the shed, an extension, because it wasn't long enough for the young birds. And er, my Dad asked me again, and I told him I had an idea. If he got some chicken wire, and put over the top of the roof first, then he put some erm —canvas over—and laid the piece of wood on the top of that, so it would slope, and put some—er—tiles or something like tiles on the top, so it wouldn't be blown off, it would be easier for it. So he done that, and it worked all right. And he finished building that, and I painted it and that, and I thought I done that good as well. Then this last bit, another extension, the shed was getting ri- right big then. I tol-, I asked my Dad if I could cut the hedge back a bit so we could build a bit more on. And then—we started building it.—And what my Dad was doing, he, as he was putting the chicken wire up on the side, he just nailing it up with half-inch nails, and bending them over. I told him "If you put another piece of wood on top of the chicken wire, so it would just make an overlap, you know, the two pieces of wood with the chicken

wire in between, so it would make it stronger." We done
that, and that made it look nice and neat. And we painted it.
And the shed's green and black, and it's about sixty feet long.
And we had to cut a hole in the asbestos in the side of the
shed for the pigeons to get in and out of that bit, and dug the
garden round it, and made it look ever so nice . . . . He's got
a hundred, a hundred and fifty pigeons.

'I thought when I started it, "I'm going to make sure this is
going to be nice when I finished". Then when I see it at the
end my Dad took a photo of it, and it was, like when we first
started and when we finished, and it was much better, and it
made their garden look nicer. And it looked more like a
home. And er—I just, my Dad was ill, he was in hospital for
two weeks. I looked after the pigeons for two weeks and
. . . . go racing when I get older.'

$$\text{(Boy}_{14}\text{, Group C, 16}\tfrac{1}{2}\text{)}$$

'When we was in the Old Time Music Hall we really, everybody was a star, you know what I mean? Even if you was
doing a little part you was a star. Well actually I had quite a
big part, me and Tracey, and I was so nervous. I made myself
really, I wouldn't go on at first. I said "I can't go on. I can't
go on. I'm, you know, I'll go on there and that's it, and I'll,
I'll mess it all up and everything. I'll, I'll never get it."

'I was still nervous up until the last night. And I really,
really enjoyed myself. But afterwards everybody was saying
"You really done well", and everything. And when I thought
about it, I thought "I must have done well. I must have done
really well", and I was really pleased with myself. And I used
to sit down and think "Well, you really done well" . . . . It
was really something that I really thoroughly enjoyed. It wasn't
something that I did just because I was pushed into it. It was
something I wanted to do, and I enjoyed doing. And because
I enjoyed doing it so much I did it well.

'I was still nervous the last night. And um, everybody was
cheering and that. They were wanting us to do it again, so
you realized how well you must have really done it. Oh, it
was terrific. I think that the best thing I've ever done in my
life, the Old Time Music Hall . . . . I was really, really
enjoyed myself, and I really think I did well in the end.
Because I got so much confidence. I mean, I was nervous, but
I was so confident in a way, that I felt I just went up and sang
it all off like I knew it off by heart, and I been doing it about

ten years. I think that's about the best thing I ever really, really done well.
'There's not many times that you see everybody so happy. But when—I mean you occasionally see different people happy at different times, but not everybody's happy all at the same time. Whereas at that Old Time Music Hall everybody was happy behind stage, all the people who watched it were really happy, and it just give you satisfaction that you'd really pleased someone. You'd done well.'

(Girl$_2$, Group C, 17½)

In conformity with the prevailing values concerning what is appropriate for the two sexes, the greatest opportunities for girls to use their talents, while remaining acceptable generally among their peers, lie in expressive activities not far removed from their main role position.

'I said I wasn't really keen on the idea of ballroom dancing. And this boy asked me to give it a try, you know, that I'd never really know what it was like until I'd tried it. So we went along, and I found it very good. And, oh, I've been going every week now. And while we was there he's introduced me to a lot more people who are like him, you know.
'We have ballroom lessons for an hour, so that's um, you know, really quite good. We all, because we enjoy it, like. And we have, we—dance for an hour. Many of them are taking their Guilds in it, you know. Um, I've just qualified to take mine so I, I'm hoping to do that in fact.
'Before I went to ballroom classes, I thought it was not a very, you know, I thought it was for—creeps, you know, someone who—like pansies or something. I didn't think of it as a, you know, worthwhile spare-time hobby, you know. It was more discos for me.
'There's more grace in ballroom. And there's um, there's a lot more—thinking. You've got to think about your movements, so there's a lot required in it. But, I mean, you can't just go in and do anything, pat. It needs thinking about.
'I find I'm thinking more about—situations than I ever did. You know, I was sort of rash. You know, quick decisions. Now I say to . . . . and think what would be the best way. You know, I find I'm—getting along a lot better now.'

(Girl$_3$, Group B(M) 16)

There is a range of technical and mechanical activities open to boys, and which perhaps have the strongest appeal to some who find social life difficult, especially making relationships with girls. Work in this area may be deeply absorbing, requiring heavy and prolonged commitments in time and money.

'My Dad bought this old Imp for twenty pounds, and we was deciding to do it up for me, you know, in a year's time. But my Dad found we had difficulty, and we were, Dad said it was mine, so I had to decide what I was going to do with it, you know.

'We sent away for a set of door sills, and we got them. And when we took the old ones off we found that the floor was coming away. So my Dad, he's er, he's a—toolmaker, and he's got hold of some angle irons to hold the floor up. And er, that's really all it, at the moment the bodywork is rusty and . . . . some filler and er, all it needs is a little bit of mechanics on it and it should go, mechanics on the engine and it should go. Apart from that it's all right.

'If there's a job that's got to be done and I know how to do it my Dad just lets me get on with it so he can do something else. But if it's a job that he—that I'm capable of doing but, you know, I'm not sure how to do, my Dad'll tell me how to do it, and he'll keep on coming back and checking up, to see how I'm doing.'

(Boy$_8$, Group B(M), 16)

'About Christmas time sort of decided that I'd set myself up as, as a disco . . . . and um, sort of try and run a disco. After Christmas I had to get the equipment, build the deck and that. And about, just before Whitsun holidays we, we did our first disco.

'I like—I'm not terribly good at dancing, but I like music. I like playing music, and I thought it would be a good idea. And I like—electronics, and building things. And rather than doing useless things that were just for decoration I thought, "Why not build something I could use, and perhaps earn a bit of money out of it?"

'It j-just about pays. You have to buy about five pounds of records a week, to keep up with the charts and the expenses that, and the output we get, we don't make any money . . . . If we didn't want to improve it we would be breaking even lovely.

'We've got two decks, the basics. And I've got a mixer, which is the first time I've used integrated circuits, which are a bit, a bit dicey, because they're a bit delicate . . . . hundred-watt amplifier. It all fits into one big ca-cabinet. And what you call a sound-to-light converter . . . . when the music plays, at certain frequencies, the bass, middle and the treble frequency, if the music is on that frequency it flashes a light, and if it's not on that frequency the light's off. So the lights flash in time with the music. And I put these in the main cabinet, and the whole thing weighs about two hundred-weight.'

(Boy$_7$, Group B(M), 16½)

Despite wide social class differences, both in the objective character and the actual experience of 'informal work', there seem to be two main exceptions. The first is participation in a three- or four-piece 'band' whose main repertoire is rock music; this is an overwhelmingly male activity, often requiring great patience on the part of the girlfriends of those involved. The second is the theatre, where for obvious reasons there is no sex discrimination, at least in the activities on stage. In part, no doubt, the satisfactions of acting are those of being a focus of attention, and close involvement with a group that shares a common task. It is tempting to infer that the theatre has a fascination for another reason, related to the position that adolescents occupy in relation to society as a whole. Boys and girls from the whole range of backgrounds are required to spend a great deal of time, especially during the early teenage period, in a kind of limbo; their social life is largely of their own making. Competence here requires a well-developed hermeneutic skill, and positive abilities not unlike those of an actor; some adolescents are aware of discrepancies between their different roles. It is possible, therefore, that the theatre has an immediate relevance to everyday life, the contingent nature of which is also often recognized.

For adolescents the great significance of 'informal work', as compared with the greater part of either the school curriculum or full-time employment, is that it is their own. They are the ones who initiate it, direct it, take responsibility for it and carry it to its conclusion. Thus even if it is done clumsily it is often judged to have more value than activities set up on their behalf by professionals. 'Informal work' is one of the major ways in which boys and girls can come to a deep personal understanding of their tastes and capabilities, experiencing their spontaneous creative activity. It is plausible to assume that this has a great influence upon the development of the project, since it is on the basis of such intuitions that a person begins to formulate a conception of what he or she might become. If so, the quantitative aspects discussed at the beginning of this section have a particular significance. This research indicates that in this respect girls have a very different type of experience from boys. Even within group A, where the opportunities are most obviously present, only about half of the girls made reference to their own productive life, and the proportion diminished towards the 'lower' part of the social class system. It is hard to avoid the inference that those who have never experienced themselves as productive beings on their own account during adolescence undertake projects that are to that extent impoverished.

Preparation for Employment

At some point during the early teens a boy or girl will inevitably encounter the question of future employment. The topic may arise in conversation within the family, or with friends; it may be presented in a more formal way, for example through careers talks at school. Eventually, whether the issue is perceived as that of planning a career, getting a job or simply deciding when to leave school, choices are involved.

The interview data yielded five main categories relevant to this question:

1 item 3, category 1: decisions relating to career or occupation;
2 item 3, category 2: academic decisions, mainly to do with choice of subject for study at school, but also including any affecting attitudes to academic work;
3 item 12, category 1: decisions related to the future, especially career; educational decisions related to the future;
4 item 15, category 1: taking seriously the future, getting qualified;
5 item 15, category 2: taking academic work seriously.

As in the case of 'informal work', the totals for these categories may be taken as a very rough indication of the salience of future employment in the consciousness of boys and girls at different points in the social stratification system. Since the topic was an admirably safe one for discussion with a stranger, it may occupy a slightly larger place in the interview data than it merits as a representation of the concerns of adolescents in everyday life. Conversely, the non-mention of decisions related to future employment may have particular significance. The frequencies of choice within the five categories, and the totals, are shown in table 7.2. These figures indicate that any crude notion of a 'present orientation', applied either to adolescents as a whole or to those from particular class backgrounds, cannot be sustained. However, the fact that about a quarter of the whole 'sample' failed to mention the topic, even during a period when their future has become problematic, is striking. In the case of group C girls, especially, it seems justifiable to infer that a considerable proportion are not giving serious attention to their future, perhaps because the concerns of their day-to-day existence are so pressing.

Table 7.2 Frequencies in categories dealing with 'preparation for employment'

		1	2	3	4	5	Uncorrected total	Total per 20 participants in each cell
Boys	A	5	2	1	2	3	13	15
	B	10	3	2	4	3	22	15
	C	13	3	3	5	2	26	16
Girls	A	9	0	2	6	0	17	18
	B	9	6	6	4	1	26	17
	C	10	2	0	2	2	16	13

A more detailed study of the accounts indicates a small number of main patterns in the way adolescents take decisions about their future occupation. Considering the small size of the sample and the variety of subject matter covered in the interviews, the data on this complex topic are far from substantive. It is possible, however, to describe certain broad features, and to give the sketch of an overall picture into which other pieces of research may be fitted. The five clearest modes of relating to the question of future employment which emerged from this research are as follows.

1 Some of those from middle-class backgrounds have an obvious concern about their future, and clearly recognize the importance of making adequate preparations for it. They either envisage a definite career ahead of them, or at least have distinct aims relating to further or higher education. It is characteristic of their decisions that these are made, not so much as a result of the rational consideration of a wide variety of possibilities, but on the basis of actual experience: this is taken to be sufficiently convincing evidence to direct them in their choice.

'I'm not particularly good at school, and I honestly didn't know whether I was going to get no O levels or, you know, all six. I needed to go back—and er, my father wanted me to get, to get an A level to go to college with, to take up farming. But I, I have never liked school, you know. I wanted, I wanted to leave school and get a job, you know, whether on a farm or elsewhere. I had to decide at the end of the

previous year whether I was going to go back, so they could
make arrangements. And erm, I honestly hadn't got a clue
what I was going to do. I said I was going to go back—and I,
I convinced myself I was going to get four O levels. In the
end when they did come through I got three O levels and a
CSE Grade One, which was, you know, just enough.

'I think I, I stayed on because my Dad wanted me to, not
because I wanted to . . . . I think in, in ten years' time I'll
think it was the right decision. But now—I'm short of money
all the time and I don't think it was.

'At school you've got to go to work every day, and it's the
same, same routine.—And you don't, you don't get many
privileges, like the lads who all go to work now. They work
for British Rail, they get a free pass, they're going on holiday
next year for nothing, on a free pass. It's things like that
make you feel a bit jealous, you know.

'I'm only taking two A levels . . . . to taking three. I've got
to get one to, to go to college. So that's definite, and even
then I might not get in if there's too many applicants. I've
got, I, I could do with two. I'll go to college, and take er—
there's a special course for farmer's sons. And then my Dad
wants to retire pretty early so, er, he'll introduce me to his
farm. I'll be about twenty-five, I should think.

'I take, take a pretty big interest in, in politics now, hoping
that, you know, some allowance will be made to farmers.
Because um, obviously if they become state farms I don't
think farmers will have the incentive to—try as hard as they
would if they, they own the actual farms.

'I want to get my hands on that farm, and as far as I'm
concerned, as, as long as I can get that farm, you know, get a
good living, you know, that's all I'm concerned about.'

(Boy$_8$, Group A, 16½)

'My father was a businessman . . . . my grandfather started
the business, and my father took it over. And originally as a
career, naturally I suppose, I um, planned to go into business
myself. My father wanted me to, I think . . . . but he didn't
push me. I was not old enough to know really what I wanted
to do. Erm—but I find going into business um, unsatisfactory
now, with, um, greater knowledge of life. It's um, politically
it's unsatisfactory for me. I'd like to um, be able to look back
upon my life with satisfaction, rather than um, a feeling that
I'd done nothing.

'I was very persistent with wanting to go into business. I
never knew what it was my parents—my mother and my stepfather would keep asking me what did I mean when I said I
wanted to go into business. I didn't really know myself, you

know. Um—I liked the idea of—develop—developing something on my own initiative. But I thought of things as objects,
as machines, rather than as people. You know, the human
aspect didn't come into it really. And when I became, well
suddenly I went um—on holiday with a friend who had asked
me. He had asked me to go on holiday with him at the last
minute. Um, and on holiday I bought some books, Communist Manifesto etcetera. And most of it's a load of rubbish
but, I became politically more aware suddenly. And—I
became increasingly more interested in medicine as my stepfather told me about his life and his relationships with his
patients, aspects of his work, and so on . . . . um dealing with
human problems and—Of course it's very unsatisfactory I
think—um, economically of course, but I was interested, and
I thought it was a worthwhile um, way to spend my life.'

(Boy$_4$, Group A, 17½)

'There were several opportunities open to me, and er,
probably during my fifth year I decided definitely what I
wanted to do, started looking around—and er—other than
that I can't think of any, that was about the only time that I
decided that that was what I wanted to do.
    'I am going to teacher training college, not too far away
from home, and er, going to do a three-year certificate of
education. I want to teach young children, infants . . . . I've
had quite a lot of experience with them, although I haven't
got any brothers or sisters of my own. The play-group which
we ran, we ran at school during our fourth year . . . . I did
that in our fourth year. And we also went to a local primary
school, and we used to enjoy it tremendously. Then lots of
my friends have got young children so . . . . holidays I spend
one or two weeks with them, and go baby-sitting quite
regularly . . . . five, five to about seven. I think . . . . they're
always willing to learn, and like to learn new things. They'll
be prepared to listen to you, and er, like you to enjoy life
with them as well.'

(Girl$_3$, Group B(N), 19)

2 Other boys and girls, mainly from middle or upper-middle-class
backgrounds, show a very different reaction. They have a strong,
and in some instances even oppressive, awareness of the future,
but lack any clear basis for resolving the problems that it presents.
Generally they have begun to question conventional middle-class
values such as the importance of having a safe career, and hence
the necessity to become highly qualified as quickly as possible. In

the light of their own experience the social life-world within which those assumptions are held has a diminished credibility; the consequence is a kind of *anomie*, a bewilderment at the variety of possibilities that the future holds, and a sense of not being ready to make a firm commitment. At the same time there is a realistic awareness that decisions must be made, and that in due course some means of livelihood must be found. Attitudes of this kind are possibly more characteristic of girls than boys.

'I'm definitely taking a year off. That's about the only thing I know, um—because I just think, well I just think it's essential. I mean, I think it's a bad idea to go straight from school to university. I er—I think one year off is really very important.—I'm not quite sure—I intend to do a bit of travelling um—I'd like to do the Greek Islands, perhaps South America—that's a bit more ambitious. Um—I'm not sure I'd really, I mean, I'd really like to go somewhere. A bit of work perhaps, and then hopefully university. Then I don't really know. I'm dreading it.

'I mean, I sort of vaguely know vaguely what I want to do, but I don't want to commit myself, but—I'd probably like to do, to do something with the theatre um—not acting I don't think, in fact I know not acting—um.—Or I'd like, perhaps like to direct films or something.—But I certainly do not want to go in for a nine-to-five office job. I just—well I mean, OK theatre or films or whatever will probably be nine o'clock to nine o'clock, rather than nine o'clock to five o'clock, but—I just couldn't bear, I really just couldn't, I'd really just go spare if I had to do a kind of office job type of thing—I don't know, I just couldn't er—I just can't. Haven't got the temperament, I don't think. Um—I don't know, going to have to give it a bit of careful consideration I think, it's not that far off. But I can put it off for about four years, five years um.—I know what I don't want to be—which is a doctor, or a nurse um.—I don't know—a bit hard really . . . . For instance I know people who—know exactly what they want to do, will go on to medical school and then will go into research or be a doctor, simply because that's what you do when you come out of medical school. And I know people who want to be actresses and—um—who know what they want to do, but—um—or perhaps who just want to kind of leave and become housewives, or you know, well no, that's a bit rude, but have kids and devote their lives to that. But I certainly don't want to do that. I mean, I think I'd like to have a kid or perhaps two kids, but not until I've got a career off the ground. I mean, that's what, I think that's what I'd put first, sort of um, er—I mean, a lot of people find it incredibly rewarding to have kids, but I don't think I—I think I'd find it rewarding, but I don't think I'd find it rewarding enough.'

(Girl$_{17}$, Group A, 17)

'I haven't any—real, you know single interest in er, anything in particular. I, I've, I like children. I had thought of, um—teaching, but, er, my sister's gone in for that [Laughter] and she's in her final year at college and she put me off it slightly.

'University, mainly er . . . . because there again I haven't got many sort of ideas of what I would do with a degree afterwards. And er—I suppose student life attracted me um—and since then I've had second thoughts. [Laughter] Um, polytechnic . . . . I've been thinking about an HND course. Um, I thought it would be a good idea to get a basic er, business, er, a business training behind me, and which I could sort of branch out later on, perhaps give me time to decide—on, more on what I, I want to do. But there again [Laughter] I've had second thoughts on that recently.

'Nothing has really sort of struck me to make me really—sort of, you know, think "Yes, I'd really like to do that", as yet.'

(Girl$_2$, Group A, 18)

'I'd always thought "Something always turns up, something will turn up". And so I hadn't really bothered much with getting a job. I was too preoccupied from when we formed the group, about late May, early May perhaps. From then until the end of the A levels I was more taken up with—playing in the group than I was with anything else.—And, er, I didn't put much effort at all into the A levels.

'When I got them I thought "Well, now what?" And my father'd been going mad. And I'd just been ignoring him almost. He'd been going on "Oh go and get yourself a job", you know, "You're not doing anything. Get writing to folk." And I, I'd just never bothered. I feel as if I couldn't care less. But I never actually—I never thought to myself, "Oh, stuff the job". I never thought like that, consciously anyway . . . . I just never bothered with it, although it wasn't a case of not bothering. It's—I knew it was there and it was important. I just didn't do anything about it. And I'm still in, in that position. And I don't know what I'm going to do. I don't know what I want to do, really.

'I don't want to lea- go away from home. I, I've a lot of commitments. I like it here for a start, even though I'm not on brilliant terms with my parents. I'm, I don't—hate them or anything, you know. I can live with them. And I've a girlfriend here. I've a group. And if I get a job I'd get a job round here. If I go to university I'd go to one locally, but I wonder if it's possible. Or at least live somewhere round here. I'm not particularly bothered about actually living in our house. It's, I like the district, I like everything about it. So I see no reason to leave it, because I've—well, ever- everything works here. So why not? That's my reasoning.

'The prospects of being on the dole doesn't worry me all that much because I've never, I've never had a full-time job, so . . . . it's nothing really. And I know a lot of people just doss around for a year before they decide what they're doing. A last year of freedom, almost. Erm—so it doesn't worry me that way. But I'm, my father's very worried. And he, he knows that I could—be making something of myself, and I'm not. And because he's worried I'm worried, for him almost.

(Boy$_3$, Group B(N), 18)

3 Most of those in this group are from lower-middle-class backgrounds, together with a few from the working-class. The immediate form in which a choice presents itself to them is usually whether to continue with academic work or to look for employment at the first opportunity; behind that is the larger issue of whether or not to try to form a career. Some boys and girls who decide to prolong their education have definite aims in mind, whereas others have only a vague awareness that by 'getting qualified' they will give themselves better long-term opportunities.

A number of factors seem to be involved in the decision, among which the question of a career may not necessarily be the most salient. There is the matter of whether the social life of school is tolerable; whether there is sufficient money for current needs; the plans of friends; obligations to the family; the availability of jobs in the locality. One necessary (though not in itself sufficient) condition for a decision to continue in education seems to be that a boy or girl should, at some point above the age of about twelve, have had intuitions of competence within the school system; without that, the personal project is developed in some other way. But for those who do remain at school the currency of 'qualifications' becomes highly valid, and there is little bewilderment at what the future might hold. Unlike those in the previous category, the range of possibilities they envisage is relatively restricted and highly practical. The likelihood that they will find employment is high; careers guidance at school is particularly well adapted to their position.

'I was, I was a bit unsure about whether to stay on at school, but, um, mainly I think because of my parents, because I thought it was, it was taking them for granted a lot, you know. Because, I mean, they've kept me at school for, well, five, ten years, and um, and now to keep me on at school for another two years, it's, I think it's asking a lot of them. And —and I, I was, you know, I was pretty uncertain whether to stay on or not. But with the jobs as they were I thought, if I got more qualifications, then I got more chance. And, and my Dad didn't say much. [Laughter] I got no sort of encouragement or disenc- and that from him, but . . . . he didn't sort of comment at all. He sort of left it up to me. My Mum, she said that if you, sort of, if you needed the qualification for a job then and you get, you know, if you had an aim in mind at the end, then it was all right. But she was, I think she was pretty uncertain really. Don't think she really wanted me to stay on, if the truth is known. But I made the choice.'

(Girl$_5$, Group B(N), 17)

'I thought that leaving school at sixteen would be too much of an emotional upheaval for me. I might suffer by it. And also a lot of my friends were staying on as well, and also I also needed a couple, two more subjects in order—now I've decided what I want to do. And I needed two more subjects in order to follow that course . . . . at O level. I'm only staying on for one year.

'I want to be an auctioneer. And the subjects, I've only got three O levels, and . . . . is five. And I need maths and English this year.

'Auctioneering is my part-time job. I work at an auctioneer's on Saturdays, doing sales and things. And I've seen the type of work that he does, and he's talked to me about it. And—he's offered me a job, and says it's there when I want it. And I've seen the type of work that goes on, and I like what I see. And I enjoy working there.

'In the job, it involves meeting people, and I li- enjoy meeting people. And I, in doing this job going round the place I know an awful lot of people because he puts on, er, implement sales. Farmers, and I know farmers . . . . and we get a, and he lets, you know, have a go at auctioneering . . . . and, erm, booking for them, booking things . . . . cashing up, and general things like that, and helping setting out the sales, all aspects really. And, I, I, and also I work and he's also an estate agent, and I work in the office, and, and I, I do plans for him, copy plans and things. And I feel I could do well, and I enjoy doing it, things like that.'

(Boy₇, Group B(N), 16)

'I started on these three subjects, applied maths, chemistry and physics. As I said, for O level I found them easy, but for A level they were completely different, they were much harder. And about three years ago I had a very good er— think about what I wanted to do as a job, and I narrowed it down to office work. Now I've narrowed it down to banking. So as I realized I was doing these three subjects, they were difficult, they were going to be absolutely no use to me for what I wanted to do, my career, even if I didn't go into banking, because I know I want to do office work when I'm old, when I'm er, about eighteen, go out to work. I'm, I've decided on that because I'm—I usually stick to my decisions. I realized these subjects were absolutely no good at all. Also I found them difficult. So I had to give up all three. That was at half-term. And after half-term—I had, or rather during half-term I had a good think about it. And er, with er, Mr Spencer, he's my er—year master, we had a good talk about this and it was decided that I do economics, geography and statistical maths, because these, as well as er, being a great help to me for what my career, were also er, a bit more— better, easier shall I say, to do.'

(Boy₁₀, Group B(N), 16)

'I did the CSE in biology and got a grade five, er three, sorry, for the CSE. I was very pleased with that, you know. I was really amazed, didn't think I could do it.

'I was always thinking "Oh well," you know, "I'll do it but I don't think I'll get anywhere. I'll try my hardest" and, you know, but I wouldn't get anywhere. But for English I got two fours and I thought, you know, I'd fail that, and—that was the only, the only three exams in which I got . . . . I took six and I failed the other three.

'It was that, not being, you know—the position that the rest of, you know, the members of the fifth form, fifth form, not getting jobs and all getting married off and things like this made me think "Oh well, I'm not going to be in the position that they're in." I'm going to get, you know, come back, get more exams and get a job, and have a career in front of me. I think that was it, you know, why I stayed on, I think, more than anything else.

'One of the girls, she left at Easter, and she's still looking for a job now, and she gave up and got married—because she couldn't get a job. She was so depressed, she couldn't get a job or anything, so she went out and got married.

'A girl I used to go to school with, her brother got married when he was only nineteen. He just doesn't seem happy at all, and I thought "Well, he's got married so young and he doesn't, you know—he's not so happy." So I thought "Look at him. I wouldn't bother. I'll wait until I'm older."'

(Girl₂, Group B(M), 17)

4 This group is in some respects the obverse of the third, since it consists of those who decide to leave school at age sixteen, but are still thinking in other terms than merely 'getting a job'; it does, however, contain more boys and girls from working-class backgrounds. The most characteristic instance here is the person who takes an apprenticeship, being willing to accept the commitment to an extended period of training, perhaps including college work, for relatively little immediate financial reward. It is here particularly that there is an expectation of satisfaction in employment at a level that is comparable to the experience of 'informal work'. As in the previous case, the range of options considered is fairly narrow; decision-making is relatively easy.

'Most of my friends—are serving apprenticeships and some have gone in, have got steady jobs—I think the majority of them are at college, which is sensible in my opinion, to go to college. There's the usual, ones that are the drop-outs, these typical ones who—break windows, smash up bikes or vandalism. They're, they're out of a job at the moment, they'll be earning say fifty quid and "Great, I'm earning more than you. I'm at Joe's All-Night Cafe, I'm on fifty quid a week." They don't realize they'll be on fifty quid a week when they're thirty-one, and they'll be on fifty quid a week when they're sixty, you know, and so on. They'll be on the same money all the time just for washing dishes in Joe's Cafe or something like that. Whereas I'm on, say, twenty odd quid now, when I'm fifty or forty, or thirty or forty I'll be on seventy, eighty-odd quid a week. And I'm getting a decent education. I've got a trade behind me. They get a kick out of Joe's All-Night Cafe, they've, they've got no trade to fall back on . . . . There's no point in just working at Joe's All-Night Cafe to wash up for fifty quid a week. And if they're not that they're on the dole, Social Security.—And they seem to think if they can get money, get away with not working, "Oh, great. Oh, I don't have to work, I've got money." But nine quid a week is no fun, because I was on the Social Security for three weeks, from the time I left school till the time I got a job. Which I was entitled to, because my, my apprenticeship didn't start for—from 27th May to 5th September. I got a job in between, and until I got that job in between I had to have Social Security . . . . I was drawing that Social Security for my Mum, my bike and my savings, so—I wasn't drawing it for myself.'

(Boy$_{15}$, Group B(M), 16)

'In the fifth year, we have careers officers coming in every so often, and we have careers talks on a Friday. And we were all sitting there sort of thinking "What kind of job do you want?" Well, there's two jobs I gone for, and that's receptionist's or hairdresser's, apprentice hairdresser . . . . what did I want to do when I leave school? And he gives me this form, you know, to fill in, to send away to college, day-release college. And they want me to go back after Christmas. And I've to put my name down and see if they can take me after that. Anyway I hope to get this job because—it, it was important at the time, because, you see, my Mum wanted me to, you know, she said "Be a receptionist and it will be easier". But I wanted to do something with my hands, you know. I want to do a trade.

'I go to my haircutter and watch the people round you. And you just sort of get the scissors and do this and do that, and it looks fantastic. You know, it's great, I just love it. You know, I want to do this.

'This boy I go with now, his sister, she used to do the course, she left. She, she only did it for two years. She found it too much for her, you know . . . . so she just left, so she said it's very hard and, you know, terrible money at first. But once you got through, she said, should be great.

'Once you start you'd be on about twenty-one, twenty-three pounds per week, even if you're really good. But again the money doesn't bother me. It's just something I want to do . . . . You'd meet the girls in the shop and, you know, if you're working in a unisex shop you'd meet the fellows as well. And, you know, you get to do, towards the people that come to have their hair done, they'll get to know you, and they'll say "Oh, I want Sandra to cut my hair", kind of thing. And they'll come to know you and you'll know them.'

(Girl$_4$, Group B(M), 15)

'Just as I was leaving school I wrote off for numerous jobs,
but er, I was given two interviews and offered two jobs. One
was in a factory doing something like what I'd be doing now
anyhow, and the money was really good, for my age. And I
was offered a job at a smaller firm where I am now, and the
money weren't quite so good, but I liked the idea of a smaller
firm with not so many people to work with, so you can get to
know everybody. Whereas if you're a great big factory you
can be working there for two or three years, and one day
somebody will come up to you and say "Who are you?" when
they work down there on the shop floor, like. So—I decided
in the end that um—I'd take the job with not quite so much
money, but a better atmosphere and everything . . . . I just
like the idea—because there's only three or four of us in my
workshop anyhow, in which case I know just about everything
there is to know in the workshop, where to get parts and that
sort of thing. And I know all the people, and er—all of them
I see socially, out of work . . . I prefer to work with someone
that I've perhaps seen out of working conditions, in the pub,
something like that, rather than sort of work with someone
that I don't really know and probably wouldn't be likely to
know for a few years . . . . They're all older than me. Um—
one's twenty, one's twenty-two, one's twenty-seven. Two are
married, one's engaged . . . . but they all sort of find time to
come out with me.'

(Boy$_{22}$, Group C, 17)

'I'd left school and I um—applied for a couple of jobs, and as
things went I wasn't doing too well because a lot of the places
said I needed more experience. And um—I wrote back to
them and said well, if anything turns up that they thought I'd
be capable of doing, would they let me know. And, I was
asked if I'd like to take up two positions, at the same time.
And the first job was a bit more money, but it was just for a
copy-typist, and I thought I'd get a bit bored with that,
because I like to have a change now and then. So I took on
um—the position of being a guinea-pig at the other one,
because they're trying out a new commercial scheme.
   'It turned out for the best because now what I'm doing is
I'm a trainee secretary and I've, the training I'm doing, I go
round all the different departments. I started in personnel,
and I actually take over the, I train with the actual secretaries
in the offices for two weeks, and then for the rest of, more or
less for the next three months I'm left in the office on my own
to cope with all the situations that arise. So I'm getting full

experience of work of what any other secretary will do, and I also go for shorthand, day release and night school . . . . It's more interesting than just doing straightforward copy-typing . . . . My training's for three years and then after my three years, what they've said they'll do is, I'll go in and work with the secretary I've started off with from personnel. And then if and when a secretarial position arises, ... then I'll be offered that position . . . . it's good money even though the pay at the other job was better.—My friends all get better pay, but in the long run I think I'll work out that I'm the one that better off, because I'll probably get a higher wage than them in the long run anyway.'

(Girl$_{19}$, Group C, 17)

5 There is, finally, a proportion of boys and girls, virtually all working-class, for whom during adolescence there was never a serious question about whether or not they would stay on at school beyond the leaving age. Since they are expecting to gain no qualification that would alter their occupational prospects, the main issue is more likely to be whether (if they are old enough) to leave before the summer exams in the hope of finding a job in advance of the main spate of school-leavers. Some of these, especially boys, have actively rejected the school system and its approved channels for directing people into employment, and inhabit social life-worlds that have developed alternative constructions of the realities of school (cf. Willis, 1977). It would be simplistic, however, to suggest that all those who leave virtually unqualified see their schooling exclusively in this light. Even among those whose main role was to be hard and uncaring, bravado was inclined to fade in an individual interview, as was described in chapter 3, and regrets were sometimes expressed at the failure to make more use of schooling.

For those in this group the issues involved in choosing a job are relatively straightforward, since it is mainly a matter of finding any kind of occupation that is reasonably well paid; there is little expectation of satisfaction from the activity itself. In some cases the help of relatives already in employment is enlisted; simple pragmatic factors, such as the ease of travel to and from the job are important; locality is often of outstanding significance, some adolescents preferring unemployment in their own home district to moving even a few miles away.

'I was always kicking everyone's head in at school, you know what I mean? Didn't care a fuck like.
'I don't think, if you don't want to go to school—I, I don't,

I don't think you should, because I reckon you could learn more than what you can at, staying at home than what you do at school. Because you don't learn nothing at school, or I didn't when I was at school.

'If you can read and write and you don't want to—go to college or—you know—or, you know, get a job in an office, you know, or something. I don't, I don't think you should go to school. Put it this way, all we had to do is . . . . if, if you don't, if you want a job in an office you want to stay on, all right? And if you want to go to college you had to stay on for GCEs and, you know, and er, you know O levels and all that. But—if you, I, I don't want to go to college . . . . and I don't want a job in an office. You know what I mean, I don't want to—be one of those stuck-up people, you know what I mean, "I've got six O levels" and this and that, like, you know what I mean? And er, any job'd do me, like.'

(Boy₁, Group C, 17)

'I'm leaving at Easter—yeah. My auntie's, she's trying to get me into a job in a factory where she works . . . . in um— egg packing thing, station . . . . Rather work in a factory like that and be with people all the time than work in an office or something like that.

'I do cleaning for—a bloke who lives up our way—um—I get two pounds a morning doing that. That's quite good as I've saved up that and when I leave school, like if I leave at Easter, then in the summer I should have enough money to get a motorbike, if I keep saving.'

(Girl₁₇, Group C, 15½)

'When I left school my, my Dad had a job lined up for me, which was landscape gardening. And, um, I went to the man to see if it was still available, and he said "No". So, um, I went home and told my Dad and he told me to go straight down to the careers office. I went down there and, um, see Mr Collins. And he give me some jobs. There was roofing, don't like roofing because I can't get on the heights. And he give me, um, Woolworths and Walls', which is the sausages and things like that. And, er, I went to Woolworths and they told me that I couldn't, er, have the job; I don't know why, all right I think. And then I went to Walls', same thing . . . . because at school I didn't get on well with teachers, because they kept rushing me . . . . And, um, so they sent me to special classes at school. And the last job I had was, um, just working in a shop weekends. That weren't much good, though, so I went down to see Mr Collins again. And he just give me, I heard him saying to this girl whether she'd like to work down Valley Products. She said "No", so I asked Mr Collins about it, and he told me go down and see the manager. So I went down to see him and, um, he told me to start on the Monday.'

(Boy$_{14}$, Group C, 16½)

'The majority of people round here are, are good people, you know. You know, I don't mean good in the sense that they don't steal or nothing, but I mean, you could go up to a person and you can start talking to them.

'About ninety-nine per cent, or let's say ninety-five per cent of them are brought up round here, and know what life's all about. Because it's an hard, it's an hard place round here, you know what I mean?

'We, we prefer to go in a, to a warehouse or something, like, and get in there and take off some geezer who's got money. You know, if he owns a warehouse he got money, and the insurance covers it, doesn't it? You know, so he's all right, he doesn't lose really, does he? Well he does in a way, he loses good, but he gets the money for it, doesn't he?

'You know I, I wouldn't move out of this area, you know. This is, it's a fantastic place. I wouldn't like to live anywhere else.'

(Boy$_{11}$, Group C, 15)

Within this five-fold typology the clearest examples of values being used at a conscious level are by those in the third and fourth groups. Here there is a relatively circumscribed area of decision-making, which is comprehensible and largely within the control of the adolescents themselves. Some of the considerations that are brought forward, however, are only marginally concerned with positive decisions about a career. In contrast to this, those in the first two groups can take their time, and the range of possible choices is immense. One response to this is simply to settle for the known, in some cases through actually building on an existing role. The other main alternative seems to be confusion; arguably those who find themselves in this state are the more realistic, in that they are taking the truth about their situation more fully into account, though some are actually paralysed by their own insight. Values are involved in the choices made by those in the fifth group, but in a different way; for these are not so much consciously held as present in the social life-worlds that have the greatest salience for them. The conception of a broad 'value-orientation' towards either the present or the future seems to be inadequate for the description of adolescents. If these terms are to be used at all, they should be applied to specific social life-worlds; for it is possible for a boy or girl to have an 'orientation' of one kind in one context, and of an opposite kind in another—without necessarily perceiving any serious anomaly.

The Experience of Paid Employment

In the previous section it was possible to make comparisons across the whole range of social backgrounds included in this study, because until the school-leaving age all adolescents are in some sense preparing, or being 'prepared', for employment. However, only about half of the school population leaves at the age of sixteen, and the majority of those from middle-class homes do not finish their training until they are outside the age-range included in this study. Arising from this fact alone, it is evident that there is a very deep dichotomy in the character of the social experience encountered in later adolescence; there is some mitigation in the fact that boys and girls would like to have an income of their own; and in the prevailing conditions, where employers are often glad to find a source of 'cheap labour', for which they will not have to take long-term responsibility, there has been something of a boom in part-time jobs for teenagers throughout the range of age and social class. This section, then, mainly deals with specific points about adolescents' evaluation of part-time and full-time jobs. Indirectly, it is also concerned with certain aspects of the way in which the personal project develops in relation to their experience of employment.

Part-time Employment

Almost all adolescents find that they are in need of money. Even if they are given an allowance by their parents, they would generally prefer to derive as much income as they can from their own effort, thereby asserting their own competence and independence. Provided that the pay is sufficient virtually any kind of work is acceptable, since it is not taken on as a long-term commitment. In some cases, by the time a boy or girl reaches the age of fifteen the part-time job has gained a greater personal significance than school; even if it is not outstandingly pleasant, it is at least an achievement that has been personally initiated.

Those who continue their education beyond the school-leaving age (by far the majority of whom are middle-class, or in process of becoming so) are often able to find a more substantial job than the stereotypical paper-round. Even so, they generally do not expect to find great intrinsic satisfaction in their part-time work; they are well aware that they are not destined to a similar kind of future, and do not identify themselves closely with their temporary occupational role. Against this background their assessment of part-time work is often favourable. Besides the pay and its associated benefits, there are several other sources of satisfaction; in particular, a job provides knowledge of a world that might otherwise be inaccessible, a taste of reality that contrasts strikingly with school, where most of the formal activity consists of the manipulation of symbols. While they may be critical of the conditions of work, they nevertheless value the chance to engage in it.

'This, er, bloke came into the garage and, um, he was, I was checking his oil and water. And he seemed quite a miserable sort of person and, um, came up to him and he told me, he told me, you know, that my hair was, er, too long to work in front of the public, or something like that, and I was dressed too scruffily. And I thought, I turned round and said "What's it got to do with you?", you know, that type of thing. And of course there's a, there's a man- , the manager, the managerial staff on the garage that they come round from site to site, and, er, they get you doing things you know. And they, they're supposed to, it's like a Mafia. It's a cheap, it's a cheap English company, that's sort of similar to American companies in a way. Everything's so cheap and, you know, it's like plastic. And they're only out for what they can get and that type of thing, which offends me, I suppose, a bit. But, er, but when he, when they do come round it's, er, er, the, they sort of tell immediately, tell the miserable little person on the forecourt to start running about and, er, you know, checking everybody's oil and flogging as much as you can, just sort of, just so, just so that they can get their pay packet at the end of the week, you know. I don't like people, er, who come in and start making trouble for the cashier, because she's got a big job. She's got till, and she's got the panel with all the pump readings on. And she's got . . . . she's got, got her toe on them, because if anybody drives off, then she loses the money. It's the company's policy that if anybody drives off without paying for their petrol, she's got to pay for it because it's her fault, that, er, it's her fault that, um, they've lost the money in the first place, which isn't at all good. And then one of the company policies is that if she's down on the till when

all the pumps are matched up and the oil sales, and all the
sales of the whole garage all matched up with her, her till
figures, then if she's down, that she has to pay the difference.
'It's quite a cheap, a cheap and nasty company, actually.'

(Boy₂, Group A, 17)

Whatever may be the case with the work itself, the accompanying social experience receives an overwhelmingly positive evaluation. It is possible that interpersonal relationships at school
provide a background model, against which the reactions of
people at work are unexpected. Whereas some middle-class boys
find difficulty in establishing a *modus vivendi* with work-mates,
this appears to be the case less often with girls; part of the
explanation probably lies in socially conditioned sex differences,
though there is also the fact that a more restricted range of part-
time jobs is open to girls.

'I started the job in the spring, mainly selling to tourists—and
it was one Saturday afternoon . . . . about two o'clock on a
Saturday afternoon. And I was, you know, I was a bit lost at
first. [Laughter] I didn't really know where to go. And um—
I'd been told to report to the woman, which I did, and it just
seemed to snowball from there on. I enjoyed the work I was
doing, and—people were always saying "Hello" to me, people
I didn't know, but who obviously knew me, because I was a
new person there. And everybody was just so friendly and,
and helpful all the time that—it, you know, within five
minutes of getting there I wasn't really feeling depressed any
more.'

(Girl₄, Group A, 17)

Among the negative reactions to part-time employment there is
one that has a common basis: it is a sense of being exploited, of
being given a disproportionate amount of work or responsibility.
Objectively, this arises from a difference in perceptions of the
role. The part-time employee believes in equal treatment; those
who are in the workplace full-time may well think that he or she
'deserves' to be heavily loaded during a working week of
perhaps a quarter of the normal length, and an employer can
hardly avoid the opportunity to make use of a person who (initially
at least) is strongly disposed to be co-operative.

'I used to work on a market, which I enjoyed. But they used,
used to make fun of me a lot. Well they didn't really make fun
of me, they just used to make jokes, and I couldn't, I

couldn't take it really, you know. It's, they used to make
jokes on anybody, but I couldn't take it. They used to treat
me as though I wasn't as old as I was, or as old as I thought
I was, anyway. Er, I didn't like that, and, and I wasn't being
paid very much. So I, I finally decided to ask for a rise, or,
you know, st-stick my neck out and say "Get out", which
isn't, which at that time wasn't the sort of thing I'd do,
although I do do that—kind of thing now. You know, I'll say
"Right", you know, come to an ultimatum. Er—but I asked
for the money and he wouldn't give it to me, so I left.'
    [Later he found a much better paid job in a supermarket.]
    'Gradually I worked my way—into the back, which is just
cutting cooked meats, and . . . . because nobody else would
do it, I think, rather than any other reason. I've been doing that
for about a year now, if not over. And it's, well I do get
bored with it, but it's a job. You know, I just accept it as a
job. I mean, I'm not doing it all the time. So I, I accept it as
that.
    'I enjoy the actual work, you know, getting everything
right. The trouble is, coming on to it, that I, I get the feeling
that, perhaps wrongly, though not always wrongly, that I am
doing—a lot of work, you know. All the work is in with
mine, and the other people aren't, and then I'm the one that's
given more work. For instance, when we call on Friday night
there's me and another lad who works on, does the bacon,
who come in, students they call us, because we only come in
at weekends, and there's the lad who's working there all the
time. I mean, I'm very good friends with him and I can't
blame him, but he's been working there all, all week, so he
doesn't want to do anything, you see, when the other lad
comes, and he's cutting bacon and there's not much to put
out anyway. So what happens is they're standing there talking, you see, a lot of the time, not all the time but a lot of the
time, while I've got to put all these cooked meats out. And
then as soon as I get the counter filled up they, they want
someone in the counter, you see, to work on the counter. So
they say "Go on the counter, Dave", you see. And, and I
don't like working on the counter, I must admit, and they
don't like working on the counter. That's why they send me
on, and it makes my blood boil, you know, to see this sort of
thing.'

(Boy$_5$, Group B(N), 17)

'It's all orders, and "Oh, you can lock up to-day, and close
the safe, and put the alarms on", and, you know, and I got to

do all the work for them, until it's all locked up and—things
like that, you know.

'The others are there most of the time. They should know
how to do these things, you know, instead of putting the
responsibility on to me. See, if anything happened they—
wouldn't get the blame. It would be me, because I have to
lock up. The girl that runs the shop, um, she's ever at me,
you know, "Oh, will you be able to work tonight?" or
"You'll have to come in tomorrow for me because I want to
go out. I'm getting my hair done", you know. And they're
pressing on me, you know, "Well you've got to come in to
work, got to come in to work." They wanted me to work all
the half-term week and I refused, because during the summer
I worked all week and all day, and I got twelve pounds after
that. And I was so disgusted I told them, you know, you
know, "You're not, you're not having me as a slave" . . . .
And I just worked the hours in which she fastened to and I'd
agreed to, and no more. So she's never asked me since to
work any overtime for her.'

(Girl$_2$, Group B(M), 17)

The interviews provided rather less material on the topic of part-
time employment from younger boys and girls, especially those
from working-class backgrounds. In part this may be because of
the smaller range of jobs available to those in the early teens; it is
also possible that some jobs may not have appeared sufficiently
important to merit discussion. As with 'informal work', however,
any opportunity that provides the sense of being an agent and
being in control is clearly of great importance.

'I—told my Mum I wanted a job, but I didn't say where or
anything, you know. I just said I wanted a job. Well, she put
my name down on a list at work, you know. And, erm—then
erm, the next few years after that, because I've been on the
list for ages and ages, couple of years after that, I got a letter
through the post saying that, saying that, erm, saying that I'd
got, got an interview on such and such a day. And I went
down there and I got, done the interview, and I did all right.
I just done some of the things I could do. And erm—I got
the job. It involves me serving up and, the garden centre.
And, you know, I'm sort of the boss, on my own, up in the
garden centre, because nobody else—likes that job, other
than me . . . . I decide where to put things if, you know, if
there's new stock in. They say "Where do you want it?" and I

say "Oh, leave them down there and I'll see where to, where
to put them", you know. And I price them and everything,
and I serve people—And there was another thing that got my
confidence, in speaking to people and serving them.
  'I know that I ca-can do the job, and I know that I, if—
when I do leave school, I got a job there. Because they said
if, when I leave, I can get a job . . . . But, um, satisfactual to
know that I've got the job and nobody else is, you know. My
friends are always wanting jobs, and I've got one permanent.'
                                                   (Girl$_{11}$, Group C, 15)

The opportunity for short-term exploitation is also high,
because employers may well have few scruples in their dealings
with those whom they believe to be relatively powerless and
uncritical.

  'When we first went out selling I found it was sort of, it was
  OK, you know. We went to different areas each week, away
  from the town and stuff . . . . We could make, you know,
  couple of bob commission on it. So I didn't mind at first, you
  know, walking a long way, which I didn't mind. I quite
  enjoyed it as it was out in the open, and meeting a lot of
  people. And then they started advertising for new people. So
  the van—started getting full pretty quick, because me and my
  mate, we been there a long time. We used to stop . . . .
  dropping us off anywhere, but basically it was in the same
  place, where we just couldn't sell anything. So when we—we
  couldn't sell anything we said to him "Don't put us on there,"
  we said to him, you know, "We just can't sell anything round
  here." So he put us in the same place the next week.
  'On my very last Saturday I was working from ten o'clock
  in the morning till two in the afternoon. I made thirty pence
  commission, and it cost me thirty pence in bus fare. So, you
  know, I just, I just worked a full day for nothing.'
                                                   (Boy$_{13}$, Group C, 15)

Full-time Employment

Because of the way the 'sample' for this research was constructed,
much of the data on this topic refer to the early experiences of
employment, when the memory of school still provides a set of
background expectations for relationships within an institution.
The simple fact of having a job is highly valued, especially in a
time when this cannot be taken for granted; shortcomings that

might be intolerable under other circumstances are often accepted out of necessity. Moreover, an adolescent's identity is often invested to some extent in his or her occupational role, especially when this involves a long-term commitment. Factors such as these must be taken into consideration in interpreting accounts of full-time employment. In making a self-presentation to a stranger a boy or girl cannot afford, so to speak, to be too critical, because the personal implications might be damaging. In fact, the material on this topic conveys an overwhelmingly positive impression, and in some cases even shows evidence of a strong traditional 'work ethic', with a marked tendency to criticize those who do not follow it.

As in the case of part-time employment, participants in the research were more expansive on social aspects than on the work activity itself. Conversely, there were relatively few accounts of conflict with overseers or employers as compared with teachers. In part, no doubt, the accentuation of the social is an artefact of the research method; nevertheless, there is strong ground for thinking that in the early years of employment it is often the social experience that is most highly valued, and that failure in this domain rather than in the work itself is one of the greatest sources of apprehension. The first months of employment are of particular significance, since these set a standard for future expectations. Some adolescents are very anxious when they begin their first job, especially if there has not been a precedent in part-time employment.

'When I first started work I wasn't sure what everyone would think of me, you know. And it was my first day, and I was a bit surprised that people were really nice to me—I did get on well with people. It seemed to get better as it went on— rather than worse, as I thought it might do . . . . very apprehensive because just before that, well a while before, I was still at school, but I'd broke my leg, you see. That's what really made me take on a job. I felt I didn't feel like going back to school, and it was in a big firm, you know, wasn't as though it was a small office with a few people in. There were a lot of people in it . . . . It's in a building society, a clerk.
'When I first walked in I walked in with personnel manager. I thought "Everyone's going to stare at me, you know, bcause I'm new." When I think, when I'm settling down at my desk and I see someone walking in, I just think "Well", I just carry on with work, you know, "Suppose you think back to when you were first there." So you try not to stare at them, just get on with your work . . . . I think of myself in

same position, yeah, and I thought, "Well I wouldn't like everyone to be staring at me", so I just get on with my work and try not to make them feel embarrassed. So I suppose that's what everyone was thinking when I first started, you know.

'I was just nervous—same as I'd been if I went to any place, I suppose, after school. I mean, it was such a big jump from school to work. I was afraid I might blow it all in—say wrong things.'

(Boy$_{11}$, Group B(N), 19)

'I work in an office, and I work an accounts machine. And when I got there at first I was so nervous that I wouldn't get on with anybody. It was terrible. I used to sit there, and I used to not say a word. And for about three months I was there, and I never said hardly two words to anybody. So I thought, they all thought I was quiet, and I wasn't getting on with anybody really, because I wasn't talking to them. Well, after I'd been there about six weeks we started to chat and that. And I'm the youngest person there, and they're all about forty-odd. And they're nice, really nice people. And I think I get on really well with them now, but at first I was so worried about it and I think I made myself not get on with them, because I was too nervous to talk to them. I used to think "What shall I say?" but now I just say things instead of sitting there thinking "Well, sh- should you say this or should you say that to them?" So they're just, like, friends really.

'Monica, like, she's very, she's a really nice person, but she's er—she's very, she jumps, not jumps at people, but she's very strong-minded. And if she makes up her mind to something she'll not change. And at first I thought I was going to get on, you know, not too well with her, but after a while I think me and her are really best friends out of everybody . . . . she's a bit older than my Mum.'

(Girl$_2$, Group C, 17½)

The satisfaction derived from the social relationships at work has two outstanding and related features. One is that of belonging to a group that is engaged on a specific material task (and is thus less introverted than many typically adolescent groups). The other is that of being treated as an adult; that is, as a person who does not need to be looked after, who is able to make decisions and take responsibility. In this context even the exercise of a very circumscribed range of choice, or a very limited degree of power, is significant.

> 'I used to have another mate I went around with, came up this club—about the biggest bum around he is, and he—I wasn't able to get a job when I left school, and he went out and got one and he didn't even try, and he got in a timber mill.—And if he worked hard enough after six months he had the chance of an apprenticeship. And he didn't work, he just sat around doing nothing—and I was on Social Security slogging my guts out.—And my old dear jumping down my throat, "Why don't you get out and find yourself a job?" because she thought, you know, getting a job was easy—and er, always jumping down my bloody throat. And er, he got the sack in the end. I got one job as an apprentice electrician—I kept that one for a few weeks and then it just all went to pot . . . . they couldn't pay for my fees to go to college, but they could keep me on. But I said "No, no, it's a boring job."
>
> 'I gets on all right with the biokes in the yard. In the yard we have a great laugh, I likes it in the yard . . . . Well those blokes don't sort of treat me as a nipper. I'm a lad, but he don't sort of say "Oh you stand there and I'll do the work for you", the sort of how I've been brought up, "Come on. You do this, you do that." Like this bloke called Fred says "Do you like painting?" And this bloke called Fred, he gives you the choice of what not to do and what to do.—And I always says "Yeah", because I likes the bloke so much. I says "Yeah, I'll do it for you".'
>
> (Boy$_{23}$, Group C, 17)

Whereas (at least in the early years of employment) the sense of social enrichment is widespread, and not closely linked to the type of occupation, satisfaction deriving from the work activity itself is more restricted. Predictably, it is particularly associated with 'caring' jobs, and skilled manual labour; as is illustrated by the following two extracts, the first from a girl working in child care, and the second from an apprentice joiner.

> 'I got this job, I decided, well—"My money, I've worked for it", er—and now I don't need to sort of ask anybody for, to buy anything for me. Because if I want something I can save up for it for myself. And er—you know, I sort of felt as though I finally mattered . . . . and something that I was not only paid in er—money, but also the reward of doing it, the sort of enjoying myself . . . . in comparison with everything

really—being on the dole, being a student—you know, because—this job I have to take decisions, you know, all the time.'

(Girl$_{13}$, Group B(N), 17)

'I was out of work for six weeks, you know. The whole family was getting worried for me, like. And then this job, job come up. So I thought, "Well, I'd better take it", you know, just to be on the safe side.

'I never thought I could do it, you know . . . . Oh, when I done it at school, sort of, it was one big joke—you know, with everybody else there, throwing chisels about, and, you know, it really dangerous. Here it seems all right. Down on the site, you know. Specially when you got all the old blokes that you're working with, great laugh.

'I never thought I had enough patience to do anything— you know, because I could never make make-up kits and things like that. When people saying, you know, "Just put the rafters up on the roofs" and things like that, "If they don't fit first time, take your time and do it again, and do it again." It sort of gives you confidence in yourself. And when you've done it right, it sort of gives you a sense of achievement, you know.

'Person I was apprenticed to, he was a good craftsman, he was very good. And everything he done had to be perfect, you know, whereas a lot of the young people say "Leave me the painting so you can catch the work", right? But everything that he done had to be right. So, sort of, I was learning from him. Everything had to be right.'

(Boy$_{15}$, Group C, 15½)

A person who is entering employment for the first time has little basis for evaluating the situation in which he or she is placed. Moreover, since the relief at having found a job is so great, there is little incentive at first to develop a critical standpoint in relation to it. As time goes on, however, it becomes possible to be more reflective, and to admit that there are many ways in which it does not bring satisfaction. In addition, a boy or girl has the opportunity to compare experiences with friends, and in some cases to make direct comparisons through having been in more than one job. One of the first negative features to be openly admitted is boredom.

'My job's mainly secretarial, but I don't like it because it's in a factory as well. I mainly just pack goods up, which I don't

like doing that. But today I sort of skived out of it . . . . it
gets boring, same things all the time . . . . used to be a lot of
secretarial, but now all the orders have calmed down and
there's not much to do . . . . so I'm looking for another job
at the moment anyway . . . . Draughting, um, graphic
designs, or something like that. Applied for some, but they
keep saying "No". All the qualified people get it. It's not fair,
I don't think . . . . some people left school in May, still
haven't got jobs, so I'll keep mine until I can get something
better, not just drop it now . . . . I left in May last year,
didn't get a job till—er, November, yeah, couldn't get one
until then, so I'm not going to lose it now. There's still people
without jobs. Feel sorry for them all, you don't get much on
Social Security.—I didn't like being on it anyway . . . . Just
get lazy really—I didn't though, because my boyfriend owns a
strawberry farm. Went down and helped, got more money,
which I shouldn't have done. [Laughter]

'I'm disappointed that I didn't get a drawing job, but I'm
still trying, so there might be a chance, I don't know . . . .
like I wasn't disappointed at school. But once you leave and
I couldn't get a job for all that time, I really got disappointed
and wished I'd done this and done that, but when I got a job
they sort of disappeared, most of them. But—but now I
haven't got a drawing job I've still got to look—a little more
disappointment, you know, in not getting there. I'm disappointed in the job now, don't like it, it's boring.'

(Girl$_{22}$, Group C, 17)

Virtually all adolescents have simple constructs readily available
for evaluating an occupation in money terms. It is only gradually,
however, and mainly through direct experience, that a more
sophisticated understanding of the wider social relationships of the
workplace develops; in adolescence there is a tendency to view the
structures as immutable, rather as the child, according to Piaget
(1932), tends to regard moral authority as transcendent.

'I went to work at a factory, you know, a bed factory. And,
you know, they promised me this and that. They promised
me, you know, "You'll go on to staff when you're old
enough". Anyway, I were machinist for first twelve month or
so. And after I'd learned that, you know, I'd learned about
all these machines and how they worked, all, you know, with
me working on them, you know. We learned how to strip
them down and this and that. And then they moved me from
there to go and be a sort of a trainee staff. And this is where

it got me, because I went and I did this staff job. Though I weren't on staff myself, you know, it were a staff job. And I did that for twelve month maybe, and then I went back into welding department where I'd been previously . . . . my brother took my job and . . . . he went on staff. So all they wanted me for, was sort of cheap labour. He were on staff, you know, staff salary . . . . and that sort of got me. — And I gradually found out that the job I were doing, all they were doing were kicking you from one wall to another, and they were just using you as a means, you know, to satisfy them. So I left that firm altogether and I went to work at a firm — well it's a sort of warehouse. The money's not as good, like, you know. It's about a fifty per cent drop, as much as that.

'I enjoy my job a lot better where I'm working now, because it's more of a free-and-easy — it's a sort of clerical and manual job as well, like, you know. It's not a lot of manual you know, you don't sort of push and pull things. I just sit down . . . . I just check orders, you know, to make sure they're all right to send out . . . . But it's not enough, though. If I were offered a better job I'd take the better job, you know, but it's just getting a better job this day and age, you know.'

(Boy$_{11}$, Group B(M), 18)

It may well be mistaken to regard the conservatism of (mainly working-class) youth in relation to employment as a general personality characteristic, or simply as a realistic response to their lack of power. The main cause may well be cognitive rather than 'motivational'. At school there is a period of over ten years for boys and girls to explore the social relations, and to develop what they regard to be appropriate forms of action. The situation at work, however, is unfamiliar; neither school, nor family life, nor relationships among peers provide an adequate model for understanding it. Initially therefore it may well be necessary for a person to regard most of the authority relationships as fixed, in order to have a framework within which to map out the immediately relevant social environment. It is only after a person has developed a sufficient understanding of this domain that a more radical outlook on the conditions of employment might be expected.

Reactions to Unemployment

As may be apparent even from the interview extracts already used in this chapter, anxiety about employment prospects has become a major feature of the way adolescents view their future, especially

when the time for taking action draws near. Conversely, there is
virtually no indication that unemployment would be considered a
desirable alternative to having a job, even if the remuneration were
comparable to a normal wage.

'I never realized it was so important. I suddenly realized "It's
only four weeks tomorrow that I leave, and with job situation
like it is I can't get one—it's just impossible." Mary's got
one, Mary's got one, my other mate's got one, but I haven't
got one. They just seem to be lucky. But I've, might have one
that starts in September if they take me . . . . They're
opening a new Littlewoods and it'll need people. If I get that
in September and I can't get nowt else I'll just have to go on
Social until September . . . . I ought to try and get a part-
time job or something till then, and earn something . . . . It
feels a bit rotten, it does.—When my first wage comes, I can
get a load of clothes, but if I go on Social . . . . I've got to
give my Mum . . . . I'll take two off, you, you know, when
you're not having much.
  'Careers officer says to me "What do you want to do?" I
says "I don't mind. I want to work in a shop or on a cash-
out." I want to work really on a cash-out, that's easy enough.
[Laughter] So she says "Well, we had one girl wanted at a
supermarket this morning, but it went, just now." I thought
"Just now, Oh God", you know "too late". So she says
"There's nowt else", so I says "Right" . . . . So I wrote to
lots of places . . . . I'm not bothered, I just want to find
something . . . . There was a job advertised in a shoe shop,
but when I went today it had gone . . . . I feel mad, feel like
sitting down and crying—I'm mad, it doesn't half get me mad
. . . . I says to Mum "There must be something the matter
with me." Mum says "There must". I even tried a biscuit
factory . . . . I'll just keep trying, I mean, a sixteen-year old,
you don't want to be on Social, well I don't . . . . I want to
get a job, I want to start off right when I leave school. Some
people get a job. They only stick it out three weeks and they
leave, and then I won't know nowt about it . . . . Even my
grandmother's friend tried for me where she works, but they
don't want school-leavers, want eighteen-year olds. All they
want is someone that's had that fifteen years' experience.
That's no good for me.'

                                      (Girl$_{10}$, Group B(M), 16)

When a boy or girl personally accepts the label 'unemployed',
the subjective environment changes; it becomes a state of in-

activity and lassitude, where personal powers cannot be adequately used or expressed. This perhaps seems strange, since during their schooldays adolescents also have long periods of unstructured time to fill, and handle their position with considerable ingenuity. The two situations, however, are not fully comparable. 'Normal adolescence' has become an accepted part of the everyday world; even if its characteristics are not always commended, its presence is at least recognized. Over the years adolescents have developed a variety of ways of giving meaning and structure to their lives; arising from shared answers to the problem of occupying an anomalous position with regard to the rest of society, values have emerged for the direction of personal life. In contrast to this, adolescent unemployment has not yet received wide social acknowledgment. For those who experience it the roles and values relevant for an earlier phase are not adequate; sufficient time has not yet elapsed for satisfactory answers to this new problem to have evolved, and then to be handed down from one generation to another. At least for indigenous English adolescents, it seems that there are no social life-worlds specifically adapted to the unemployed condition.

'Being on the dole isn't exactly much fun . . . . You know, first two days were great—after that I hated it—because the only people I met during the day who were my friends, but er—were people who were on the dole as well. You know, we'd all sit around all day, sort of, "There's no jobs there", you know. Everyone else was looking in papers—but they don't have my kind of jobs in those papers, so it didn't work. —You know, because we'd all meet in the youth club where I used to work in the evenings . . . . and um—you know, we'd all get chucked out in the afternoon and all congregate, you know, at somebody's house, just sit around and watch telly or all go home to our separate houses and be bored.—You know, most of us admitted that our highlight of our week was going to collect our Social Security money.—It was the only day during the week that I actually really dressed up—it was silly really, as nobody I knew would see me. But, I'd get up at seven o'clock in the morning. Didn't need to, didn't need to get up until about nine o'clock. But I thought er, well "Start the day off well", and er, get dressed and—I'd always get around half an hour early and wait, sort of, around before going in, take the slip of paper and go and cash it.'

(Girl$_{13}$, Group B(N), 17)

'There's no buildings, scaffoldings, there's no work for

scaffolders. And they had to lay eight of us off, eight
scaffolders, and I was one of them, like, you know. Eight out
of fifteen blokes. That's fifteen blokes . . . . and they lay
eight of us off. So, so that's what happened.

'I was working with my brother and my uncle, and then
they laid eight of us off. Now I don't worry about that. I just
got no interest now, I mean. I was working, I was earning
good money, I getting up to go out to work. Now they laid
me off and I, really, I just ain't worried now, you know what
I mean? As long as I get my Mum's money and I'm all right,
you know what I mean?

'I can tell you what we going to do tomorrow. From twelve
o'clock onwards we'll come down here to the Club. If we,
they let us in, which mostly they don't, they just turn us
away, we come up here and we play football from twelve till
three o'clock. And we get bored off with that, we just hit one
another [Laughter] or we play, or have a game of snooker.
Or, like me, I like a drink. I could, I might go into the pub
up there till three o'clock, come down here and have a game
of football. Then we go home, have something to eat, come
down here, have a game of football, or go down the pub. So
what we doing really all our life is what we want to do, is
listen to a few sounds, like you know, go down the pub, have
a good drink, get a bit drunk, like, and have a game of
football. But the only part, bit about the drink bit, is where
you get the money.'

(Boy₃, Group C, 18)

From the standpoint of those who have been successful in
finding a job, the position of the unemployed may well look very
different. There is a marked tendency, among boys especially, to
lay blame on individuals, and to take little account of the
'objective' state of affairs. Reasoning inductively from their own
experience, their view of the situation may appear completely
valid. And there is little incentive to adopt a more elaborate view,
since if responsibility is clearly attributed to individuals, their own
sense of being in control is maintained.

'People have said, like, "Why do you want to go to work so
quick? Why aren't you enjoying yourself first?" And when I
see that, it makes me sick. They said "Why don't you go on
the dole?" That makes me spue, because people say it's, if all
people can do is sit at home and rely on—on the dole money
to keep you going—well, I think people need adjusting.
Because—I, er, politically I don't—er—care much for any of

it, except for the bits, I suppose. I don't know whether this sounds silly or what, but—but you hear about the rise in unemployment, I think some ways that could almost be nothing, really. —As soon as I left school and I went to look for a job, other than what my Dad was trying to sort out, there was just so many jobs. And I thought, "Well, blimey, I've come out of school and I've only got two O levels, but I know I want to work, and I don't want to sit at home and draw dole money every week at the same time, you know." And if I did do that, oh . . . . I just can't bear the fact that there are so many jobs and yet, there's people sitting at home and they think "Because I'm at home and drawing money, it's more than I'm getting at work." If everyone went back to work or went and got a job, eventually they'd find something better and um—money would come their way, I'm sure it would. Because it's happened—I don't know, you know, it's happened to me. It's happened to me because I've gone looking for a job, and that's what I wanted to do . . . . and because I've got a job it's allowed me to do a lot more than I ever could have done.'

(Boy$_{27}$, Group C, 18)

'You could tell the people who were going to get jobs, and who weren't. Even though I sort of mucked about at school, I could never see myself sort of not getting a job. I always thought I had it in me to get a job, to do what I wanted. I could tell who was going to get . . . . you get the local yobbos and that, kids who are lazy. You know yourself who going to get a job . . . . A few of them weren't clever enough—a few of them were too lazy, they didn't have the right attitude.
'I felt I'd done well getting a job—I got it, I got it with ease. I was really pleased the way I just sailed through. Really, it was no sort of big gap between school and trying to find a job. I just applied and got it straight away.'

(Boy$_{28}$, Group C, 17)

As a general hypothesis it may be suggested that the character of the project of any individual is deeply affected by intuitions about the nature and extent of his or her personal powers. This probably applies to some extent even in the private realm, but much more where the product of personal activity is valued by others who appear in some way to represent society to the individual. Employment, for all its deficiencies, at least provides an arena for social development, and an acceptable general role. Widespread adolescent unemployment, however, is a relatively new feature in advanced industrial societies. In due course (if, as seems likely, conditions comparable to those of the late 1970s continue), those involved will resolve their predicament. Out of the available fragments new social life-worlds will be constructed; new types of project will develop, and means will be found by which some sense of personal identity and worth will survive. That these will be seen as a threat to established order can hardly be open to doubt.

8
The Development of 'Self-Values'

The previous three chapters have described values related to specific kinds of context in adolescent life. Generally the level of abstraction at which values are consciously held is low, and there are indications that most boys and girls do not make clear or extensive correlations between their actions in separate social life-worlds. As will be clear from the many extracts already given, the accounts provided abundant evidence concerning the way adolescents see themselves, and the kind of people they wish to be or to become: this is the domain of 'self-values' (Rosenberg, 1965). This chapter takes the analysis some way further, and on to more speculative ground, by commenting on some of the processes in adolescent life that appear to involve a person's self-image deeply, or possibly to change it. Clearly a study of this topic has a close bearing on the larger question of personal identity, and the controversies about its relationship to adolescence.

The remote origins of the self-image are, presumably, to be found in the earliest days of childhood, when a boy or girl begins to learn from 'significant others', and from the general character of the social and material environment, about the kind of person he or she is assumed or judged to be. The ability to conceptualize this is only rudimentary during childhood. Livesley and Bromley (1973) give evidence that by the age of about ten the child has generally learned the principle of invariance, and begun to apply it to people; abstractions are made from several instances, and somewhat crude ideas of traits and habits have developed. This, it might be suggested, is the dominant mode of thinking about persons in early adolescence. At this time there is generally a rapid increase in social experience; the number of different contexts in which a person sustains roles, or relates to others at the perspective level, increases. Associated with this there is a greater capacity to envisage the standpoint of others, and with it the ability to be more objective; it becomes possible to make self-references almost as if the subject matter of these were another person, and hence to engage in reflexive evaluation. The mode of acquisition of self-values, and the associated processes related to the way in which a sense of personal identity does or does not develop during adolescence, are still obscure. On this topic, as with many others, there has been very little detailed social–psychological research concerned with the character of everyday life and the way this impinges upon the person. Rather than treating the problem blandly, and simply trying to elucidate a developmental sequence, a realist methodology could pose the basic question in the following way: 'What types of circumstance in everyday life might a person face, and as a necessary part of solving the problems which they present believe that it is necessary to choose to be one kind of person rather than another?' In other words, questions about self-values must be asked in dynamic rather than static terms; and in keeping with the model outlined at the beginning of this book any answers must assume the person to be perceptive, active and reflective, even if not always well-informed or logically precise. Relevant material was associated with all the items from the interview schedule, and especially nos 4, 7, 13 and 15, which have an obvious self-reference. Considering the wealth of data, the treatment given here is very incomplete. However, for this general study at least five main types of experience can be identified as having particular significance for the development of self-values. Since there is variation in the way these relate to boys and girls in different parts of the social stratification system, there appear to be several main patterns of development. The picture is considerably more complex than a straightforward linear sequence, though it is far from being outside the range of systematic inquiry.

Having and Maintaining a 'Character'*

This issue arises with particular urgency for those who spend much of their time in the company of others having a similar age and background. The problem is that of being a member of a group with shared values, and yet at the same time being able to sustain a

---

*The rather vague term 'character', meaning a distinctive style of social action, is used here because the possibly more appropriate term 'social identity' has been developed by certain social psychologists, notably Tajvel (1974), in a specialized and different sense.

sense of being a person distinct from the others. Perhaps it is significant that when the question of personal identity was raised in a 'validation session' (see page 117), the 'consultant' immediately construed the question in these terms. He also suggested that the problem appeared to be more pressing for boys than for girls. The tenor of the evidence in chapter 5 is in concordance with this, since it is more common for boys, especially those in the lower part of the social stratification system, to associate in groups during early adolescence. Those who have close dyadic relationships (the girl and her girlfriend is a particularly common example) do not experience the problem of 'being different' in the same way. From the closeness of interpersonal perspectives each one has a much more detailed and refined knowledge of the way in which he or she is an individual, clearly defined in relation to at least one other person of the same age.

Having a 'character' is not a new question at the threshold of adolescence, but is presented in a new form. At home the situation is much more simple. Except for the rare case of identical twins (for whom the problem may be acute), roles in the family are clearly demarcated. Each new member finds a ready-made network of relationships within which certain positions are already occupied. Each person knows who he or she is in relation to the others; this, together with differences of generation, and of age and sex among siblings, means that very little conscious effort is required to be distinctive in comparison with the others. When a person begins to participate extensively in adolescent social life, however, there is no ready-made solution. Two main types of perception influence the way the problem is resolved. There is, first, the personality of the individual concerned: that is, on the basis of past performance each person will believe that some types of 'character' are easier to play than others, and that some are virtually impossible. Second, there is the availability of positions; if a distinct place in a group is already occupied, or if there is another strong contender, it might appear to be wiser to adopt another 'character'.

To many boys having a 'character' is a value in itself, regardless of the actual content. Besides being a means, so to speak, of verifying their personal existence, it often helps in maintaining a defence against pointed personal attacks. In terms of content, middle-class boys have a far wider range of acceptable options than their working-class contemporaries, including being intellectual, artistic, athletic, political, poetic, 'mad' and mystical. Under some circumstances 'character' may even be more highly valued than popularity.

'Over the last, last two years, when I started gigging, you get to start being recognized on a small scale, which I am in school really . . . . I'm sort of a character that everyone knows. I'd say I'm quite popular, it all sounds very big-headed, which I am. When, when you're doing gigs and things, being told how good you are and how great you are and how good look now, when you playing this . . . . it's great and that. That also begins to sort of take you over to the point where you, you treat other people, well I treated other people very badly. I treated myself very badly because I was sort of this entity, this this thing and um—and I also sort of fell apart.

'It's a sort of strength of character in a way if you go around thinking as I did,—I mean, if you carry it to extremes it's, it's got to be damaging, but if go around thinking, you know, "How good I am", then if people tell me what a bastard and I and whatever, then it's not going to affect me too much, I'm not going to get into deep depression and sadness because everybody hates me, I just don't care.

'I clown about a lot, I've got a big mouth in lessons. I just, which is mainly, it's, it's not because I want everyone to laugh at me, it's just I get so bored. I keep myself alive by insulting people or whatever—I can, I can never take anything seriously.

'I've got a bitter streak in me, I mean, if someone falls over I've, have hysterical laughter. Mind you, it's probably a sort of exhibitionist thing. I want to be cruel, because that's attention. I put a lot of my actions down, because I want to be the centre of attention and so—I pick a fight with some, start telling jokes or I shout a lot or—and it works. But I don't think that way, I only think that way when I'm, like, being serious and thinking about myself, like now . . . . it's not preconceived at all.'

(Boy$_{15}$, Group A, 17)

Among working-class boys the total range of 'characters' is often narrow, and more restricted by stereotypical expectations attached to maleness, though there are many subtle stylistic variations (cf. Marsh, Rosser and Harré, 1978). In some cases wit, fighting skill or other practical competence (including that of disrupting the school system) is the primary basis of distinctiveness. The possession of a powerful 'bike', and skill in handling it, can take on a strong symbolic significance. The extent to which a boy can be idiosyncratic in developing a 'character' of his own requires careful judgment; to be successfully deviant is a considerable gain in status, though to fail is a disaster.

'I was supporting Arsenal at the time and I decided to change to lower division clubs, fourth division. Everyone was, uh, supporting the local heroes and I was supporting a team at the bottom of the fourth, third division. There was no one else in the whole school who supported the same team. I used to think great of this team, I still do because they're doing well now . . . . Watford . . . . and er, I used to get the mickey taken out of me, but I used to stand up to them as much as I could.

'I wanted to be different, I didn't want to be one of the rest. Everybody—Liverpool won the champion one year so everyone immediately supports Liverpool, and say, Manchester United won it next year, they'll change to Manchester United . . . . At first it was hard as people just keep on and keep on taking the mickey, you know. They wouldn't listen to it if you sort of try and explain and talk about it, they just weren't interested . . . . Individual, got a streak of individuality in me. I don't like to be, I don't like to follow, I can't stand people who follow other people just for the sake of wanting to be "in with the boys", that sort of thing. It's never really mattered to me. I have to do this . . . I just do what I want.

'Everyone's got their own identity, everybody's an individual, except for one. He's a follower, nobody likes him anyway, he's a bit and all. You usually find the dim people try to latch on to someone. He's latched on to Showaddywaddy and David Essex, boy, and the pair of them together, they're a right couple! Everyone gets on to me about Watford.

'It all relates back to Watford somewhere as that's my whole life, Watford. Watford and my work. I believe in Watford. Watford to me is my religion.'

(Boy$_{28}$, Group C, 17)

Because of class differences in styles of behaviour, it can be a serious mistake for a boy to try to develop a 'character' that is perceived by others as an inappropriate expression of who he is. In some cases, especially among older boys, this is strengthened to a value set on personal authenticity; there is a sense in which it would be weakness or deceit to depart from the 'character' that has been adopted.

'This boy comes from one walk of life, and I come from another one. And he tries getting into the way, sort of thinking, that I am. But his parents, you know—his Dad's got his own business. He wears a leather jacket and he rides a bike, but that's as far as it goes, if you see what I mean. He never completely gets into it. He hasn't got a clue about money, his parents give him everything he wants.

'I don't go out of my way to be friendly to someone, I just start being my normal self, I don't change from one day to the next, one day I'll talk to someone, the next day I won't. If I talk to them, I'll talk to them again. If I go out with one girl, I don't see why I should change what I am just because she wants me to. If I start changing then people will sort of say I'm two-faced or something, like, when you're with them you're one sort of person, when you're not with them, you sort of change. They'd say "Oh, he's only putting on an act, he ain't like that really." But I don't, I just sort of act like I normally act. I don't seem to change, so everybody treats me as I am.

'If you are something, it's a waste of time sort of denying it. I don't see the point in it. If you have to keep up all these false identities and everybody you see, you have to try and be different, it doesn't work—so I never try. My father says to me "Don't you want to wear something different from that and make a good impression?" What's the point of going out dressed in a suit if I don't usually dress in a suit? They won't know me for what I am.'

(Boy₁₃, Group B(N), 18)

Even so, in many cases the kind of 'character' adopted by boys is relatively crudely drawn, and played with little initial sincerity; it is, in the original sense, a role. With girls, however, it is often a matter of greater subtlety. A 'character' may well be taken up as a result of interactions at the perspective level, and tends to be a particular interpretation of the 'nice personality' discussed in chapter 6.

'People I, I've, I've heard people say that—I'm the sort of maternal adviser type. So immediately I think "Ahah", start turning into the maternal adviser type, even though I never thought of myself that way before. And I don't think I was, just—really it was that I had a couple of successful relationships with men, and people—somehow believed I could impart the secret of success to them, and came to me for advice, which I was willing to give because it made me feel good, when they asked me. And er—other people have—have said to a friend—"Oh—you're the kind that really turns men on", casual sex and this marvellous life. She's turned into a whore. It's people—are—they think that, they like seeing the picture that others see, and think it's quite a nice one and turn themselves into that picture.

'I, you, have a fixed position in our group, so as everybody has a purpose in it somehow, although—I think a lot of them are unconscious of it.—And, as I said, I am the one people talk to. And there's a girl people to talk to about their sexual fantasies, because she's very sort of racy and—interested in that sort of thing. And—er—well everyone has a slightly different position in the group.

'There's erm—there's the one really intellectual person with whom, you know, if you feel like a discussion or argument you go to him and talk to him. And, er, er, my friend from private school who is very pretty and silly and naive, and she's the one they feel like protecting, they bring out their protective instincts upon. Well all of us do, male and female. And erm, there's the, the couple of very daring people who— instead of having to risk our own lives, we can watch them risk theirs, you know, on their big bikes and sprites and things. Erm—there's one person, one boy who balances with me, he's a depressive. He's co-, attempted suicide a couple of times, and he talks to me and makes me feel uneasy, and he talks to another girl and has the same effect on her . . . . I think I need him more than he needs me. He just needs someone to talk to—really, and someone who won't make a joke out of it, like he has found other people have.—And there are jokers that keep us amused into the small hours of the morning and things like that.—Really we all need— several people in the group fulfil a need even if we don't need other people.

'I haven't worn jeans for a very long time. I was the first one to stop wearing jeans, because somebody said that I was —turning into a woman. I thought "Oh lovely", and stopped wearing jeans. Um—people have said that I'm patient and placid, and really I'm not. But I wouldn't show anybody my neurotic side now, because I like the idea that I'm patient and placid.'

(Girl$_8$, Group A, 16½)

'When I was at school, you know, I got on with every one of my teachers and I had loads of friends at school, you know, get on with them. Now, even down town I know everybody down there, all the little kids, and all the older ones . . . . they get on well with me. I've never—argue with anybody, except Pat who lives with my dad. I've never, sort of, fighted with anybody—and well, Tuesdays and Wednesdays, I used to go with my Nan to bingo, you know. All the old people

liked me so I, more or less everybody likes me, more or less
it seems, you know. —Even kids like me, you know, when we
have them at—come into the shop, I always get a smile out
of all of them, and you know, their mothers stand there
astonished because I get a smile out of them. It must be my
face, it's so funny. [Laughter]. Even in my school report they
said "Gets on very well with people", you know, "Very
cheerful person".'

(Girl$_{20}$, Group C, 16)

This research did not indicate the proportion of boys and girls
for whom the desire for social distinctiveness is a major concern;
nor did it reveal in a direct way why, for some at least, this should
be so important an issue. One possibility is that it is a direct
consequence of the changed view of the self in relation to others
that occurs during early adolescence. The child has strong ground
for thinking he or she is unique; the social world is relatively
restricted, and the ability to see another's point of view is limited.
During adolescence, however, as social horizons are widened, the
person begins to appreciate his or her insignificance in relation to
the whole, and realizes that there are many others who are in a
similar position; in other words, as developmental psychologists
have shown, the standpoint becomes far less self-centred. It is
paradoxical that one of the first responses to this awareness should
be a mode of behaviour that to an outsider has many of the hall-
marks of egocentricity. A person who successfully maintains a
'character' has developed a major resource for personal identity.
Even if this is subsequently rejected, residues from it inevitably
remain in the personality, affecting performance at a later stage.

Handling Damaging Perspectives

Like the problem of 'character', this also arises as a direct result of
the wider range of social experience that generally becomes
available around the beginning of adolescence. During childhood
a boy or girl is well known at home, and has gained an overall
impression about how he or she is perceived. Since the information on which this is based is itself derived mainly from observations
of action in a restricted set of circumstances, it may well be partial
or inaccurate. Nevertheless, in the absence of equally convincing
alternatives, perspectives at home form a major contribution to
the self-image. When, however, a boy or girl begins to spend
significant periods of time in other social life-worlds, and particularly if these do not overlap extensively with that of home,
fresh sources of data for the self-image become available. New

associates who have not had the opportunity to make close or prolonged observations begin to form hypotheses that are based on very limited evidence, such as first attempts at performance in novel roles; in due course the adolescent receives messages in these new contexts about the kind of person he or she is taken to be. Also, others who have known a boy or girl for a long time may well take note of instances of novel behaviour, and, in keeping with their commonsense psychology, simplistically infer that new traits of personality have developed.

In this kind of way an adolescent is liable to receive mutually contradictory messages at the level of interpersonal perspectives. In some respects this may prove to be a liberation, because there is the possibility of escaping from personally limiting attributions made by parents and others with whom there has been close association during childhood. It may be assumed that, where the new perspectives are more favourable than the old, a boy or girl will have little difficulty in assimilating the new information, and in making adjustments to the self-image. Many adolescents, however, imply that it is more common for them to be confronted with messages about themselves that denigrate them in some way; they become particularly aware of information or circumstances that might damage their self-esteem.

In the interviews three main sources of damaging perspectives were identified: parents, teachers and peers. The type of content of the attributions tends to be different in each case, and the resultant problem for the adolescent may require different kinds of tactic for its resolution.

The general topic of interpersonal perspectives between adolescents and their parents has been handled in chapter 5. As was indicated there, although difficulties in this area occur throughout the range of social class, some of the most acute forms of discord tend to be found in middle-class families. Parents may well perceive a boy or girl who participates with dedication in activities with peers outside the home as wild or irrational, because of a failure to comprehend the inner logic of the social life-world. The reactions of parents are experienced as damaging when these involve not so much the criticism of specific actions, but the imputing of more permanent personality traits. Whether such attributions are actually made by parents, or whether they are merely perceived as such by the adolescent concerned, cannot be decided from this research. It is plausible, however, to suppose that many parents themselves operate with very naive trait theories and, so to speak, inflict these upon their children. In some cases adolescents' own means of construing persons may well be more sophisticated than those of their parents.

'My father—mildly objects to me, but he, he sort of thinks, well, you know, "Leave him to it. He knows what he's doing, he ought to, anyway." And I get on with my father. The only problem there is he thinks that, he's worried about me getting a job. He, he's worried, I think, about keeping me for a while longer. He, you know, he wants some money off me. It's putting it a bit crude, is that, and I put it to him, and he said "No, it's not like that at all." But I think it is.

'I really, I get on with my father. He's all right. But my mother, well—she's not particularly bright. She's very worldly, and er—she's come to the idea that I'm evil, almost, because I go out until all hours, I come in at all hours of the morning, I go off drinking. Now previously her excuse was "You're not old enough. You'll get done by the police", but now her excuse is "Well, you're old enough, but you ought to have more sense." And she seems to think, she's never touched alcohol in her life. Her family hasn't, she's been brought up strictly, and so she thinks that because I do this I'm getting into the style of the people who she doesn't like, who go out boozing all the time, alcoholics. She doesn't know that you can have a pint and still be perfectly normal.

'She looks at life at its face value. "We are alive. Let's make the most of it, i.e. live." And that's as far as it goes. "Be alive, do the normal conventional things" . . . . She's very conventional um—so she thinks, but she's actually very unconventional in that she doesn't smoke, drink, gamble, go out at night, etcetera. But she thinks she's quite normal. And she thinks she must be right, and very upright. And, I mean, she's very religious, good woman actually. And so she thinks "Well, I'm not, I'm not bad, I'm not wrong. And he's doing something completely the opposite. Therefore he must be wrong." And I can't get it through to her that I may not be, that I might be a good person, and that I'm not always drunk, and raping women, and things like this.

'In a way I'm very, very like my father. That's why we get on. And yet, I'm also very like my mother, and that's why we don't get on. It's the bit that my father and I have in common that makes us get on, and the bit that my mother and I have in common that makes us not get on.'

(Boy₃, Group B(N), 18)

At school, of course, where academic stratification tends to follow that of social class, it is more likely that, if there is serious disharmony at the level of interpersonal perspectives, this will affect boys and girls from working-class backgrounds. Middle-class adolescents belong to a home culture that is more easily compatible with the official culture of the school. If, as is generally the case, they are successful in the school system, their self-esteem receives some degree of support; or, if school counts for very little in their concerns, at least their view of themselves is not impaired. On the other hand, those who find themselves in the lower academic bands or streams often have to face a continuous set of implicit messages that they lack competence. Naturally enough, one main response to this is to look elsewhere for indications that they are intelligent and resourceful.

'I thought I was below intelligence, I had a lot to worry about, I'd have to think more, I thought, er, all my school work was bad and everything compared with others. But really, my school work might not be up to standard, but I'm not thick.

'I come to the youth club committee. I like to be on that because I feel I'm contributing something to the youth club and it makes me feel more adult—it sounds silly, but it's a sort of feeling that you get when you're on the committee, you're above everybody else, but you're not, but you sort of feel it that you're, sort of, above-intelligence, or intelligent enough to be on the committee to put my views forward, and I'm told that I'm sensible enough to be on the committee and that makes me feel good, all these little things.

'That was when I discovered that I was, I wasn't sort of— people kept on constantly telling me, "God you're intelligent. Why do you make out you're thick? You're not", and that, and that made me feel good. But I discovered that about myself, I couldn't understand it. I was in, I went to a committee meeting, I went to meetings at school, I found that when I was in the classroom I would have a sensible discussion with somebody, and this surprised me in a way because I didn't think—I mean I was using words and expressions and things that I didn't know I knew, you know. I was saying them, they, you know, were just coming up because I just happened to be of er—I was capable of going places, but I didn't think about it, and when I finally discovered it, it was bit of a shock really . . . . That's another thing, adults would listen to me, if I talked about something er . . . . I could talk like an adult. And that, that surprised me, I was talking like an adult, you know. It came very suddenly. I was grown-up mental, not just physically, mentally much quicker than I thought I would . . . .'

(Boy$_{15}$, Group B(M), 16)

But there is an additional problem. The classroom is generally viewed by teachers as requiring interactions that are primarily at the level of role. Some working-class adolescents, however, particularly girls, tend to interpret the situation as if it were at the more delicate level of interpersonal perspectives. Thus, under conditions where disintegration is constantly tending to occur because of the lack of a common definition, a move made by a teacher as part of a standard role-performance may come to be construed almost as if it were a personal attack.

'I says "Oh yeah, we've done those problems before, in first year". But I couldn't remember . . . . then he asked me a question—about it, you know, about ten minutes later. And er, I sort of sitting there. I'd never done them before, and I got mixed up, and that's when he started shouting things, "What've you just said?" I said "What I've said before and what I say now are two different things." So that got him even more mad, and he just said "Don't throw your tantrums at me."

'I thought he was making a show of me. When we come out he said "Well if you can't do that, young lady, you do these multiply sums", multiplication, one times one—and all that. And he sort of throwing the books, you know . . . . he was throwing it. And I said to him "I don't have to work if I don't want to. And you're not going to make me."

'It was just because he asked me that maths. "What number goes there?" he said. I said "What are you asking me for? There's plenty of others. Ask them."'

(Girl$_7$, Group C, 15)

The third main source of damaging perspectives is a boy's or girl's own close associates. Anyone who, in the terminology of chapter 6, 'moves out' into the social life-worlds of adolescence is thereby implicitly committed to paying particular attention to indications from peers about how he or she is being perceived. For reasons already discussed, girls especially tend to become experts in operating at the perspective level; the price is that they may become highly sensitive about the reactions of others towards them.

The subject matter of damaging perspectives may be virtually any aspect of the person. It may, for example, have to do with appearance or physique.

'I've got a bit of a dark, you know, a dark hairs across the top of my . . . . and it looks like a moustache. And it never bother, never bothered me at all in the juniors—and er, you know, just didn't get skissed about it. But when I came into this school . . . . "She's got a muzzy, look at her, look at her, our muzzy woman", and everything, they were saying.

'Just went home and said "I've got to get rid of this," I said, "They're all skissing me about it at school." My Mum said "Er, well, you never, never bothered about it before, have you?" I said "No. Well, I've never been skissed about it before like this." She was saying "Oh it's nothing. Look at Liz Taylor, she's got one" . . . . "Don't want to be like Elizabeth Taylor, and I want to be like myself, and I don't want to have a muzzy."'

[With the help of her mother she tried to remove it with a depilatory cream.]

'But it grew again. And, you know, I got skissed again. So I did it, you know, I removed it again . . . and um, but now I don't bother about it. If anybody skisses me about it I say "You're jealous because you haven't got one", you know. It doesn't matter any more.'

(Girl$_8$, Group C, 15)

Alternatively, it may be some aspect of perceived character or style that received adverse criticism.

'And, er, one day, these friends, er, they were just talking generally about, er—whether it was right to tell other people their faults, you know, straight out and all that. And, er, any-way they came round to me and they were sort of saying, er, "You're terribly vain, Judith". [Laughter] I think they sort of struck me like, er, you know, a streak of lightning [Laughter] sort of, erm, because I'd never actually been told that before. And, erm, when I look back on it, erm—I, I think it really struck home to me, that fact that I was vain. And I realized I was vain from that time onwards. And, erm, made me more aware of that fault, because before I, you know, I hadn't, er, I hadn't really seen myself as vain at all.

'I was very cut up about it at the time, they told me, erm, because, er, I thought in a way they were all, well, they all agreed on it. And then I felt a bit sort of cut off from them. And, and I, I felt they were sort of—um, putting themselves above me and I, I automatically hit back with, you know, perhaps a few mean things, telling them er, more maliciously, what, what I thought of them than they thought of me. But erm later, erm, it really quite, quite upset me, you know, the fact that, erm—they thought this and the fact that I, I saw this later to be true, you know.'

(Girl$_2$, Group A, 18)

Rather less commonly, the subject matter of damaging perspectives may be a person's beliefs or opinions.

'We're all known to be crazy, for the things we get up to. But sometimes we have, you know, serious talks, going home from school and that.

'They were saying you should die because you should, if someone kills someone he should in turn be killed. And I saying "This is stupid because—um, not only—the fellow who's getting hung suffers, his wife and kids also suffer . . . . And er—I think it's wrong because sometimes you can't really be sure the fellow's done it. Sometimes, you know, he may not be guilty and a few years later . . . . And I don't think it's fair on the judge exactly, you know, to sentence people to death. Some judges might sentence one fellow to death, and another fellow, another wouldn't, and things like that."

'I felt like a stranger really . . . . sort of um, I really can't describe it—in some ways I wanted to sort of believe—in hanging, sort of so I wouldn't be like an outcast. But I just couldn't, you know.'

(Boy$_{13}$, Group C, 15)

It may tentatively be suggested that, although damaging perspectives from fellow adolescents are experienced as powerful and painful at the time, their effect is relatively impermanent. For during early adolescence, especially when the prevailing mode of construing persons has not become firmly committed to the principle of invariance, perspectives are relatively transient, and therefore a boy or girl has the chance to make a swift recovery. It is the attribution of distinctive traits that presents a particular problem, and this appears to be far more typical of adults' reactions. Indeed, some adolescents may become so highly sensitized to this possibility that they draw inferences even from the reactions of strangers.

'You're sitting on a bus and getting, you're sitting at the back just laughing, you know, not doing any harm . . . . and, you know, "Teenagers, they're all the same". People, they're sort of not aware of what you do, you know. A lot of friends do voluntary work, did help an awful lot, you know. —They're not aware that you've got views on anything, or—you're just a teenager, you're noisy, you know, you're a pest. [Laughter] I get very annoyed. My parents aren't so bad, but occasionally you get their friends who say, you know, teenagers are all the same, you know, they don't appreciate anything.—I feel angry, but I never do anything. I can imagine why people do, why people do actually have to go against society and rebel, because you know it gets so it's expected of you, you know, you can see why people do begin to behave like that if you get it often enough. I suppose it must be worse for boys, you know, if they walk around in a gang, but you find that even things like shopping with a friend at Christmas, you go into a London store and they're watching you, you know, "She's a teenager, she's going to shoplift", however respectable you look. It is pretty annoying.'

$$(\text{Girl}_{19}, \text{Group A, 18})$$

For anyone whose mode of construing persons has not developed as far as a clear trait psychology, the existence of damaging perspectives, while unpleasant, does not pose a logical problem. However, to those who accept the assumptions implicit in every-day language and everyday interaction, that each person is a kind of unity describable by means of a set of traits, it may well appear that a logical issue is involved. The whole range of perspectives, some favourable, some less so, cannot all be right. The obvious solution is to accept some, and reject others. It would appear that many adolescents are inclined to take messages about themselves more seriously from their peers than from adults; and in keeping with the rest of humanity to accept perspectives in concordance with their 'self-values', while rejecting others. Thus where per-spectives from peers are favourable and those from adults are not (as, for example, in the case of some middle-class girls in relation to parents, and some working-class boys in relation to school), the mode of resolution is simple. The problematic cases are more likely to be those where perspectives from peers are damaging. The analysis of this issue is beyond the scope of this study. It may be hypothesized that a person can survive as a social being only by accepting some perspectives, even if unflattering; but that he or she will urgently look for another way of recovering self-esteem.

A more complete resolution of the problem of receiving mutually discrepant perspectives requires a mode of construing persons that is much more complex than a commonsense trait psychology. Those who reach that stage become able to under-stand that the basis on which they had felt it necessary to make clear choices between perspectives was incorrect. It may then be possible to abstract elements from the whole range of information and achieve a higher-order resolution, in which both construals made by other persons and the character of situations is taken into account. Personal identity is then no longer a matter of accepting what is given, but is open to some degree of choice. Conceptually, this requires an advanced level of formal operational thought in the social domain. Within the age-range of this study, it seems that this is a characteristic of very few. And it is likely that a considerable proportion of the adult population never develop that degree of sophistication, since they function adequately in social life by conceptualizing in a more concrete way.

The Severing of Social Bonds

It is usually during adolescence that a person comes for the first time to face decisions of a serious kind, whose effects may well reverberate throughout the rest of life. The obvious paradigm case here is the choice of a career. However, as was suggested in chapter 7, the salience of this can easily be exaggerated, and the issue may well present itself in a disguised or transmuted form. Whenever a major decision is consciously made, and something of its long-term implications are realized, 'self-values' are involved. For the question 'What should I do?' subjectively appears to entail such questions as 'Who am I?', and 'What kind of person do I wish to be or to become?'

The previous three chapters have given some indication of the wide range of decisions that commonly occur in adolescent life. In terms of form rather than content, there is one type that may have particular relevance to 'self-values', and hence, indirectly, to the formation of personal identity. This is the kind that involves the relinquishing of some activity, the cutting off of previous associations, the resolution to dispense with some existing means of support. The emphasis here is often negatively on breaking, rather than positively on commitment. For many of the circumstances in which adolescents find themselves were not created by their own deliberate action, but are part of the ready-made world in which they found themselves; and it is often the case that involvement in social life or the development of particular interests is gradual, unmarked by any one decisive step. To break away, however, means a definite choice: a movement from the known to the unknown. It involves risk, perhaps requiring a person to rely at first upon inner resources rather than social support; and it is logically possible only in the light of reflection on what a person wishes to be or to become.

Biographically, some of the first situations of this kind have to do with the giving up of childhood pursuits. For most boys and girls the transition to the form of social existence defined as adolescence is a simple forward movement, in which new activities appear naturally to displace those of an earlier phase. Occasionally, however, a deliberate decision is involved; there may well be a certain nostalgia for what is left behind, and yet a recognition that its passing is inevitable.

'My Grandad, I don't know how it came about but, anyway, he bought me this pony. "Oh well, that was great", you know, um, and I got the riding hat for my birthday and um— I was dedicated, but my friend was, she was even more dedicated than myself, she cleaned out, she did everything. And um, even though I was only twelve, you still got work to do at school and um—my friend could do it but I couldn't, I couldn't combine both. At thirteen I was just starting at a new school and um—the girls were mocking me about having a horse. You know, I mean, they didn't. And er, I was trying to do my homework, riding the horse. I mean, sometimes I'd feel like giving my homework up and riding the horse, and I had to make a decision. Did I want to be, did I want to make a career and go to college and do a secretarial course or something? And even at thirteen it's a big decision . . . . It was only a pony, and I was growing up rapidly from—you know, I'm tall like my father. So um—I looked a bit silly stuck, sat on the horse . . . . So it wasn't totally just "I'm going to get rid of him because I can't do that and my homework." And um, my grandfather said "Would you like another one?" and, you know, "A horse this time?"
'And I said um, "Thank you, but no. I want to go to school", I mean "go to college". So bearing it in mind, thinking that I've given the horse up, I've got to work hard at the course I'm on, otherwise I've could have kept my horse. So if I don't obtain any results I've wasted these years. I could have just carried on with the horse, and just worked on a farm, etcetera.
'I've sold him. I'm still keeping in touch with the girl, but it upsets me because when I shout the horse, his name's Ginger, I get, he's the other side of town, and um, the other day I went and I shouted "Ginger" and he wouldn't come to me. Oh, and I felt so awful, to think that he was my horse and now it belongs to another girl.'

(Girl$_1$, Group B(M), 17½)

'I acted childish up to a certain point, and I think it was—around May. And then I just started to grow up, and met more, met more older people, and sort of looked at their attitude to life and their personality, and sort of imitated it. So it was in a way a change of direction from childishness to another way. I built a model, a war model, you know, little hills and I had little soldiers and tanks, and I used to like playing with that with my mates. But now I've grown out of it and life seems to be changing, and now it's still a bit—wobbly, and not sure which way to go.

'Bike chasing, I still like to do it occasionally, but I haven't got a bike. And I think my brother will be going through that. Like to go out with him, go back to them days . . . . Now is the time to grow up, for some reason or another—I've decided I will. There's still problems in that, though.

'I like to be young, you know, act . . . . three years ago—I just can't, people just don't seem to let you, you grow up with you, just grow up and go round with a solemn face. It's depressing, you change from one attitude to another. People are saying maybe you should do this, you should do that. You just got to pick a personality up somewhere. You got to act your own. Other people know your personality, but you don't. Some of them tell you straight out "You're stupid, grow up", and all that—I seem to be doing that now. I haven't been told that this would happen. We used to—I like to be treated as a—older person, as a young man and that.'

(Boy$_9$, Group C, 15)

There is a common stereotype that suggests that adolescents are in a state of rebellion; it is the obvious mentors who are considered, such as parents and teachers—those who offer their prescriptions from a role-position far removed from that of the adolescent. The tenor of this research, however, implies that the genuine assertion of autonomy is a relatively rare occurrence, because many boys and girls, especially during the early teenage years, simply exchange one type of authority for another. Those of approximately the same age often appear better guides, because they are more able to show what is appropriate not only in a symbolic, but also in a concrete way. When, as occasionally happens, a specific model or authority is rejected, it may well be a very significant moment in personal development; for it requires a person to look to some other source of help, or to develop more general principles of action that are in accord with existing 'self-values'.

'I think again with my sister. We used to like the same things and do the same things. When I was little I used to follow her about and think she was, you know, right, and copy everything she did. When I was about twelve she used to, when I think now! She used to tell me to do, and I'd just go and do them! . . . . One day she told me to do something and I said "No". She was really shocked, and after that I just do what I want. I enjoy myself more, but I can do what I want to, not follow her. After that we had arguments, because I don't think she could accept I wouldn't do what she said . . . . Now I just accept that we have different ideas.'

(Girl$_{10}$, Group A, 16)

Such a move is relatively easy; but it is hard to leave a social group and its accepted way of life.

'I started off, it was with Doyle. There was nothing to do. We used to have a laugh properly, the load of us, but—you couldn't really have a laugh properly. So, you know, we used to get a bottle of cider and drink that. And you wasn't paralytic drunk, but you was a bit drunk and you'd, you know, enjoy yourself on that. We used to have a right laugh, things we used to go at. They thought we was lunatics, we used to go up to people in the street . . . . But after a while it, it really horrible, cider. I don't know . . . . It's all right if you're having a glass, but if you're drinking a whole bottle down it's repulsive stuff—and not only that, it, after a while it don't have any effect on you. And—there's quite a, quite a few people round here taking pills, smoking gear and that. And so we, you know, first of all we started off having a couple of joints, but they don't really get you out, you know, they just make you feel—nice. And we just used to take a couple of pills.'
[The involvement in drugs deepened, until one time she accidentally took an overdose of a pill of unknown character, and had to be taken to hospital.]
'And the next morning I was being godmother to my little cousin. So I got in the church and I stood about out of my head. You have to give the baby's head to the priest, I turned round and gave him his feet. [Laughter] So anyway, it was all right that day. And then—my Mum and Dad, like, we had a really big sort of talk, you know what I mean, and that . . . . It just ain't worth it, and nothing really, because when you're like that you can't erm remember what's happening. So—I just

stopped. You know, we all stopped after that . . . . if I'd have stopped before, I'd have been, I wouldn't really have wanted to, I'd have gone back on them after a while. You know, but then I wanted to, I didn't need to do it any more.

'One night my old mates said, you know, "Why don't you come out?" because they knew I wasn't going about with them, but they also knew—I'd stopped going about with a friend who I started with just after then. And they knew I was staying in. And they said, you know, "Come out round to a disco." And I said "Oh, I'll think about it." And I really wanted to go. But I thought "If I do and then—I'll probably get back into going about with them again." So, you know, I didn't, and that's really—put, you know, I've stopped it completely.'

(Girl$_6$, Group C, 14½)

Some of the most taxing decisions that an adolescent has to make are concerned with personal relationships. Often when an association is brought to an end it is because of some clear breach of the code outlined in chapter 6. There are some cases, however, where a person simply comes to judge that a friend is 'not suitable' in some way. This means, in effect, that there is disharmony of interpersonal perspectives; the characteristics of the friend, and the messages he or she conveys, are no longer in keeping with the person's 'self-values'.

'A year ago, a year ago we stopped seeing each other. And my parents had never liked him, or any of that. And I think I only went out with him just to annoy them. He, erm, he lives in a village round here. He wasn't particularly—he left school when he was sixteen, he hated school, never took any exams. He worked in a factory. He hated everything when he was not in the pub, but, something, I liked him . . . . as a friend, but, I knew that it, it was ridiculous. And they never said, you know, "Don't go out with him", but I always knew that they didn't approve, you know.

'I, I went out with him for eighteen months, two years. And then suddenly a year ago now, a year ago this week, I decided, er, "This is ridiculous, this is going nowhere. This is just me trying to rebel against them for no reason, because they're not trying to stop me." Just seemed pointless. I seemed to have proved my point, could do it if I wanted to, could do what I want to. But I didn't want to. So I, I stopped, you know, seeing him.'

(Girl$_5$, Group A, 17)

It is almost a truism that adolescence involves a dilemma between the attractions of leisure-time activities and the serious demands of school; although the salience of this issue can be greatly exaggerated, there are some boys and girls who do experience a dilemma of this kind. It is most typical of those whose social position and future prospects are by no means assured, and yet who have sufficient awareness of their competence to take the idea of qualifications seriously.

'I had to turn down a play, see. The er, the person who actually runs the theatre—is a schoolteacher and quite intelligent, you see. And she . . . . and she, she's so lucky in as she can carry, put her mind to quite a few things at once, you see, which is very unlike me, because if I do something I've got to do one thing, you know. And I've got to concentrate on that. Now I was taking exams at the time, and she'd asked me to be in a play. Now er, it was a question either of pass the exams or do the play. So er, I plumped for the exams, which anyone should do. And er, she couldn't see why er, I couldn't do them both. But it was quite a big part that she was offering me at the time. I would have like to do it. But er, I just couldn't learn the script and learn my work for the exams as well.

'She thought that everybody—she never actually took people individually. She used to think of everybody as intelligent as her, you see. So er, she expected me to be able to do the lot. That's why I had the disagreement, I had an argument with her about that. And er, it just ended up that she wouldn't talk to me for a while [Laughter], usual thing.'

(Boy$_9$, Group B(N), 16)

In ways such as these the deliberate severing of social bonds becomes, in effect, part of a larger choice: that of being and becoming one kind of person rather than another. Anyone who does refer to self-values, and attempts to make decisions by using assumptions about what he or she is like, is beginning to postulate a personal identity, even if on the basis of partial or incorrect information. It must be said, however, that such occurrences appear to be relatively rare within the age-range of this study. The main patterns of movement in adolescent life, differentiated as they are in relation to social class position, do not generally necessitate decisions of this kind. 'Strength of character' (in the old-fashioned sense) is not a highly valued or frequently sought attribute, nor is it likely to be under the prevailing social conditions.

Developing an Autobiography

The previous sections of this chapter have shown how certain kinds of predicament in social life require a person to reflect, and in that process either to consult existing self-values or to postulate them for the first time. There is also a different kind of issue, not so directly related to action, that becomes significant during adolescence. By the mid-teens a person has had a long enough period of life within memory, and a sufficient range of experiences, to have begun to acquire an autobiography. At the same time, and as a result of processes of the kind discussed in this and the previous three chapters, the capacity to interpret events, and to be objective about the self, has developed to a considerable degree. One question that arises for anyone who ponders on his or her life-history has the following form: 'How is it that this person who has changed so much, who has coped with such a variety of social conditions, can nevertheless in some sense be the same?' This research did not involve any attempt to discover how frequently, and under what circumstances, this kind of problem is raised; though it seems likely that it is more familiar to those who have the chance of privacy, to those who are not participating (at least for a while) in close relationships with other adolescents, and to those who have had to move from one social milieu to another. Whatever may be the case, it is evident from the way the interview task was handled that many of the participants in the research had an abundance of autobiographical material ready to hand, and that reflection on the apparent paradox of personal continuity and change was no novelty. Here the main emphasis of the accounts was on the vicissitudes of social life, and changes in attitude or interior state.

Some boys and girls are able to recall a distinct change in the style of their social behaviour as they took up the socially defined role of 'adolescent', associated with the assertion of independence from parents, and 'moving out' into new social life-worlds. Although, as has been indicated, there are some instances where a deliberate and considered break with childhood pursuits is made, it is far more characteristic for the transition to be unreflective, its significance only being realized at a later stage.

> 'My life must have changed in some certain way when I became a teenager—thirteen, fourteen-ish, something like that. When my mate was fifteen, you know, and he was starting to rebel, I started to rebel with him, and I started to do what I wanted to do. I stayed out later than I do now—it just happened. I never thought about why I done it. It just

something that happened. I didn't plan, sort of, say, "When I'm thirteen I'm going to rebel against what everybody stands for"—just the way I turned out. If I was in a different city, in a different area, I might be a different sort of person.

'I suppose everybody does it, don't they? When you start changing, start growing up, as they say—my parents shouted, couldn't understand it. They didn't have any control over me at all. I was worse than I am now. I didn't have any respect for anything then—I used to, sort of, say "I'm going out." "When will you be back?" "Don't know." Didn't really care what time I got in, or whether I went to school or anything. I didn't seem to care.'

(Boy$_{13}$, Group B(N), 18)

One of the most frequently mentioned aspects of personal development is the acquisition of social skills: being able to meet people easily, talk, make friends, interpret signs of success or failure, promote relationships, effect reconciliations. The strong emphasis on this topic in the accounts is itself an indication of the high value that is attached to success in the interpersonal domain.

'Social life is very important to people. I mean, I know quite a few people that, um, have hardly any social life um, mainly because, I don't know, if it's their family, they have, you know, upsets in their families—or whether it's, it's they just don't feel like being sociable to people, or they find it difficult to communicate with other people, whereas I find it easy— um. I must admit, um, I never used to find it easy, I used to be very shy, but that was when I was young, you know, when you usually go red or hide behind your mum, used to say "Oh, she's shy" and that used to make it worse. So—I don't know—I suppose that's really the way I've changed in my life . . . . I think that's the main thing actually. If a person isn't confident in their own self, you feel that you're always going to be looking out for things. They always say to you "Well, go out," you know, "Enjoy yourself." And most people wouldn't think to go out as they don't know what's going to be ahead of them, they don't know what to expect, because no one's ever told them, and they usually just shy away, you know, and think "No I don't want to go." And they usually made ridiculous, you know, excuses up, "No, I don't feel very well" [Laughter], you know. You can tell it a mile off. You shouldn't really push because I think, I mean, nobody ever pushed me. I came round myself. It wasn't really until in my fourth and fifth year when I had interviews, you know, at the careers library, career days, that I became confident in myself. I thought, "Well, I can talk openly, what am I so worried about?" So the direction, you know, the change of my direction in my life is probably because, you know, I can speak openly now. Speaking about myself to people, which I want to be able to do, because if I do, you know, to be a hygienist I want to be able to speak openly to people and not always repeat the same conversation, I mean, pick up other people's interest and talk to them when they come into the surgery.'

(Girl$_{15}$, Group B(N), 16)

'I discovered that I was new, in a sense, that I'd changed, that I was new in their town, their school really. It's off the subject a bit, but—yeah, I felt there was something in me that was coming out now. I was, and whereas before I wasn't so, so outspoken. Because the first three years in my school here was like—for a start school was new, we were the first proper year. All the other years were an amalgamation of other schools, but our year was the first proper year. So we were all goody-goodies with the tie, you know, and we was all done up smartly and we didn't want to get out of time in a lesson. But slowly that went out as other years came in.

'That was when I first noticed that people—well I got on with people, and like, I didn't stick out like a sore thumb, but I was, I could get on and that. Um—I didn't fade away if I was in a room with people.'

(Boy$_{27}$, Group C, 18)

Adolescence sometimes involves sharp contrasts in achievement, both between different social life-worlds and within any one of them. When success follows after failure there is no pressing problem for a person's self-image.

'Just then the teacher told me that he was fed up with me. He said I'd never get anywhere when I got out to work. He said, you know, I mean, "You'll have to adapt to work," he said, "and if you carry on like this you'll never get anywhere," he said, "You'll end up at the dole office." And that annoyed me because I know that I'd been working part-time, and I'd got all right there with everybody sort of thing. And um—you know, I just flew off the handle.—I was really mad, swearing, cursing . . . . I felt that he said too much. A lot of things he said to me were quite unnecessary.

'Well, er, with going to school and everything, as I said, I went through a depression and everything seemed like to me that I was going down hill, you know, I was getting right to the bottom. And as soon as I got out to work everything started coming back up again, you know. And, now, you know, I'm on top of the world, everything's going right. Actually I'm thinking that something's got to go wrong pretty soon. I mean it's never been like this before. And, um as I say, I'm still coming up now. I mean, I can come up a lot more, but I feel personally, myself, that I'm up about as far as I can go now. So—you know that quite pleased me to find out that after going for so long, about six or seven months go down and down, getting worse and worse, to suddenly to get right back up again within a few weeks. When I started work and it got better all the time, you know, I was really pleased. It did me the world of good—I've got a lot of my pride back. Because with going down and down all the time, people used to come up and take the mickey about me at school, skiving, having arguments with teachers, that sort of thing. If ever we were sat somewhere someone would always bring up that, and you know, just felt when I started coming back up again people used to say to me "You're doing alright at work" and I'd say "Yeah" and they'd say "Yeah, well I'm not too hot at work at the moment, I've had an argument with someone." And I'd think to myself then, "Well, I'm all right".'

(Boy$_{22}$, Group C, 17)

On the other hand, experiences of failure or rejection following after success are far harder to assimilate, posing a serious challenge to a person's self-image.

'To start off with I was working for this newspaper. I was working for nearly five months, when I . . . . I was doing the advertisements for the printing side. So I was there, I was working there for over five months. But then I started passing out, and having blackouts, which made, which meant I wasn't allowed to work. But they held my job open for quite a period of time, but, you know, they couldn't hold it open indefinitely because, you know, I'm not supposed to be working now. So they closed my—you know, they said "I'm afraid, you know, that we'll have to take someone else on, but we'll give you a good reference" and all this, which I thought was fair enough, because they held it open. I been, just recently I been getting really fed up, you know, of being out of work—been moping about the house, all sorts. So I decided to get another job. Well, I love children, so this seemed to be the ideal job. I saw it advertised in one of the employment agency windows. So I rang them up and they said "Yeah, come for an interview". So I, I got it, you know, after 'phoning them up. Then um—I started. I um, I was looking after twenty-eight children. The girl I was supposed to be working with was in ho- hospital. She'd been taken ill, having an operation. So twenty-eight kids on your own, from two to three-and-a-half, when I wasn't supposed to be working, was a bit of a handful. So I was doing it for two weeks. At the end of two weeks they said "Oh, we're not going to be needing you any more because, um, we got somebody else to take your place." Which, it didn't so much annoy me, it mainly upset me because um, it was just for, they used me for two weeks, doing all the heavy work, you know, let me do all the hard work. The money I was getting was pretty grotty anyway.

'I think I managed quite well, considering I haven't got any qualifications. There wasn't no serious accident, you know. Kids fall over there all the time, but, you know, there was nothing serious happened that went wrong. I think I managed considering, well because the, I had eight new children, brand new from the nursery, which is a bit hard to cope with, because they scream from morning to night, you know. That was the whole time, you know. In the evening, bedding them down, everything. Twenty-eight kids, the average is six to a person, you know, that's the law's average. So considering I was looking after twenty-eight when I was supposed to be looking after six for the first—I think I done quite well. [Melancholy laughter]'

(Girl$_2$, Group B(N), 17)

Many adolescents, especially in the early teens, describe feelings of being different from others; experiences of this kind provided the largest category derived from item 9, 'When you were right on your own, with hardly anyone taking your side'. It is as if a person's awareness of inner states, which includes variations of mood, self-doubt and feelings of apathy and depression, has little congruence with the general manner in which others present themselves. There may also be objective circumstances which give rise to a sense of being unique. However, as a result of forming close friendships, and of meeting a wider range of people, some boys and girls gradually come to realize that they are not so different as they had first inferred.

'Well, like, my father walked out when I was two—Er, when
I was eight Mum remarried, but during when I was younger I
was different, because I lived with my grandparents and I'd
got no father and um—I couldn't even remember anything
about him to tell anybody else so—I was different. Funny, in
a way it affected me more than it did my brother. Because
my brother, he remembered him, and he didn't want anything
to do with my father. In fact he, I'm sure if he saw him now
he'd punch his face in. Where it's different—you know, I'd
love to see him. Um, then the psychiatrist said, because that's
the person who tested me . . . . all the things in your background that you don't really remember, like change of schools
when I was very young, being bullied from the age of eight
until you are sixteen, didn't exactly have a lot of good on to
you. Um it all, you know, affects things and that, you know,
like the ways my spelling and confidence. Um, then when I
went to college there was only one person there who was from
my same school and she was my friend. She was, you know, a
really good friend, the best one I've got really. So—she
wouldn't bully me or anything like that, you know, so I'd got
no worries on that score, and no one knew what my background was like. And in fact we found out that our class was
the most mixed-up class we've ever got. There wasn't one
person there who had a stable family background. You know,
we were really worse than some of the children we looked
after—so I finally found out, you know, I'm not so different
in having a stepfather and what-have-you. It's sort of—so I
didn't have to hide it, and you, you know, didn't have to brag
about it either because it was just accepted.'

$$\text{(Girl}_{13}\text{, Group B(N), 18)}$$

Being physically uprooted is another type of experience that can
have a profound effect upon 'self-values'. It provides the opportunity to compare one social setting with another; there is an
enforced separation from friends, and often a feeling of isolation
until new friendships are established.

'I was very resentful when my parents decided to move,
because I was getting on well at school. I got lots of friends,
and my whole life was based there, and I was in the middle of
getting eight O levels. And the situation was that I was going
to have to move, going to have to move schools, and er—it
was just one big upheaval. I wasn't looking forward to it at
all . . . . I was going to stay behind with my Gran and all
sorts. In the end we moved, and I just had to go with them.

'I had lots of friends. I'd go out every weekend, be out Friday, Saturday, perhaps Sunday as well. I had a boyfriend that I didn't really want to leave. This town seemed the end of the world away, you know. It seemed so far away, and such a tiny place.

'I missed being with my friends, going to parties, and having freedom, being able to move around. Whereas here I had to rely on my father to take me out, you know, providing transport to get somewhere, because a lot of my friends here live outside town, which means there's no buses.'

[For a short while she continued to travel in to her old school.]

'Even though I'd got friends there, I felt as though they'd rejected me because I'd moved, and I was living here. And I wasn't included in them any more. And I felt really alone. They just . . . . and although I could stay away over the weekend I was never asked if I wanted to go to a party . . . . "Oh, you don't live here now. You don't want to know us." And it was just a barrier between us—which um, made me feel really alone, and I felt that everybody was against me.'

(Girl₁, Group B(N), 17)

Perhaps the most dramatic changes of all are those that involve the loss of a parent through death or divorce. Here one of the most enduring parts of the taken-for-granted world, against which other vicissitudes can normally be measured, itself becomes unstable.

'When I came back off this week, from camping, my Dad said to me my Mum's ill. So I stayed up with her, me and my Dad —and kept her covered up to keep her warm. And then, then we all went to bed. Next morning my Dad got up about seven, because he went to work. I stayed up with her, got up . . . . my Dad was up all night with her. And I got up in the morning and sat with her. And she said to me, because my Mum didn't like the doctors, and she said to me "Don't", if my Nan comes up, "Don't get the doctor." So—my Nan come up about nine o'clock . . . . come up about nine o'clock and she said "Mum, your mum's ill today", and she says, I says "Yes". She goes "Well she, she looks really rough. You'd better get the doctor." I says "Mum told me not to get the doctor", and just as I said that my Mum went into a coma. And my Nan said "Well if you don't, your Mum's not going to be here." So—I went down the road on my bike and I got the doctor, and the doctor come up, and my Dad come in just as the doctor got there. And he gave her an injection, and my Dad went for the ambulance. And as the ambulance come, my Mum died. She di-died of bronchitis and asthma . . . . seen her worse before—she died.

'My sister was just getting married, and that left just me and my Dad at home, and—nothing seemed to go right after that.

'If we was in for a row we'd talk it out, me and my Mum and my Dad, to see what one's right. But now we can't do that, and if there's any trouble my Dad's got to be there on his own, you know. He hasn't got nobody to turn to.'

(Boy₁₇, Group C, 16)

By mid-adolescence some boys and girls have reached the point where they are able to evaluate the consequences of earlier actions and decisions. There begins to be a sense that irrevocable choices have been made, and that certain options have been closed for ever. The most characteristic topics mentioned in this context are failing to make use of opportunities at school, not developing talents that had been evident at an earlier age, and allowing health to deteriorate. Although, objectively, it might be judged that in such cases adolescents are often victims of circumstances, there is little sign of such a viewpoint in their accounts: it is possible that in accepting responsibility even for actions that are injurious, a person can more easily maintain a sense of being in control.

'In some lessons I've missed pieces of work that I really have to know and remember. And I think truanting stopped me from getting on a bit better than what I did in my exams. I could have stayed in, could have done a bit better. I think it was a mistake. I'll leave at Easter. I don't know hardly anything.

'When I leave school I know I'm going to get a bad reference, and I think it'll stop me from getting a job. So— when we go back in September I think I'll stay in school, even though I'll be fed up with it. I'll know that I've done right to stay in then, might get a better reference, and get a better job with it.

'I've been offered to take one CSE in geography, and I won't take it . . . . it means I'd have to stay on. Same for child care, I'd have to stay on . . . . don't want to do that.

'I've been asked to take my O levels in art. I won't take that. I don't think it's worth it, couldn't even draw . . . . this person what takes us for drawing and that, he said to me, "Well, you're wasting your own—talents" and all that. I said "Well, it's just my problem", said, "I just don't want to take

them, because I don't want to stay right through, right till
summer. Prefer to leave" . . . . It may be harder, I think,
than staying on, to get a job. So I just tell him I won't take
them. Just leave them.
    'At first when I was in the third year I wanted to be a
secretary, but they wouldn't allow me to type then. [Laughter]
So I couldn't take that. Then I wanted to be a designer, and
can't be bothered with drawing and all that now. So I just—
leave it now. Still like to be one . . . . I'd need my O levels
and A levels and CSEs and all that for it. So I know, I know
can never do that unless I went to, er,—er, night school and
got a pass in that. But I can't be bothered going to one. So I
just leave it. I'll end up working in a shop. It's work, it's
money.'

(Girl$_4$, Group B(N), 15½)

'I used to run for the school all the time . . . . and I used to
run for the school . . . . not normal running, cross-country.
And I was only good at that, weren't good at nothing else.
And I was always in school team, you know. And Steve never
used to do games, and I used to get friendly with him, and I
thought "Oh, I ain't going to do games this week." And then
this lad he went down and then started smoking. And then
my asthma got bad. So—I give up sm-, er, running. And I
thought it was clever giving it up, you know. Er, when I look
back at it I'm disappointed, you know, because I'd rather be
—running.
    'I used to have the pace, you know. I used to be able to—
get that pace to keep going, but I can't get the pace. When
I'm running over and that, I can't get the pace. Just give up.'

(Boy$_{19}$, Group C, 16)

Thus adolescence often involves experiences of contrasting
character, reflection upon which may well require a modification
or elaboration of the self-image. Of course assimilation is very
rarely carried out at a formal-operational level; far less does it
commonly involve the sophistications of psychological or sociological theory. It is probably more common for a person to make
sense of autobiographical material simply by drawing on certain
features, heightening their significance at the expense of others
and using these as key interpretive tools. The evidence of chapter
4, as well as the more detailed study of the accounts, suggests that
social success, and circumstances where it is plausible to postulate
the existence of personal control, are particularly significant for
the organization of personal history. Autobiography is thus never

static; its character changes with age, both depending on existing 'self-values' and in turn contributing towards their creation.

Giving Accounts to Others

Many adolescents draw attention to the satisfaction they derive from meeting new people; in youth clubs and pubs, in connection with hobbies, in changing schools or in moving from one district to another. Such situations may well require a person to give some kind of informal self-description, so that there can be a minimal basis for developing a friendship. Adult life often provides more permanent conditions, such as the relative stability of institutional roles, which allow time for the gradual development of acquaintance; it is often the case for adolescents, however, that relationships must be established quickly, if at all. In the flux of social life there is little opportunity for an extended autobiography, or for a person's actions to carry their own message; instead, there must be a resort to abbreviations.

When a highly condensed self-description is required, it seems probable that two overriding considerations are involved. First, whatever fragments are included, they should be such as to show the person in a way that is in accordance with existing 'self-values', or at least not exhibit too large a deviation from them. Second, they should, as far as is possible to judge, be adapted to the hearer. (This does not necessarily imply that the presentation should be pleasant.) Granted these, giving an account might involve making a selection from certain situation-specific regularities in conduct, and putting these forward as if they were persistent traits. Alternatively, a person might amplify one or more of his or her social 'characters', and postulate these virtually as if they constituted a personal identity. Collages that are assembled in order to meet the demands of particular occasions not only serve their immediate purpose, however; a person can, almost literally, talk himself or herself into the sense of having a personal identity. At any rate, it is plausible to suppose that the degree of consistency implied in self-presentation often exceeds by far that which actually obtains in everyday life; and that those who are constantly giving brief accounts of themselves can even be deceived by their own sincerity.

This feature of adolescent life requires no illustration here. The participants' behaviour in the research exemplifies the process in action, and the material already reproduced from the tape-recordings gives indications of typical content. It is clear that given an appropriate setting boys and girls from a wide variety of backgrounds, and throughout the age-range commonly defined as 'adolescence', are highly competent at giving accounts of themselves. Of course, the conditions of the research interview were different from those of ordinary social existence. Probably the interview was more demanding, in that it involved an extended account, and required the participant to be far more explicit than would be necessary in interaction with peers; on the other hand it may have been easier, in that there was a responsive and captive audience, and there would be no opportunity for subsequent checks on veracity. Despite differences such as these, this inquiry reveals something of the character of accounts in 'natural' settings, and the hypotheses put forward in chapter 4 about the mode of self-presentation in the research are directly relevant to parallel processes in everyday life.

Patterns of Personal Development

On the basis of all the evidence brought forward, and particularly that which is contained in this chapter, it may tentatively be suggested that there are several main patterns according to which the self-image develops during adolescence, depending mainly on the prevailing character of a person's social experience. Five such appear to be as follows.

1 Those who live almost entirely in mutually compatible social life-worlds, who do not experience markedly discrepant perspectives, and who have suffered no major dislocation in their personal experience. The majority of this group are from settled middle-class homes; they do not 'move out' extensively into the company of peers, or if they do this occurs relatively late. Personal identity is not a 'problem' to them, because there is no reason to question the information about themselves that they have received. The proportion of the total of adolescents in this group may be of the order of 10 per cent.

2 Those who inhabit mutually incompatible social life-worlds, but do not reflect on their experience, perhaps having little opportunity or desire for solitude. They take up different 'characters' as required. Since their mode of construing persons does not involve strong assumptions about personal consistency, their own inconsistency is not experienced as a 'problem'. It would appear that very many younger adolescents, perhaps of the order of 70 per cent, are in this group, and that a considerable proportion continue to experience themselves in this kind of way right through the adolescent period.

3 Those who are subjected to markedly discrepant perspectives, including some that are potentially damaging. There is a 'problem'

here, in that they have a strong motive for rejecting certain messages about themselves. A common solution is to accept as correct only information from some sources, while rejecting or re-interpreting the rest. Their personal identity thus is their favoured 'character'. A considerable degree of consistency is achieved, but at the expense of specializing in certain areas of their lives, and leaving others relatively undeveloped. Examples here include a small minority who devote themselves to academic or technical pursuits while remaining relatively asocial; and those who fare badly in the school system but become highly competent and original in their own social life. There are probably more boys than girls in this group, which may perhaps constitute 10 per cent of all adolescents.

4 Those who are 'on the move', never staying for long in any one group of friends, or in a close relationship with other individuals. As a result, they are constantly having to explain themselves to others, and become adept at doing so. Personal identity is, so to speak, assembled on demand, but does not exist in a more substantial way beyond the level of story-telling. The most striking instances here are among boys and girls who fall into the hands of the law, child-guidance or the probation service, and spend successive periods of weeks or months in different social environments. In proportion to the whole, this group is very small.

5 Those for whom personal identity is genuinely a problem. This may be because of living in social life-worlds that provide alternative definitions of appropriate action for particular circumstances; it may arise because a person has become sincerely committed to incompatible roles; or it may be the result of severe dislocations in personal life-history. The 'problem' is the more acute if parents or others who are highly respected have conveyed the message that consistency is important. Then, even if the content of the values attributed to these sources is rejected, the form may still remain: that is, there is still a belief that consistency of some kind, albeit in a deviant life-style, must be attained. This research suggests that this also is a small group; those who belong to it are likely to be from middle-class homes, to have had wide social experience, and to be in the later teens. At any rate, clear indications of a 'problem' of personal identity, perceived as such, were given by no more than 5 per cent of the whole 'sample'.

> 'I never used to have a set character, because of course after this sort of breakdown, sort of thing, I was in a bit of a dazed mood, and I was for many years. So I used to, instead of having one character, I used to take on the character of the person I was talking to, so that I could talk to them on their

level. And I think that's how I more or less shaped up. It, I think I do that to some extent now, although I think I'm beginning to get a character of my own.

'It would surprise me if anybody knew who they, who they were—I think one's got that many facets. That's one of my, my—you know, oh what do you call it? But I'm quite certain that you've no set character. I think you, your character—changes in your environment. I think, well, as I say, I've got one character at school, and I've got one character at home, although I've noticed that recently they've been coming the same. But even so, er, I've been, I've noted it in other people as well, that they're not the same at school as they are at home. And in many other cir-circumstances as well. I think—that I used to do it, consciously, I used to consciously, um—take on their characters, you know, or try and mould in to them, to the person that they expected to speak to, um, rather than—be me as I thought I was.

'I've had in the past, being at school, taken on that many facets, that I don't know which one really is me, and I don't know how to approach it.'

(Boy$_2$, Group B(N), 18)

The typology put forward here is speculative, and the suggested proportions even more so, though both are consistent with the general tenor of the data; no doubt this provisional analysis will require modification and extension in the light of further research. The main point, however, is that the idea of a 'search for personal identity' as a dominant underlying concern of adolescents in an advanced industrial society such as England in the late 1970s cannot be sustained. It is relatively few for whom personal identity presents itself as a 'problem', to be resolved by intensive research or reflection. For the great majority a mode of social existence that is functionally adequate is sustained some other way.

9
Appraisal

This book began with a brief review of two major psychological approaches to the general study of values; it was suggested that there was a place for a different kind of research programme in this field, whose data would be much closer to the realities of everyday life. A loosely constructed model of the person, suitable for the purposes of critical description, was put forward, together with a sketch of how values might be envisaged as being 'attached' to persons in a variety of ways. The evolution of a research method, designed as a means of obtaining data on some aspects of values in adolescent life, was then described. Four broad topics have been examined, with particular attention to differences in experience caused by social class position.

Much of this work has been tentative, since it is the first large-scale trial of a new research instrument. The method appears to be well suited to the life situation of those in mid-adolescence, enabling boys and girls from a wide range of backgrounds to talk very freely about themselves, and so (generally in an indirect way) about their values. In the processing of the data there has been an attempt to handle material from open-ended discourse with some degree of rigour, but without falling into positivism; evidence from the actual carrying out of the research has been used, as well as that derived from the accounts themselves; and categorized, semi-quantitative data have been applied as a check or control on more discursive interpretation.

The research method is vulnerable to two main types of criticism. On the one hand, those with a taste for more classical approaches might well point to its extreme openness, and assert that its discriminative efficacy has not been clearly demonstrated. On the other, it might be claimed that research of this kind does not come close enough to the real social and material conditions of existence to show how patterns of thought and action are related to these. Considering the purpose of this type of research, I believe that criticisms of the latter kind have the greater weight. Indeed, probably one of the most fruitful extensions of this inquiry would be in detailed work with adolescents located similarly in the social system, in which case much more of the 'fine structure' of the data could be examined and interpreted. Here, however, there was a compromise between the extensive and the intensive design: This increased the scope, but also set limits on the way data could be handled. Such a tactic was necessary, perhaps, for an initial inquiry, though its weaknesses need not necessarily be taken forward into further studies using the same research method.

My aim in this book has been to present a composite view, a general guide to values in adolescent life, amplified with a great deal of illustrative material and many detailed observations. The picture that emerges of 'normal' adolescence in England during the late 1970s has many differentiations. One way of illuminating this is to adopt a fairly complex model of the person. Thus each boy or girl is to be regarded as occupying a number of social life-worlds. Some of these are closely integrated with adult life, whereas others involve meanings and values that are distinctive to youth. In many cases the different social life-worlds function in a complementary way, so that a person can move from one to another without a sense of discord or unease; in others, however, there is sufficient discrepancy for a boy or girl to infer that there is a 'problem' to be resolved. The character of particular social life-worlds varies greatly, for example with social class position, locality, and any ways in which a person has chosen to specialize. Out of this rich range of possibilities the variegated character of adolescent life is constructed. There is no suggestion here of adolescents constituting a new type of social class, or of a single pervasive 'youth culture'. The observations made in this research, however, do not contradict those of specific subcultural studies, though two qualifying comments must be made. First, since most boys and girls do not belong to clearly defined subcultures, subcultural phenomena cannot be used as major keys to the interpretation of 'normal' adolescent life. Second, for those who do belong to a subculture, it can be misleading to characterize their existence solely on that basis. As Murdock and McCron (in Pearson and Mungham, 1976) have pointed out, subcultural membership is among a range of possibilities of adaptation available to those whom society has defined as adolescent.

Clearly, there is a danger in taking one main observation from a study such as this and highlighting it in preference to others. But if any single recurrent feature were to be selected, it would be the strong concern about competence in the interpersonal domain that is shown by boys and girls throughout the whole range of social class background, and perhaps especially by those in the middle part. The expression of this concern does, of course, show many stylistic variations. Those who are in their teens at this point in history are in a situation for which there is no clear parallel. They have been denied (at least until the age of sixteen, and maybe for some years beyond that age) the opportunity to give much of their time and energy to constructive involvement with the material world; they have generally not found that of the intellect either attractive or convincing; politics often appears incomprehensible, and beyond the possibility of meaningful involvement; as a result they have turned to their immediate social environment and attached to it an almost obsessive importance, developing some of their clearest values in this domain. Putting it in another way, many adolescents are involved, because of the circumstances that constrain their existence, in a prolonged, unstructured and highly informal course of 'sensitivity training', which neither they nor many of the adults who are involved with them recognize as such. As a result they tend to be very perceptive of others' reactions towards them; they are deeply concerned to be known as those who 'get on well with people'; they are acutely conscious of when things are going against them; failure here is the ultimate disaster, to be avoided at almost any personal cost.

Other research, notably that of McPhail *et al.* (1972) and Ward (1976), has drawn attention to similar features in adolescent life, though without comment on its significance in structural terms. For while this concern about human relationships is obviously commendable at one level, it may also be viewed as a reaction to a condition of perceived powerlessness, and estrangement from the main forward movement of society. It is in the interpersonal domain where, above any other, it appears to be possible to develop competence and control. There are techniques that can be learned by experience, and constant feedback from the reactions of others to indicate success or failure. There is a rich but not overwhelming store of knowledge available from solutions that have proved satisfactory in the past. Here a person can have a realistic chance of success, using social skill to overcome the barriers imposed by age or social class. At least since the work of Durkheim it has often been observed how a society can undergo adaptation, producing the kind of people, and in the right proportions, for its emergent needs. Here, the cynic might observe, is 'post-industrial society' in the making. If the main style of forecast is correct it will require only a small proportion of highly trained and work-oriented executives, while the majority are engaged, formally or informally, in bringing services to each other, or simply in existing without any part in the process of production; for the latter group an awareness that remained at the interpersonal level would be ideal.

There are pointers, however, towards a different interpretation. The participants in this inquiry did not show much resemblance to the adolescent of the popular stereotype: they were not mindless consumers, practitioners of violence and sensuality, rebels against all authority, degenerate, feckless or lazy. The feature that emerges most strongly, both from the carrying out of this research and from the tape-recorded data, is the way in which so many adolescents are concerned to be effective interpreters and performers in the social environments that are personally significant for them. The apparent conservatism, shown particularly in attitudes towards locality, sex roles, employment and the family, may be viewed as a temporary cognitive necessity, facilitating the mapping of immediate relationships. Just as with the professional who participates in a research programme, certain hard-core assumptions have to be fixed, in order for systematic investigation to proceed at all. Similarly, such fundamental values as freedom and justice are generally encountered during adolescence only in relation to highly specific issues; it is rare to find a person correlating such experiences in different social life-worlds, or making abstractions towards more general principles or ideals, because there are more urgent issues to be faced.

The conditions, however, for acquiring a political understanding of their situation are already present, and to an increasing degree. For those who are driven by the prevailing social conditions to spend much time in each other's company, and who learn to communicate effectively with each other, are beginning to objectify the world in which they live. They are engaged in mutual raising of consciousness. At present, so it would appear, that process is often curtailed; awareness remains at the interpersonal level, because before there is time for further development such contingencies as training, employment and marriage intervene. But the longer the period over which 'adolescence' is extended, the greater is the likelihood that boys and girls will also come to sensitize each other to the political implications of their position. The problem of how to structure social life and maintain self-esteem when unemployed is still largely to be resolved; solutions will no doubt be found, and they will not be the same as those that have emerged for the younger adolescent age-range. Here is the seed of a new kind of radicalism: not the middle-class revolt of youth in the 1960s, but a form of consciousness that moves upwards from the interpersonal, and that could begin to provide the cultural framework for fundamental social change.

Finally, something must be said about the problem of objectivity in relation to research of this kind. It is virtually a truism that if a piece of work is to count as scientific its findings should not be dependent on the idiosyncrasies of particular persons, but be available for testing by others. (To make this assertion is not, of course, to deny the importance of creativity, or the necessity for personal responsibility in scientific practice.) In research such as that described in this book the question of scientific status presents itself in a peculiar way, arising from the highly personal and interactive nature of the research method, and the form in which data are finally presented. Very little in this research has had the character of simple routine. The elucidation of the accounts themselves has resembled the reconstruction of a passage of prose from fragments in which many letters were missing, or an attempt to envisage the shape of a solid object from its shadow. Within the data there are many signifying features that at first are opaque to the researcher. As material on the same kind of topic is gathered together from participants in similar life-situations, patterns gradually become apparent. Once one of these is tentatively discerned, it can be used for understanding the details of individual accounts. A procedure of this kind might be described as hypothetico-deductive, though it accords most closely with the characterization of scientific practice given by Polanyi (for example in Grene, 1969), where he suggests that 'scientific knowing consists in discerning *gestalten* that indicate a true coherence in nature'. When this is applied to the social world there are, of course, many possibilities for misperception. We may have attributed coherence to the phenomena where in reality there was none, and failed to grasp coherence when it was genuinely present.

How, then, is objectivity to be achieved in research such as this, so that it may qualify as science? A positivist methodology guarantees its scientific status through the fact that others may use the same research instruments on a similar sample; straightforward if technically complex induction is the main procedure for generation of non-commonsensical theory. The common result is that the practice of psychological science is left to experts, and the rest of society have to take their word for it. Here, however, the position is different. The data may have been difficult to obtain, and the carrying out of the research may have involved particular skills and opportunities. It would also be desirable to have 'expert' replications. But the end-product of such work is a set of findings that is available to the non-professional, since they are presented in a concrete form, and can easily be related to the phenomena of everyday life. The 'realist' research programme, as was pointed out in chapter 1, looks to two main kinds of evidence, actions and accounts, on the assumption that a person generates these from a single stock of social knowledge. With the minor exception of evidence derived from the process of carrying out the research, this inquiry has been entirely concerned with the accounts that the participants have given of their everyday lives. The action is available for all to see: at home, in the street, in youth clubs, at school, at work, in the pub—all the places where the 'normal' social life of adolescents is enacted. This book has been concerned mainly with a description of the meaning of some of this complex range of phenomena. The generalizations, typologies and illustrations offered in the last four chapters may serve to enlarge understanding in those who view adolescent life from 'outside'. And when some aspect of a boy's or girl's behaviour remains unintelligible, the everyday observer could do worse than adopt informally an approach similar to that used in this research, which in many cases led to extended personal explanations.

The critically minded lay person is often inclined to be sceptical about the social research carried out by professionals, preferring to rely on common sense, and on direct personal knowledge of phenomena. Such a view is sometimes justified, since anyone who holds it may well be drawing on a store of tacit knowledge that is richer than the systematized information collected by 'experts'. What is offered here is closer to commonsense knowledge than the findings of research within several other psychological research programmes, and it is intended as an addition to the common store of interpretive tools for the understanding of adolescence. For social psychology in the realist mode, of which this is put forward as an example (even if an immature one), is centrally concerned with everyday life: the resources that individuals have for the guidance of action within it, and the way in which consciousness is related to the objective conditions of existence. As such it aims at humanizing social science, removing from it any unnecessary aura of mystery, and making its procedures and findings accessible as widely as possible beyond the professional community. Those who are in the strongest position to falsify what has been presented here (even if they could not produce a comparably broad range of positive generalizations) are members of the group whom the 'sample' has been designed to represent. The data have been given by people who are themselves experts on the meaning of their actions. We have tried to present faithfully the insights that they have disclosed.

Appendix
Notes on the Conventions used in Transcripts

1 Punctuation has been inserted in order to convey the sense of the narrative. There was no clear ground for making decisions here; the general policy was to be guided by what seemed appropriate in terms of obvious meaning, rather than by the length of pauses.

2 An unusually long pause or hesitation is indicated by the sign —.

3 A small interruption in a consecutive passage (for example the interviewer making an unimportant comment), or a few words that could not be heard clearly on the tape-recording (in some cases through extraneous noise, and in others through a participant speaking very fast or indistinctly), is indicated by . . . .

4 A discontinuity in an extract, arising from a question or comment from the interviewer, or from the omission of intervening material, is indicated by a change of paragraph.

5 In order to give clarity, there has been no attempt to preserve the character or regional accents in the extracts, apart from words such as 'ain't' or 'nowt', which are clearly distinct from standard English equivalents. The general assumption is that, were a participant to read out aloud an extract from his or her interview, the result would be a form of English more or less the same as the original. However, to illustrate what is involved in this procedure, here are three extracts: presented first as a novelist might give them, in the attempt to convey the colour of a regional accent, and then in the style used in this book.

(a) *Cockney*: 'For 'bout six munts after that me Mum wouldn't believe anyfink I told 'er, but she used to check up everywhere I was goin' out an' everyfink. I felt like a cwiminol.'

'For about six months after that my Mum wouldn't believe anything I told her, but she used to check up everywhere I was going out and everything. I felt like a criminal.'

(b) *West Country*: 'De only toime it'd wurry mey was if I werr parr-loised orr—last de use o' me legs or summink, orr last an arrm. Dat I cuddn't, I cuddn't bear dart, cuddn't take et.'
'The only time it'd worry me was if I were paralysed or—lost the use of my legs or something, or lost an arm. That I couldn't, I couldn't bear that, couldn't take it.'

(c) *Liverpool*: '"Yeu god no rart to tell me whadda do", said, "You're not thad older 'an me". Yo'no, she thinks co' she goes out an' me Mum's at werk I godda star' werking in the 'ouse—an' tardying up, doin' dishes, everythin' el."'
'"You got no right to tell me what to do", said, "You're not that older than me". You know, she thinks because she goes out and my Mum's at work I got to start working in the house —and tidying up, doing dishes, everything else."'

6 In order to show the source of the extracts from tapes, the participants in each major 'cell' of the sample have been given numbers. In the case of social class group B, an additional distinction between non-manual (N) and manual (M) has been made, following the Registrar General's treatment of category III. The age of each participant is given, corrected to the nearest half-year. Thus 'Boy$_8$, Group B(M), 18' refers to the eighth boy in the manual subdivision of group B (crudely speaking, upper-working class), approximately eighteen years old.

7 In a few cases an extract makes reference to a person who is not clearly identified at the outset. In order to give greater clarity, the role-title of the person has been inserted instead of a pronoun. e.g. 'She started just shouting at me . . . .' has been rendered 'My Nanna started just shouting at me . . . .' Similarly, in a few cases the context of a remark has been made more explicit. Thus 'I was very resentful at the time . . . .' has been rendered 'I was very resentful when my parents decided to move . . . .'

8 In order to preserve the confidential character of the accounts, all personal names have been changed. In some cases a place name has simply been obscured. Thus 'Batley College' might be rendered 'the College', and 'We went to Royston' as 'We went to a nearby town'.

Bibliography

Allport, G. W., Vernon, P. E. and Lindzey, G. (1931), *A Study of Values* (Boston, Houghton Mifflin) (3rd edn 1960).

Armistead, N. (ed.) (1974), *Reconstructing Social Psychology* (Harmondsworth, Penguin).

Banaka, W. H. (1974), *Training in Depth Interviewing* (New York, Harper and Row).

Baskhar, R. (1974), *A Realist Theory of Science* (Leeds, Leeds Books).

Berger, P. L., Berger, B. and Kellner, H. (1974), *The Homeless Mind* (Harmondsworth, Penguin).

Biddle, J. and Thomas, E. J. (1966), *Role Theory: Concepts and Research* (New York, John Wiley).

Brewster Smith, M. (1974), *Humanizing Social Psychology* (San Francisco, Jossey-Bass).

Chein, I. (1972), *The Image of Man and the Science of Behaviour* (London, Tavistock).

Cicourel, A. V. (1964), *Method and Measurement in Sociology* (New York, Free Press).

Clark, S. L. (1976), 'Interviews with adolescents: a preliminary study of adolescent self-presentation in relation to popular and scholarly stereotypes' (MSc dissertation, unpublished, Bradford University).

Elliott, R. C. (1970), *The Shape of Utopia* (Chicago University Press).

Erikson, E. H. (1968), *Identity: Youth and Crisis* (London, Faber and Faber).

Feather, N. T. (1975), *Values in Education and Society* (New York, Free Press).

Fogelman, K. (ed.) (1976), *Britain's Sixteen-Year-Olds* (London, National Children's Bureau).

Gage, N. L. (ed.) (1963), *Handbook of Research on Teaching* (Chicago, Rand McNally).

Garfinkel, H. (1967), *Studies in Ethnomethodology* (Englewood Cliffs, N.J., Prentice-Hall).

Goffman, E. (1969), *The Presentation of Self in Everyday Life* (London, Allen Lane).

Grene, M. (ed.) (1969), *Knowing and Being* (London, Routledge & Kegan Paul).

Harré, R. (1970), *The Principles of Scientific Thinking* (London, Macmillan).

Harré, R. (ed.) (1976a), *Life Sentences* (Chichester, John Wiley).

Harré, R. (ed.) (1976b), *Personality* (Oxford, Basil Blackwell).

Harré, R. and Secord, P. F. (1972), *The Explanation of Social Behaviour* (Oxford, Basil Blackwell).

Henderson, L. (1972), 'On mental energy', *British Journal of Psychology*, vol. 63, pp. 1–7.

Kelly, G. A. (1955), *The Psychology of Personal Constructs* (New York, Norton).

Kitwood, T. M. (1976a), 'Educational research and its standing as science', *Studies in Higher Education*, vol. 1, pp. 69–82.

Kitwood, T. M. (1976b), 'On values and value systems: evidence from interviews with adolescents', *Educational Research*, vol. 18, pp. 223–31.

Kitwood, T. M. (1977a), 'What does "having values" mean?', *Journal of Moral Education*, vol. 6, pp. 81–9.

Kitwood, T. M. (1977b), 'Values in adolescent life: towards a critical description' (PhD thesis, unpublished, Bradford University).

Kitwood, T. M. (1978), 'The morality of interpersonal perspectives', *Journal of Moral Education*, vol. 7, pp. 189–98.

Kitwood, T. M. and Smithers, A. G. (1975), 'Measurement of human values: an appraisal of the work of Milton Rokeach', *Educational Research*, vol. 17, pp. 175–9.

Kluckhohn, F. R. and Strodtbeck, F. L. (1961), *Variations in Value Orientations* (Illinois, Row, Peterson).

Kockelman, J. J. (ed.) (1967), *The Philosophy of Edmund Husserl and its Interpretation* (New York, Anchor Books).

Kohlberg, L. (1963), 'The development of children's orientations toward a moral order: I. Sequence in the development of moral thought', *Vita Humana*, vol. 6, pp. 11–33.

Kuhn, A. (1966), *The Study of Society: A Multidisciplinary Approach* (London, Tavistock).

Lakatos, I. and Musgrave, A. (eds) (1970), *Criticism and the Growth of Knowledge* (Cambridge University Press).

Little, B. R. (1972), 'Psychological man as scientist, humanist, and specialist', *Journal for Experimental Research in Personality*, vol. 6, pp. 95–118.

Livesley, W. J. and Bromley, D. B. (1973), *Person Perception in Childhood and Adolescence* (New York, John Wiley).

McPhail, O., Ungoed-Thomas, J. R. and Chapman, H. (1972), *Moral Education in the Secondary School* (London, Longmans).

Marsh, P., Rosser, E. and Harré, R. (1978), *The Rules of Disorder* (London, Routledge & Kegan Paul).

Marshall, J. C. (1977), 'Minds, machines and metaphors', *Social Studies of Science*, vol. 7, pp. 475–88.

Mischel, T. (ed.) (1971), *Cognitive Development and Epistemology* (New York, Academic Press).

Mischel, T. (ed.) (1974), *Understanding Other Persons* (Oxford, Basil Blackwell).

Mixon, D. (1972), 'Instead of deception', *Journal for the Theory of Social Behaviour*, vol. 2, pp. 145–77.

Morris, C. (1956), *Varieties of Human Value* (University of Chicago Press).

Outhwaite, W. (1975), *Understanding Social Life* (London, Allen & Unwin).

Parsons, T. (1967), *Sociological Theory and Modern Society* (New York, Free Press).

Pearson, G. and Mungham, G. (eds) (1976), *Working Class Youth Culture* (London, Routledge & Kegan Paul).

Peters, R. S. (1974), *Psychology and Ethical Development* (London, Allen & Unwin).

Piaget, J. (1932), *The Moral Judgment of the Child* (London, Routledge & Kegan Paul).

Rogers, C. R. (1961), *On Becoming a Person* (London, Constable).

Rokeach, M. (1973), *The Nature of Human Values* (New York, Free Press).

Rosenberg, M. (1965), *Society and the Adolescent Self-Image* (Princeton University Press).

Rosenthal, R. and Rosnow, R. L. (1974), *The Volunteer Subject* (New York, John Wiley).

Rubinstein, D. (1977), 'The concept of action in the social sciences', *Journal for the Theory of Social Behaviour*, vol. 7, pp. 209–35.

Ruddock, R. (ed.) (1972), *Six Approaches to the Person* (London, Routledge & Kegan Paul).

Schofield, M. (1968), *The Sexual Behaviour of Young People* (Harmondsworth, Penguin).

Shotter, J. (1975), *Images of Man in Psychological Research* (London, Methuen).

Tajvel, H. (1974), 'Inter-group Behaviour, Social Comparison and Social Change', Katz-Newcomb Lectures (Ann Arbor, University of Michigan).

Toft, B. (1978), 'An exploratory description of the "free" speech of adolescents of different social class backgrounds, using measures derived from Bernstein's theories' (MSc dissertation, unpublished, Bradford University).

Toft, B. and Kitwood, T. M. (1980), 'An exploratory study of adolescent speech using measures derived from Bernstein's theories', *Research in Education*, May 1980.

von Wright, G. H. (1963), *The Varieties of Goodness* (London, Routledge & Kegan Paul).

Ward, J. P. (1976), *Social Reality for the Adolescent Girl* (Swansea University Faculty of Education).

Watson, J. B. (1919), *Psychology From the Standpoint of a Behaviourist* (Philadelphia, Lippincott).

Willis, P. E. (1977), *Learning to Labour* (Farnborough, Lexington Books).

Index